OS/2™

A BUSINESS PERSPECTIVE

DICK CONKLIN

JOHN WILEY & SONS
New York • Chichester • Brisbane • Toronto • Singapore

Publisher: Stephen Kippur
Editor: Therese A. Zak
Managing Editor: Ruth Greif
Electronic Book Production: Publishers Network, Morrisville, PA

Copyright © 1988 by John Wiley & Sons, Inc.

Library of Congress Cataloging in Publication Data:

Conklin, Dick, 1941-

OS/2: a business perspective / Dick Conklin.

   p. cm.
  On CIP t.p. the registered trademark symbol "TM" is
superscript
following "system/2" in the title.
    ISBN 0–471–63503–0
    1. MS OS/2 (Computer operating sys
Title. II. Title:
Operating system two.
QA76.76.063C663 1988
650'.028'554469--dc19
87-34470

Printed in the United States of America

88 89 10 9 8 7 6 5 4 3 2 1

TRADEMARKS

IBM, Personal Computer AT, TopView, NetView, and Quietwriter are registered trademarks of the IBM Corporation.

Operating System/2, OS/2, Presentation Manager, Database Manager, Communication Manager, Query Manager, Dialog Manager, Personal System/2, PS/2, Micro Channel, Personal Computer/XT, PC XT, Personal Computer DOS, ProPrinter, SolutionPac, AIX, EZ-VU, Writing Assistant, and PROFS are trademarks of the IBM Corporation.

Microsoft, CodeView, MS, MS-DOS, Microsoft Operating System/2, MS OS/2 and Xenix are registered trademarks of the Microsoft Corporation.

Microsoft OS/2 LAN Manager, Microsoft OS/2 Software Development Kit, MS OS/2 SDK, Microsoft Adventure, Microsoft Windows, Windows Write and Windows Paint are trademarks of Microsoft Corporation.

AT&T and Unix are registered trademarks of American Telephone and Telegraph Corp.

SCO Xenix is a trademark of the Santa Cruz Operation.

CP/M and GEM are registered trademarks of Digital Research, Inc.

GEM Desktop, DOS Plus, Flex OS, and Concurrent DOS are trademarks of Digital Research, Inc.

Intel is a registered trademark of the Intel Corporation.

Above Board is a trademark of Intel Corp.

AST is a registered trademark of AST Corporation.

RAMPage is a trademark of AST Corporation.

IN*a*Vision is a trademark of Micrografix, Inc.

VP/ix is a trademark of Phoenix Technologies Ltd. and Interactive Systems Corp.

PC/IX is a trademark of Interactive Systems Corp.

Venix is a trademark of Unisource Corp.

PC Mouse is a trademark of Metagraphics/Mouse Systems Visi-On Mouse and Visi-Calc are trademarks of Visi-On Corporation.

Dow Jones News/Retrieval Service is a registered trademark of Dow Jones and Company, Incorporated.

Compuserve Information Service is a registered trademark of Compuserve, Inc.

MCI Mail is a registered trademark of MCI Communications Corp.

This book is dedicated to the hundreds of programmers at IBM and Microsoft who brought OS/2 to life. You coded, tested, and recoded until you achieved an admirable balance of function and performance. But most important, you listened to both application developers and end users before the coding started.

Because of that, we now have an entirely new operating system that is as easy to use as it is powerful—a solid base for the personal computer's second generation.

Preface

On April 2, 1987, IBM made the most significant personal computer announcement since the original IBM PC was unveiled in August of 1981. The IBM Personal System/2™ effectively replaced the old PC line, bringing faster processors, sharper displays, and increased memory and storage to the market. The new Micro Channel™ bus architecture in the high-end PS/2 models paves the way for option cards and attachments designed to accommodate sophisticated applications and workloads previously unheard of.

At most of the recent product announcements, the operating system received little attention. The IBM Personal Computer Disk Operating System, better known as PC DOS, was upgraded several times without fanfare, adding hardware support for higher-capacity disk drives and local area networks. Each new release also introduced new software features such as DOS 2.0's tree-structured disk directories and DOS 3.2's XCOPY command. The DOS 3.3 version, true to form, supports the latest Personal System/2 enhancements like VGA, faster serial port speeds, and larger fixed disks.

But the PS/2 unveiling was different in another way. The long-awaited new 80286 operating system, while not immediately available, was jointly announced by IBM and Microsoft Corporation. Named *Operating System/2* ™, the "new DOS" comes in two versions: an OS/2 *Standard Edition* made up of the base operating system component, complete with 16 Mb memory addressing and multitasking support, and an *Extended Edition* featuring two additional components: a database manager and a communications manager.

The first PC generation is over. The thousands of hardware and software products that flooded the market between 1981 and 1987 are now classified as "PC-bus- compatible", "PC DOS-based", or "Family 1". Many are already being replaced by "Family 2" hardware, "MicroChannel Compatible" cards and "Full Function OS/2" programs. The second PC generation is still very young, and all of the pieces aren't in place, but it's already clear that a key player is Operating System/2. In order to appreciate the new second generation application programs, you need to know what OS/2 is all about —not down to the "bits and bytes" level, certainly—but a good general knowledge is essential. This book is written for PC users who want to understand this revolutionary software product and what it brings to the world of business, education and personal computing. It will answer your questions, help you plan for the future, and offer some useful ideas.

Dick Conklin

Acknowledgments

This book could not have been written without the help of many people at IBM and Microsoft Corporation. In particular, I want to thank Steve Ballmer at Microsoft for providing early code and documentation and Jim Archer at IBM for his technical review. Their assistance is gratefully acknowledged.

I also owe much to the students who attended my classes and seminars in the first few months after the OS/2 announcement. Those lively discussions touched on every aspect of OS/2 preparation, conversion, installation and use, and this book is better because of them.

How This Book Was Written

The manuscript for this book was written with IBM Writing Assistant 2.0, using an IBM Personal System/2 Model 60 and an IBM PC Convertible. Files were submitted to John Wiley & Sons in ASCII format for typesetting. Artwork, copy editing, and layout was done by The Publishers Network. Much of the book was written while the author was teaching OS/2 classes and seminars around the country. Thanks to the PC Convertible, chapters were written in hotel rooms, airport waiting rooms and airplanes bound for New York, Atlanta, San Francisco, Los Angeles, Phoenix and Dallas.

Contents

Chapter 3   OS/2's Multi-Tasking: Computing in Parallel   **63**

Chapter 4   OS/2's User Interface: Windows on the World   **111**

Chapter 5   OS/2 Conversion: Making the Big Switch   143

Chapter 6   OS/2 Installation: Up and Running   175

1

Introducing Operating System/2

*"The art of progress is to preserve order amid
change and to preserve change amid order"*

Process and Reality

A. N. Whitehead

On April 2, 1987, IBM Corporation and Microsoft Corporation announced Operating System/2, the product of an ongoing joint development agreement between the two companies. OS/2 is not DOS 4.0, nor is it an extension of DOS in any way; it is a completely new operating system for personal computers, designed as a platform for old, new, and future application programs (Figure 1–1). The result of years of planning, programming, and testing, OS/2 is not intended to be an instant DOS replacement. Instead, it starts with a relatively simple base and evolves over a period of time.

Application developers were the first OS/2 users, attending seminars and receiving beta test, or pre-release, copies to aid in converting their DOS programs. The OS/2 Standard Edition 1.0 was the first "street version" available to the general public, bringing large memory addressing and multi-application support to the PC world. Next came OS/2 Extended Edition 1.0, with two additional components—a Database and Communications Manager. Then the Standard Edition 1.1, with a flashy Presentation Manager windowing interface and a colorful collection of graphics and text functions was released. Finally, the Extended Edition 1.1 brought it all together: base operating system with Presentation, Communications, and Database Managers (Figure 1–2).

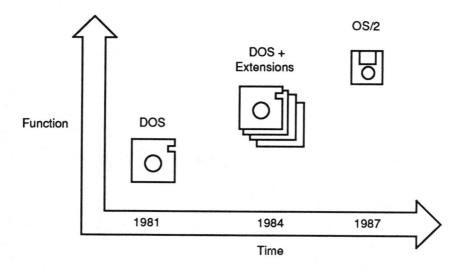

Figure 1–1 OS/2 is the latest step in the evolution of P/C operating systems. The original PC DOS was created for the first IBM PC, and has been enhanced and extended over the years. OS/2 provides the function of DOS, its extensions, and much more.

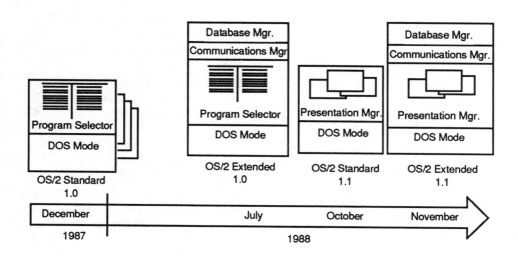

Figure 1–2 OS/2 itself is evolving with two editions (Standard and Extended) and (initially) two releases, 1.0 and 1.1. OS/2 Standard 1.0 uses a simple Program Selector interface. OS/2 Extended 1.1 combines the Presentation, Communications, and Database Managers.

RIGHT IN THE MIDDLE

The operating system plays an important role on any computer, and OS/2 provides many functions missing from DOS. One way of looking at the relationship of an operating system to the rest of the computer is illustrated by the stack of blocks in Figure 1–3. These three blocks, or layers, represent a Personal System/2 running Operating System/2 and several application programs.

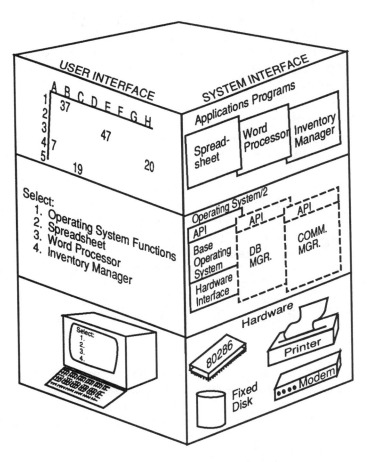

Figure 1–3 A personal computer system—computer, OS/2, and applications—offers two distinct "faces" to the outside world. On the left, the user interface consists of keyboard, display, mouse, operating system, and program screens, On the right, the three system components interact with each other through the 80286 processor, other hardware devices, the system bus, OS/2 managers, application program interfaces, and the applications themselves.

From the Bottom Up

The computer hardware: the system unit with its processor, fixed disk, memory, and associated components is represented by the bottom layer. This block has two visible "faces." The left side is the hardware's *user interface*: the display that you view and the keyboard or mouse with which you control the computer. Although occasionally you will need to load paper into the printer, insert a diskette, or switch on a communications modem, most of the time the display and keyboard act as the system's viewport and control panel. The block's right-hand, or system interface side, illustrates a sampling of other hardware elements that you do not directly touch or see: the internal fixed disk storage device, microprocessor "engine," and associated bus architecture. The computer's read only memory (ROM) chips contain permanent programs that provide an interface to the next layer—the operating system.

The Middle Layer

Sandwiched between the hardware on the bottom and the application programs on the top is the *operating system*. On the left, its user interface is represented by an OS/2 Program Selector screen with a menu of applications. On the right, three major OS/2 components are shown: the *base operating system* element common to both OS/2 versions, and the Extended Edition's *Communications* and *Database Managers*. OS/2 interfaces with the hardware layer below through the BIOS and ABIOS programs in ROM. It supports the application layer above by managing the sharing of the processor, display, memory, fixed disk storage, communication links, and hard copy devices below. OS/2's link with programs exists in the form of an application program interface, or API. The Database and Communications Managers each add their own unique functions to the API.

The Top Layer

Application programs conceptually sit on top of the operating system. In this drawing, three programs are running—a spreadsheet, a word processor, and a program to manage inventory. One program's user interface is shown on the left: a spreadsheet screen. The user can switch to other applications through a keyboard or mouse command. Each application program has been written to work with the OS/2 API below.

These three blocks of a computer system are very interdependent. The computer can run multiple applications at once, but only if the operating system manages the sharing of hardware among them. A high-resolution display is capable of windowing several graphics and text screens, but only if the application interface supports it. Multiple program tasks can drive input-output devices concurrently with reasonable performance—if the underlying computer architecture is designed to do so.

TWO BRIDGES: DOS TO THE PAST, SAA TO THE FUTURE

As a DOS user, you will find much in OS/2 to feel comfortable with (Figure 1–4). A compatible DOS Mode is built in, permitting many existing applications to run without change. Surprisingly, the DOS and OS/2 file and directory formats are identical. There are two command processors, one for DOS

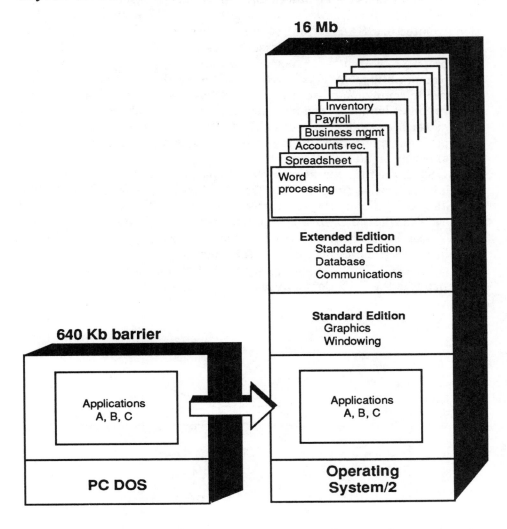

Figure 1–4 PC DOS and OS/2 are quite different. DOS supports single applications running in a 640 Kb-limited memory area. A compatible DOS environment has been preserved in OS/2, with the additon of graphics, windowing, database, and communications support for OS/2 programs. OS/2 supports up to 16 Mb of memory, and up to 12 multitasking programs.

and one for OS/2, but they share a nearly identical set of commands. An online help facility reduces the need for frequent trips to the reference manual. In spite of its many new features, OS/2 installs smoothly and operates easily. To help you understand both the level of DOS compatibility and the new OS/2 features, comparisons between the two operating systems are used throughout this book. Each chapter reviews the current level of DOS support and extensions before describing how OS/2 does it better.

OS/2 is the first software product to follow IBM's new Systems Application Architecture. SAA is a long term plan for vertical system compatibility, permitting programs to run on Personal System/2, System 3X, and System/370 computers with little or no modification. In order to achieve high software compatibility, SAA deals with much more than just the ability of a program to compile and execute on more than one system. The user interface, graphics language, communication protocols, database language, and query interface are all addressed by SAA. The durable SAA program runs on IBM personal, mid-range, and mainframe systems and it looks and responds the same way on all.

OS/2 is the first operating system to participate in SAA. Its SAA-conforming application program interface has been implemented partially in the Standard Edition 1.1, with further additions in the Extended Edition. Three of the six IBM OS/2 language compilers—C/2, FORTRAN/2, and CO-BOL/2—conform to SAA. The OS/2 Presentation Manager provides the user interface and graphics primitives. SAA query and database languages are part of the OS/2 Database Manager, and SAA communication protocols are designed into the OS/2 Communications Manager (Figure 1–5).

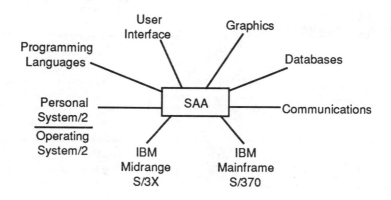

Figure 1–5   IBM's Systems Application Architecture, in order to provide software compatibility across IBM products and programs, addresses several aspects of application program development. In addition to compatible language compilers for personal, mid-range, and mainframe systems, SAA defines a program's user interface, graphics primitives, database languages, and communications protocols.

THE MEMORY

OS/2 runs on current 80286 processor-based systems such as the Personal System/2 Models 50 and 60 (Figure 1–6). It runs on older 80286 PCs like the Personal Computer AT and XT/286 models. It also runs on 80386 machines, including the Personal System/2 Model 80 (Figure 1–7).

Figure 1–6   The IBM Personal System/2 Model 50 is the smallest PS/2 to support OS/2. This desktop model can have up to 7 Mb with the addition of memory adapter

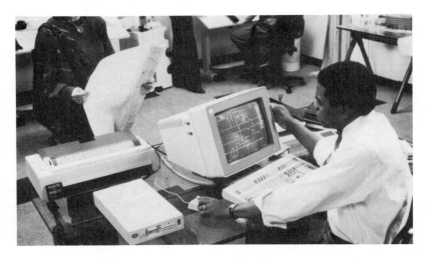

Figure 1–7   The IBM Personal System/2 Model 80 is the top of the PS/2 line, offering up to a 20 MHz clock speed, 16 Mb of memory, and 628 Mb of fixed disk storage.

The 80286 and 80386 help OS/2 overcome a major DOS limitation: the old 640 Kb memory ceiling. Now programs can be many times larger—using up to 15 or 16 megabytes of real memory. When several programs exceed a machine's real memory capacity, their inactive segments are swapped to disk so that they can continue to run uninterrupted (Figure 1–8). OS/2 does this by exploiting the built-in 16 Mb addressability and memory management provided by the 80286 processor's Protect Mode.

If the DOS Mode installation option is taken, OS/2 reserves a portion of low memory for DOS programs. While this reduces the execution space available for OS/2 programs, it does provide a compatible environment in which DOS applications can run. Whenever a DOS Mode program gets its turn, OS/2 switches the 80286 processor to 8086 Real Mode. This gives a DOS program the familiar surroundings it needs: DOS 3.3-level features, 8086/8088 processor instruction set, and real memory addresses below 640 Kb. OS/2 Mode programs, on the other hand, use the 80286 Protect Mode and reside above the 1 Mb memory boundary.

In addition to running old DOS and new OS/2 full-featured programs, the operating system also supports a hybrid category called Family applications. OS/2 Family programs are written to use a subset of OS/2 function, at a level compatible with both DOS and OS/2. An OS/2 Family program is compiled in such a way that it can run under either operating system. This

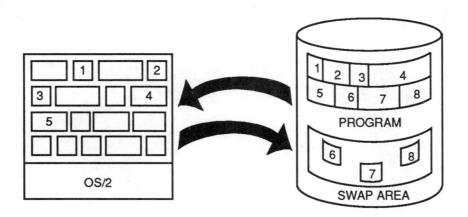

Figure 1–8 Operating System/2 manages every program as a collection of segments, each up to 64 Kb in size. When multiple (or large) programs exceed a computer's installed memory, OS/2 dynamically moves these segments, placing inactive ones in a temporary swap file.

means that a single version of a program can be maintained by a developer and stocked on a dealer's shelves. But it also means than some OS/2-exclusive features such as large memory addressing and Presentation Manager serv-ices like windowing cannot be used by a Family program in order to maintain DOS compatibility (Figure 1–9).

Many programs will be written to take advantage of OS/2 exclusives. The large memory space, for example, can yield many benefits. Generally, a programmer can build more "smarts" into a program if there is more memory to work with. Programs run faster when they don't depend on disk-resident subroutines. Additional memory can also improve performance through disk caching. A program is easier to use with built-in menus and help libraries to guide the user. Some applications mix graphics with text to illustrate program options and improve user "friendliness." OS/2's Presentation Manager supports application windowing, high-resolution, multi-color images, and a selection of optional character font styles and sizes. These are all desirable features, but they require more memory than text-based programs.

The data work area for an OS/2 application, like the program itself, can be much larger than under DOS. This means bigger spreadsheets, longer documents, or more database records in memory at once. The sorting of a large file, for example, can be done much faster if it can fit entirely in memory, instead of sorting smaller sections and merging them. Several spreadsheet tables or book chapters can be combined if sufficient memory is available. An inventory program processes transactions quicker if the spare parts file is memory-resident .

Chapter 2, *OS/2's Large Memory: Beyond 640 Kb*, explains how large memory is managed, compares it with today's DOS methods, and shows how programs will take advantage of it.

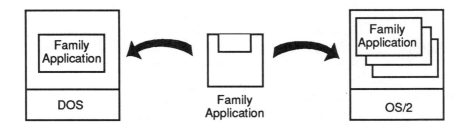

Figure 1–9 OS/2 Family application programs are "bi-model": they can run under PC DOS or OS/2 programs. By nature, Family programs are restricted to a DOS-subset of OS/2 function: smaller than 640 Kb, single-tasking, and unable to use OS/2 managers.

A MULTI-TASKING OPERATING SYSTEM

Much of the large OS/2 memory area will be used to run several programs at once. Up to 12 OS/2 full-function and Family programs, plus one DOS session, can run concurrently, receiving processor time-slices as needed (Figure 1–10). Multiple copies of the same program can be started, allowing you to switch between several reports or financial statements you are working on without stopping to save one and reload the next one each time. OS/2 saves space by not unnecessarily duplicating program segments in memory.

The 80286 processor's Protect Mode was named after its ability to isolate or protect programs from each other. Using a set of tables, OS/2 keeps track of the whereabouts of each memory segment, which programs have access to it, how recently it has been used, and whether it is currently in memory or on disk. One program cannot use a segment owned by another program unless a sharing arrangement has been established by both.

OS/2 also supports multi-tasking within a program. Several unique tasks, or execution threads, can run in parallel (Figure 1–11). This means that while a program is downloading a file from a host computer, it can be printing a report and receiving keyboard input—all at the same time. The user deals only with priority tasks needing immediate attention, without the need to wait for others that can run by themselves. Multi-tasking im-

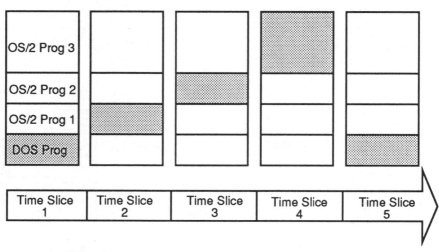

Figure 1–10   OS/2 shares the processor and other system resources with its programs by time-slicing among them. Here a DOS Mode program (currently in the foreground) receives an increment of time, followed by an OS/2 program, then another, and so forth. (A background DOS program receives no time-slices.)

proves application throughout, since a group of parallel tasks will complete before the same tasks run in a serial, DOS-like sequence.

Each OS/2 program is always either in the foreground or background. A foreground program has current control of the keyboard and display (and a mouse if one is attached). It is interactive, able to receive user input. An OS/2 1.1 background program may even share the screen with the foreground program, but it cannot receive input until the user brings it to the foreground. Background programs can often run unattended, receiving processor time slices from OS/2 as available (Figure 1–12). If an OS/2 background program cannot continue processing because it is waiting for user input or has no other work to do, it is temporarily suspended. An inactive background program simply waits there until the user returns to give it additional instructions or data, or ends the session. DOS Mode programs are different. They are *always* suspended while they are in the background.

A multi-tasking operating system must coordinate a computer's limited resources among several programs. In addition to the time-slicing of processor cycles between active programs and tasks, multiple disk files must be read from and written to. Printed output from several programs waits in the printer queue. The Presentation Manager windows multiple program screen sessions.

The performance of a multi-application system depends on many factors: the processing needs of each program, the use of multi-tasking within a program, the memory available, and the hardware capacity. Each program has some control over its priority level, but OS/2 is the final arbitrator. The user, by changing configuration file and batch file commands, can adjust some performance-related variables.

Chapter 3, *OS/2's Multi-tasking: Computing in Parallel*, describes the hows and whys of multiple application support.

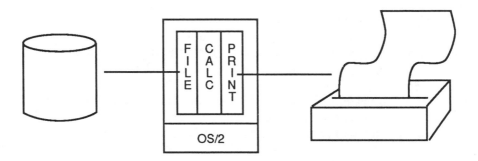

Figure 1–11   A personal computer is most efficient when multiple devices (processor, disk, printer, modem, etc.) can be used at the same time. Here, a program multi-tasks calculations, disk saving, and printing.

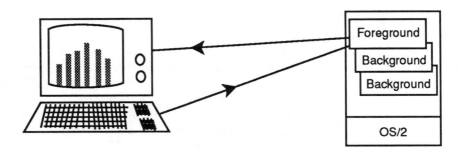

Figure 1–12   When OS/2 is running multiple programs, only one is in the foreground at a time. A foreground program "owns" the keyboard, display, and mouse, while background programs have no user interface. They are active when they have work to do, such as calculations or printing, but are suspended when they finish their work or are awaiting user input.

FROM THE USER'S POINT OF VIEW

A complex multi-application operating system like OS/2 can be made relatively easy to operate through its shell, or user interface. OS/2 1.0 provides the user with a simple Program Selector menu: a list of "known" applications (pre-installed on disk) and another list of "started" programs (some active, some suspended). You can go to the menu to start a new program or to switch to one that is already running. You can bypass the Program Selector by simply hotkeying between active programs. Control can be from either keyboard or mouse.

The OS/2 on-line help facility provides immediate user assistance via a disk-resident library. When you press the F1 key from the Program Selector screen, OS/2 provides several layers of assistance with the command or function currently being attempted. Or, you can scroll through pages of text to find the help you need. Additional explanations and recommendations can be requested for system error messages with the HELP command (Figure 1–13).

The OS/2 release 1.1 Presentation Manager™ is a major improvement to the user interface. Program selection and interaction is performed through a windowing interface from keyboard or mouse. Graphics and text can share the same screen. Optional character font styles and sizes are supported. User interaction with PM programs takes place through dialog boxes and pop-up menus, and by "clipboarding" information between two cooperating applications.

EXPLANATION: The file is already being used by another program.

ACTION: Retry the command or program later.

Figure 1–13 OS/2 provides several forms of on-line user assistance. By pressing the F1 function key while on an OS/2 screen, help with OS/2 commands and functions is provided. OS/2 error messages can be expanded and problem solutions suggested. A complete OS/2 on-line reference is also available.

Even the old "unfriendly" PC DOS user interface has been retained in OS/2. You will find it in the DOS Mode, a PC DOS 3.3-like version of COMMAND.COM, called "DOS Command Prompt" on the Program Selector menu. While in DOS Mode you can use familiar DOS commands (DIR, DISKCOPY, FORMAT, etc.) and run most DOS programs. The AUTOEXEC.BAT batch file, if present, will run when you first start DOS Mode. Or, you can start one or more OS/2 Command Prompt sessions, using the OS/2 CMD.EXE command processor. The OS/2 command prompt also gives you a DOS-like interface for its commands (most are shared with DOS anyway) and for running OS/2 programs.

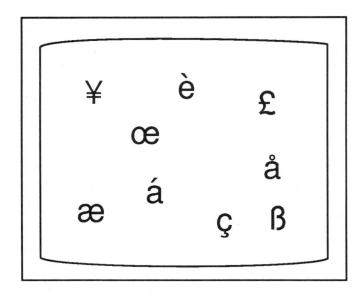

Figure 1–14   OS/2 is an international operating system, supporting several languages, alphabets, and keyboard layouts.

OS/2 is an international operating system. It supports several non-U.S. keyboards, language alphabets, currency symbols, and other local customs. Any two of the five code pages, or character sets, can be loaded, selected by an application program or by the user. The default code page, as with DOS, is the familiar 256-character set of PC letters and symbols (Figure 1–14).

Systems Application Architecture has driven much of the Presentation Manager's design. A consistent user interface (use of function keys, screen design, etc.) will be found on operating systems and application programs across the IBM product line, starting with OS/2 1.1. Graphics primitives, or commands, will permit programs to create graphs and charts on a variety of different computer-display configurations.

Chapter 4, *OS/2's User Interface: Windows on the World*, will show how OS/2 is easier to install, operate, and maintain.

FROM DOS TO OS/2

The bridge from DOS to OS/2 is not a difficult one for the knowledgeable DOS user to cross. Many PC owners will upgrade first to DOS 3.3 for Per-

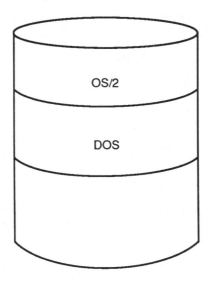

Figure 1–15   During the transition from PC DOS to OS/2, there is no need to reformat the fixed disk or erase PC DOS files. OS/2 can co-reside with DOS on the same system.

sonal System/2 support and other enhancements, and later to OS/2 when the right applications are available. Since OS/2's DOS Mode is essentially a DOS 3.3 emulator, most migrated DOS programs will find a home there.

There are some exceptions. Some DOS programs are timing-sensitive, such as those that perform communication or real-time functions. Since a DOS Mode program is temporarily suspended while OS/2 or one of its programs are running, a communications link or real-time control process may be terminated. This does not happen when a communications program runs under PC DOS alone or after it has been reprogrammed for OS/2 Mode. For this reason, some users may temporarily maintain a dual DOS-OS/2 system (Figure 1–15).

A dual system consists of both OS/2 and DOS files on the same fixed disk (DOS 3.3 command files must be stored in a separate directory). OS/2 is usually designated as the bootable operating system, so that it starts up whenever the computer is turned on. DOS must be booted from a startup diskette, which contains enough of DOS to configure the system properly. The diskette can then be removed, and DOS and its programs will run from the fixed disk.

If your existing DOS programs and data are stored on a 5.25-inch diskette-based PC, and your new OS/2 system is a Personal System/2, program and data files must somehow be migrated to the PS/2's fixed disk. This can be done directly with an interconnecting cable, or via diskettes (Figure 1–

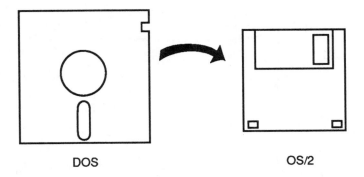

DOS   OS/2

Figure 1–16   There are several ways to migrate DOS files to an OS/2 system: diskette-copying, PC-to-PS/2 cables, over a local area network, or via a common host system.

16). Some PC/XT or AT models can have both an internal 5.25- and 3.5-inch drive installed, making diskette conversion relatively simple. The IBM Data Migration Facility uses the parallel printer cable to interconnect a PC with a PS/2. A sending program on the PC end transmits files over the cable to a receiving program on the PS/2. The PS/2 printer port can receive as well as send data, making this low-cost solution possible.

The Data Migration Facility is good for one-time or occasional file copying, where the PC and PS/2 can be placed near each other (less than 6 feet apart—the length of the printer cable). An ongoing need for file migration is better served by an external drive or a shared network server.

Since most PC and PS/2 models cannot accommodate both sizes of internal drives, an external drive can be added for file migration. An external 3.5-inch drive on a PC/XT/AT system, or a 5.25-inch drive on a Personal System/2 can be used for diskette-copying, provided the diskettes aren't copy-protected by the manufacturer. Many 5.25-inch copy-protected program diskettes can be run from a PS/2 external 5.25-inch drive.

In offices where both PCs and PS/2s share a local area network (LAN) or access a common mainframe system, another means of data migration is available. Files can first be uploaded from a PC to a shared file server or host library, and then downloaded to the Personal System/2.

The migration of DOS applications to OS/2's DOS Mode is a simple matter since no program conversion is needed, only file copying. Reprogramming for OS/2—especially to take advantage of OS/2's advanced features—requires programming skills. Very few commercial programs are distributed in their original source code format, so only the creator of an application can make the necessary coding changes and recompile the program

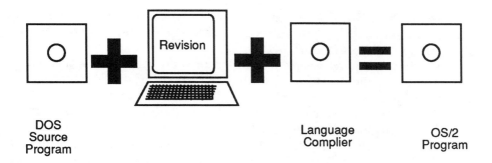

DOS
Source
Program

Language
Complier

OS/2
Program

Figure 1–17 Most existing DOS programs cannot be converted to OS/2 programs by an end user. The original source version must be revised and recompiled with an OS/2 language compiler. This requires the skills of a programmer.

(Figure 1–17). In some cases, existing licensees of a DOS program may be offered an upgrade to an OS/2 version at a reduced price. User-written programs must be upgraded with an OS/2 language compiler (IBM offers six to choose from) and the OS/2 Toolkit.

Just as today's DOS user occasionally has to modify or create a batch file (such as AUTOEXEC.BAT), the OS/2 user may also need to modify one of four system-controlling files from time to time. OS/2 creates two of these files in response to installation program options, but any further modifications or additions must be done with an editor or word processor. The OS/2 configuration file, CONFIG.SYS, like its DOS counterpart, contains several system control commands. The new STARTUP.CMD batch file initiates multiple OS/2 program sessions at boot time. The OS2INIT.CMD batch file runs as each OS/2 Mode session is started, establishing certain default conditions. Similarly, AUTOEXEC.BAT runs at the start of the DOS Mode session, starting a menu or application program just as it does under PC DOS.

Chapter 5, *OS/2 Conversion: Making the Big Switch*, describes the planning and preparation necessary for an OS/2 installation.

READY TO GO

The OS/2 installation itself is relatively straightforward. The installation diskette is booted, initiating a series of instructions and questions. User responses (such as answering *Yes* or *No* to the DOS Mode choice) establish several configuration file options. The installation program formats the fixed disk if necessary, creates directories, and copies files to them from the distribution diskettes (Figure 1–18).

The first installed program is called *Introducing OS/2,* a tutorial or short course on the operating system. Next, OS/2 and DOS programs are installed. Application installation is nothing more than copying program files to the disk, and adding their descriptive and file names to the Program Selector menu. Once installed, any OS/2 Mode application can be automatically loaded by the STARTUP.CMD batch file or user-selected from the Program Selector. DOS Mode programs can be loaded manually (from the command prompt) or from the DOS AUTOEXEC.BAT file.

OS/2 provides device support for many PC and PS/2 disks, printers, and displays. New input/output devices are installed on OS/2 1.0 by copying their device drivers to the fixed disk and referencing them in the configuration file. OS/2 1.1 aids the installation and use of new devices with a menu. Before running a program, its default printer output can be diverted to an alternate device. This lets OS/2 and its applications accommodate future device attachments without requiring operating system or program changes.

System maintenance has been improved through the use of new utility programs for capturing and printing system TRACE information. Each copy of OS/2 comes with a 90-day warranty covering fixes and replacements. Customer and dealer Service Coordinators have two IBM OS/2 hotlines (one voice, one data) to call for assistance.

Chapter 6, *OS/2 Installation: Up and Running,* details the installation of OS/2 and its applications.

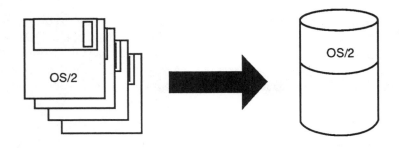

Figure 1–18 OS/2 Standard Edition 1.0 is distributed on four high-capacity diskettes: 1.44 Mb, 3.5-inch media for the PS/2, or 1.2 Mb, 5.25-inch diskettes for the IBM PC AT or XT/286 models. The installation program asks the user to answer a series of questions before setting system options and copying its files onto the fixed disk.

THE EXTENDED OS/2 VERSION

All of OS/2's features and functions are found in the Extended Edition. This version encompasses all of the OS/2 Standard Edition, plus two additional IBM-developed components (Figure 1–19). The Communications Manager collects, under one roof, communications software support previously available only by purchasing several DOS programs. Now the user can, through OS/2 sessions, simultaneously connect to a local area network (LAN), the company mainframe, and a remote data service system. In addition to the user interface, the Communications Manager provides a common application program interface for communications software.

The other new component of OS/2 Extended is the Database Manager. This brings the relational database system, popular on mainframe computers, to the Personal System/2. Using functions built into the operating system, the user can create, manipulate, and display information stored in many separate files. Database tables can be imported from spreadsheet or other file formats, or entered directly from the keyboard. Queries can be entered as Structured Query Language commands, or by using the interac-

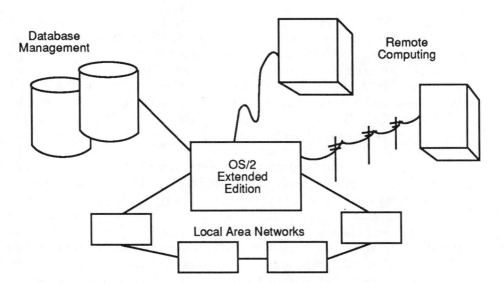

Figure 1–19 The OS/2 Extended Edition provides a full range of operating system function. In addition to the features of OS/2 Standard Edition, Extended includes support for large distributed databases, local area networks, and a variety of host communications systems.

tive Query Manager, or from programs using the application program interface. The Database Manager can handle complex inquiries, assembling information from data files stored on a local disk, a network server, and at a host system, transparently to the user.

Systems Application Architecture specifies the communications protocols and the database query language used in OS/2 Extended Edition.

Chapter 7, *OS/2's Extended Edition: Tying It All Together*, shows how this super-version of OS/2 brings mainframe function to a PC system.

PROGRAMMING?

Although this is not a book on programming, a general understanding of OS/2's programming interface will give you a better idea of its application potential. OS/2 gives the programmer many more options than DOS, and Systems Application Architecture improves program migration to other IBM systems. A consistent application program interface encourages programs that can do more and do it more easily. The ultimate beneficiary is the user.

Some OS/2 programmers will first convert their old DOS programs to OS/2 Family applications. In doing this, they will be using a subset of the full OS/2 function available, but the resulting applications can take advantage of either operating system. The reprogramming process can start by using one of IBM's six DOS-OS/2 language compilers (which are Family applications themselves) under DOS, with the final compilation and testing later under OS/2. The OS/2 Toolkit will aid the conversion process. Later, the same programs can be upgraded again to use the Presentation Manager, Dialog Manager, large data work area, and other OS/2 exclusives. The OS/2 Toolkit again assists the programmer by generating program code for difficult-to-program routines. Applications can be upgraded later to utilize the Database and Communications Managers of the Extended Edition.

Some operating system enhancements obviously require application reprogramming to be used. Other changes may be "free"—or nearly so. An example is the hardware base that OS/2 runs on. As new processors, bus architectures, and displays appear on the market, OS/2 will grow with them, adding new device drivers and an occasional new release to support them (Figure 1–20). In many cases, no program modification will be required to accommodate new hardware.

Chapter 8, *OS/2's Programming Interface: A Look Inside*, describes OS/2's API in terms of the user.

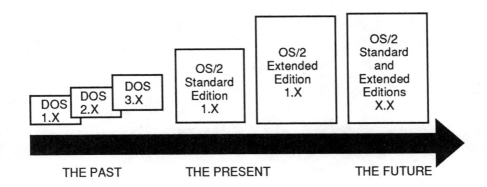

Figure 1–20 PC DOS has provided an upwardly compatible base for application program development for several years. OS/2 continues DOS's tradition of compatibility and growth with its Standard and Extended Editions, both of which include built-in DOS compatibility. IBM has announced its intention to provide future versions of all three operating systems.

ABOUT THE REST OF THIS BOOK

This book is written for users—specifically PC users who know a little about DOS. You do not have to be a hardware guru or a programmer to understand OS/2, but sometimes a little knowledge about a device driver or an API makes the big picture a little clearer. Throughout this book you will find simple block diagrams, memory maps, and screen samples designed to explain and simplify multi-tasking operating systems in general and OS/2 in particular.

As the OS/2 story unfolds, each chapter will follow a similar format. Before getting into the main part of each chapter, we will define a few terms and expressions. Then we will make comparisons between DOS and OS/2, describing DOS limitations, extensions, and OS/2 improvements. We will also highlight OS/2's compatibility with DOS and its potential for better future applications.

2

OS/2's Large Memory: Beyond 640 Kb

Perhaps the single most frequent complaint about PC DOS (especially in recent years) has been its 640 Kb memory limitation. This restriction originated with the 8088 processor used in the original IBM PC, and became, by default, an inherent limitation of DOS. When the 80286 processor came along, with 16 Mb addressing potential, a major DOS redesign would have been needed to take advantage of it. Instead, some creative DOS programmers invented ways to use more memory in spite of DOS's artificial limitation. In this chapter we will begin by looking at some of those methods that attempted to circumvent the 640 Kb ceiling (and are still with us today). Then we will see what there is about an Intel 8086 or 80286 that limits or expands memory, how OS/2 exploits 80286 features, and how this additional memory is used to advantage by the operating system and its programs.

DEFINING SOME TERMS

In this chapter we will use some terms to describe the interrelationship of three very important personal computer components: the microprocessor, operating system, and memory.

Address Register. A place in the processor where memory addresses are temporarily stored. The register size determines the largest memory address it can hold, and ultimately the maximum physical memory it can use.

Address Bus.   The set of bus wires (usually 16, 24, or 32) used to carry a memory address between the processor and ROM or RAM. In many systems, the address bus is "wider" (has more wires) than the data bus.

Address Space.   The range of memory addresses that are supported on a computer. Encompasses both read only memory (ROM) and random access memory (RAM). Limited by the processor address register, system bus, and the operating system. A system memory map diagrams its address space.

Data Bus.   The set of bus wires (typically 8, 16, or 32) used to carry information between components of a computer system. A "16-bit system" is a reference to its data bus. This is a big performance factor since it represents the processor-to-memory data pipeline.

Reserved Addresses.   A range of memory addresses reserved for internal computer functions such as the system BIOS and video buffers. On IBM Personal Computers and Personal System/2s, reserved addresses between 640 Kb and 1 Mb are off limits to the operating system and application programs.

User Memory.   RAM (random access memory) available for application programs. User memory is calculated by taking the total installed memory address space (up to 640 Kb on a DOS system, up to 16 Mb on an OS/2 system), and then subtracting memory used by the operating system and the 640 Kb— 1 Mb reserved address range.

Initial Program Load.   Operation that takes place when a diskette or fixed disk is booted at power-on. The boot record at the beginning of a disk is first read into memory, which then loads the operating system.

Expanded Memory.   A technique used with DOS to expand memory beyond 640 Kb. Bank-switching software uses a special memory card to assign banks of 16 Kb memory segments below 640 Kb. This memory can be used as a large work area or to hold multiple programs. Expanded memory is governed by the Expanded Memory Specification (EMS), jointly developed by Lotus®, Intel®, and Microsoft® Corporations.

Bank-Switching.   A technique that dynamically switches "banks," or segments of expanded memory, to addresses below 1 Mb where DOS (and the 8088/8086) can use them. Special software maps a low address range to each bank of expanded memory as needed, to simulate a large working memory or to provide multiple application support.

Extended Memory. Memory above 1 Mb on an 80286- or 80386-based system. A few special DOS programs, such as Virtual Disk (VDISK) and Disk Cache use it, but it is unavailable to most others. OS/2 uses extended memory for itself and its application programs, as an extension of the lower 0—640 Kb range.

Protect Mode. The 80286 microprocessor features this mode in addition to the default 8088/8086, or Real Mode. In Protect Mode an operating system can address up to 16 Mb of memory and perform multi-tasking. OS/2 uses the term "OS/2 Mode" to mean essentially the same thing. The term "protect" refers to the processor's ability to isolate or protect programs from each other.

Real Mode. The 80286's emulation of the 8088/8086 processors, included for DOS compatibility. OS/2's DOS Mode uses the 80286's Real Mode to create a compatible environment for DOS programs.

Overlays. Traditional programming technique used to accommodate large programs in a small memory space. Program is created in smaller sections, which are loaded into memory and sometimes overlaid to make room for other sections, under control of the application. By using overlays, a program can add function, but at the cost of performance.

Virtual Memory. Mainframe computer technique that supports programs that are larger than the total memory available. The operating system loads pages, or segments of each program into available memory as needed. OS/2's segmentation is a form of virtual memory used to manage multiple large programs in a limited real memory space.

Virtual Disk. Area of memory reserved for temporary storage. Program treats it as disk space, but reads and writes occur much faster. Used to improve performance for disk-dependent programs.

Segmentation. The 80286 supports memory segments of up to 64 Kb in size through special tables and registers. The operating system uses segmentation to manage large application programs and data work areas.

Descriptor Tables. OS/2 and the 80286 keep track of program segments through a Global Descriptor Table (GDT) and one Local Descriptor Table (LDT) per process. Each descriptor table contains a list of active (in memory) and inactive (on disk) program segments, their location, size, and status.

Dynamic Linking. Ability of operating system to load part of a program into memory and then load other segments if and when they are needed. Shortens initial program load time and saves memory by keeping little-used segments on disk.

Memory Overcommit. Program larger than all of available memory (even larger than 16 Mb) can use dynamic linking to manage its segments. Inactive data segments are swapped back to disk to make room for others. Performance improves as more memory is added.

Tasks. Concurrent program elements. Multiple tasks can run within a single application, utilizing available resources (memory, disk, printer, etc.) in parallel rather than in a sequential fashion.

Protection Rings. The 80286 enforces four security levels for the operating system and its programs, keeping applications from interfering with system software and each other.

Kernel. The "core" or nucleus of an operating system, loaded at IPL and kept memory-resident.

Command Processor. The user-interface portion of an operating system, loaded by the kernel following IPL. Includes some built-in commands and retrieves other (external) commands and programs on demand.

Cache Memory. Memory used to improve fixed disk performance. Frequently used segments are temporarily stored in memory so that subsequent accesses take place much faster.

FASTOPEN. DOS 3.3 command used to set aside memory for a disk directory. Subsequent accesses to a disk file take place faster once it is in the directory.

Well-Behaved. DOS Application program written to use published operating system interfaces. Well-behaved programs conform to IBM's "official" application program interface, making them easier to migrate to a new PC or operating system release. Ill-behaved programs are often incompatible with hardware or software design changes.

Time-Dependent. Program that depends on system clock, such as real-time (process control) or communications applications. Such programs usually cannot be suspended by the operating system, even briefly, which occurs in the OS/2 DOS Mode.

ABIOS. Advanced Basic Input Output System located in Personal System/ 2 ROM, used to provide an additional hardware/software interface for multitasking control of the Personal System/2's unique hardware and Micro Channel Bus.

THE 8088 YEARS

You really cannot blame DOS's limitations on either hardware or software alone. The microprocessor and the operating system are so interdependent and their evolutions so entwined, that they sometimes appear to be the same. The original IBM Personal Computer DOS version 1.0 had its origins in a small software company known as Seattle Computer Products. SCP-DOS/ 86™, the first operating system created to exploit the new Intel 8086 microprocessor, was later acquired by the Microsoft Corporation. Microsoft enhanced the product and then licensed it to IBM and other PC manufacturers as PC DOS or MS DOS®.

A WIDER DATA PATH

IBM chose the 8088 for its first PC, but *internally* the 8086 and 8088 are nearly identical—both run the same software and have an internal 16-bit data path, faster than previous 8-bit processors. The difference lies in their *external* data paths—the number of parallel lines (or wires) moving data into and out of the processor. The 8086 has a 16-bit external path, but the 8088's is 8 bits wide. This means that other components on an 8088 PC, such as its memory, must also be 8-bit compatible (Figure 2–1). The first IBM PC was designed around 8-bit components, which were plentiful in 1980—another factor in the selection of the 8088. (By comparison, today's PS/2 Models 25 and 30 use a 16-bit 8086 processor with 16-bit memory. With the help of a faster clock, they more than double the performance of the original PC.)

The 16-Bit Bus

A processor's basic architecture—8-, 16-, or 32-bit—has a lot to do with its speed and how much memory it can handle. A computer's overall performance, or *throughput*, is based on many factors. One is how much information can be processed at any point in time (data path) and another is how many

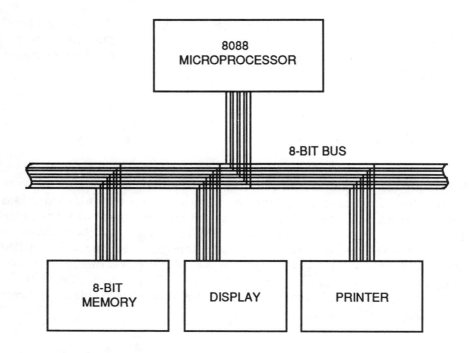

Figure 2–1   The PC's 8088 microprocessor, while it performed 16-bit operations inter-nally, supported an external data path that was 8 bits wide.

instructions can be executed during a time period (clock speed). Or, you could say that the total amount of cargo you can move between two cities in a 24-hour periods depends on the size of your truck and how fast you drive it.

Computers deal in "bits," combinations of ones and zeros that, when put together, translate into numbers, letters, and memory addresses. Eight bits make a "byte," which can be a single character. For example, the letter "A" in binary is 0 1 0 0 0 0 0 1. You could send those bits along a single wire, shown in Figure 2-2A as moving from right to left. The eight serial bits arrive at their destination one at a time, single file. But if eight *parallel* wires were used instead, a full 8-bit character could be transmitted in the same time that a single bit took before. So, the capacity of a parallel cable is approximately eight times that of a serial cable. Figure 2–2B shows a group of characters moving down a parallel cable, from right to left. The letter "A" is the first to arrive, then "B," and so on. Thus, you begin to see the advantage of a group of parallel wires, or bus. Double the number of wires and you will increase the computer's throughput, although the speed will not double. That's because

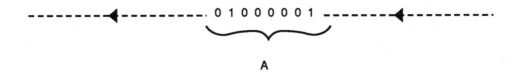

A

Figure 2–2A   A single PC character (in this example, the letter "A") is represented as 8 "on or off" bits sent over a single wire.

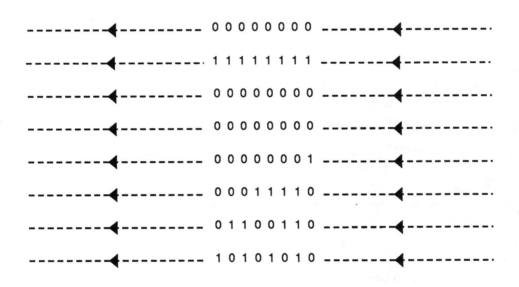

A B C D E F G H

Figure 2–2B   The same 8-bit letter "A" can also be sent simultaneously over 8 parallel wires. This permits a series of eight characters to be transmitted in the same time as in the single-character, single-wire example.

the data bus is not the only design attribute affecting performance. Other factors, such as the instruction execution rate, also contribute to overall performance.

Once you select an 8-, 16-, or 32-bit processor for your computer design, you should carry its 8-, 16-, or 32-bit bus throughout the computer. This affects the complexity of the surrounding circuitry, called "glue" by computer engineers. You will also want to use memory, displays, and other devices that take advantage of the system bus capacity. A higher capacity bus design boosts performance but raises costs (Figure 2–3).

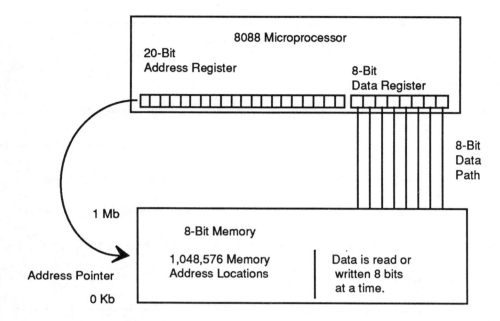

Figure 2–3   The 8088's 20-bit address register determines the highest memory address it can hold—1 Mb. Its 8-bit data register determines how much information can move between the processor and memory in a unit of time.

The Micro Channel bus on the IBM Personal System/2 Models 50, 60, and 80 is getting a lot of attention because of its potential for application performance. Actually, the bus is really made up of four types of signals: electrical power, control and timing signals, addresses, and data. The original PC's *data bus*, as we've just seen, was 8 bits wide, to match the external capacity of the 8088. 8086 machines (like the Personal System/2 Model 30) and 80286 systems (the PC AT and Personal System/2 Models 50 and 60) have a 16-bit bus. The Model 80, with its 32-bit 80386 processor, has a Micro Channel bus that is 32 bits wide and it supports 32-bit memory.

BREAKING THE 64KB MEMORY BARRIER

The Address Register and Address Bus

The size of a processor's address register determines the largest memory address it can hold, and thus the maximum amount of memory it can directly address. This register is a place in the processor where bits are temporarily stored for the purpose of identifying a unique memory location. Eight bits in binary arithmetic can represent any memory address from 0 to 255, or 256 unique memory locations (2 to the power of 8), which is obviously much too small (0.25 Kb) to do anything useful. Double the number of bits (2 to the power of 16) and you can address 256 x 256, or 65,536 locations.

Overlays

Most early 8-bit processors (like the Intel 8080 and Zilog Z-80) had an 8-bit data bus with a 16-bit address register, to support 65,536 bytes, or 64 Kb (1 Kb = 1024 bytes) of memory. In the 1970s, 64 Kb was considered more than enough for a small computer. The few programs that needed more memory used *overlays* to get around the 64 Kb limit. The main portion of a program remains in memory, and loads program subroutines from diskette as required. Each time a new subroutine is used, it overlays the previous one, thus allowing a large program to run when insufficient memory is available. The main drawback of an overlay scheme is the impact on performance from frequent disk access. Figure 2–4 illustrates memory overlays.

The PC: A Megabyte Machine

The 8088 processor exhibits some of the characteristics of 8-, 16-, and 20-bit designs. It uses 16 bits internally to perform arithmetic and execute instructions, and has an 8-bit external data path to communicate with the outside world. But even 16 bits, as we have seen, addresses only 64 Kb, and "back" in 1981, application programmers were beginning to clamor for more space.

So, Intel made the 8088's address register 20 bits long in order to support more memory. The increase from 16 to 20 bits effectively multiplied the 64 Kb upper limit times 16, to address 1,048,576 bytes of memory, or 1 Mb. Each 8088 memory address is made up of two portions: a 4-bit *segment* and a 16-bit *offset*. The segment is the address of the beginning of a 64 Kb memory segment. The offset addresses memory within the segment. Altogether, the composite 20-bit address pinpoints information—program instructions or data—stored anywhere in the PC's potential one megabyte of memory. Most PC DOS programs are designed around 64 Kb program and data segments to minimize unnecessary segment-switching.

Program code and data are usually kept in separate segments, but the 8088 does not enforce that rule. For example, a program can treat another program segment as data, and modify its instructions "on the fly." Since the 8088 was not designed for multi-tasking, inter-segment protection is not provided. Each segment occupies a fixed place in memory until the program is finished and another program is loaded in place of it, or the program overlays a portion of itself. No segment moving is performed by DOS.

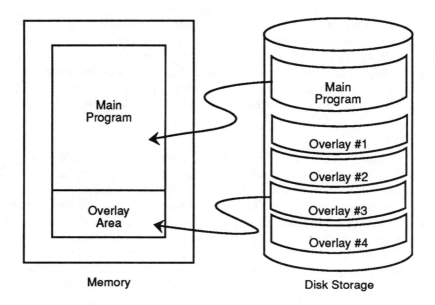

Figure 2–4 Some PC DOS programs use memory overlays to save space. The main program segment stays resident, copying additional segments into memory as needed. Overlays allow large programs to run in limited memory, but at a cost in performance.

SLICING UP THE MEMORY PIE

Reserved Memory

With a full megabyte of memory to work with, the PC's designers wisely decided to put some of it away in the "bank"—and reserved a high-end range of addresses between 640 Kb to 1 Mb (Figure 2–5) for internal computer system functions.

This reserved range includes read only memory (ROM) programs that every PC needs for internal operations. The Basic Input Output System (BIOS) program manages the flow of information inside the computer, reading the keyboard, controlling the display, handling interrupts, etc. BIOS provides a stable interface between the hardware and the operating system (either DOS or OS/2). ROM also contains the machine's power-on self test (POST) program, which tests internal components each time it is turned on. Part of the BASIC language interpreter is also stored in ROM. Other reserved memory addresses are used for special RAM, primarily the display buffers, where each screen image is built. The 640 Kb—1 Mb reserved memory

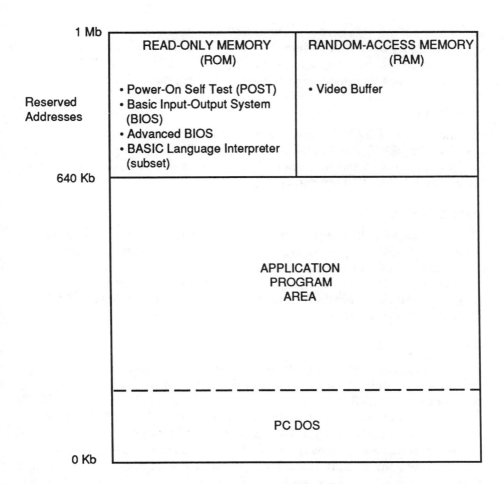

Figure 2–5 Every IBM PC has a reserved memory address range between 640 Kb and 1 Mb. This space is used by read only memory programs such as BIOS, POST, and BASIC, and as a buffer for the display image.

address range is preserved on every IBM Personal Computer and Personal System/2, and is unavailable to the operating system or its application programs.

All addresses below 640 Kb are used by RAM—mostly for the operating system and its programs. Early PC models offered memory increments from 16 to 64 Kb. Later, as demand increased, the average PC grew from 64 to 128 to 256 to 512 Kb of RAM. A portion of RAM consists of memory chips on the computer's main system board. This amount (64, 256, 512 Kb, etc.) depends on the PC model. Additional memory can be installed on adapter cards, using one or more of the PC's card slots, until 640 Kb is reached. The POST program counts memory as it tests it, incrementing the total on the upper-left corner of the screen as each segment is finished. The BIOS on an 8088 or 8086 machine ignores any installed memory that totals more than 640 Kb.

Low-Memory

Around 1.5 Kb of RAM (in low memory, beginning at memory address 0) is used by BIOS, DOS, and BASIC as a work area. The *user area*—all of memory on the system board and on memory adapter cards, up to 640 Kb—is available for use by DOS and its programs.

User Memory

PC DOS boots itself into memory first and leaves the rest for application programs. The kernel, or nucleus, loads first, then the command processor. Next DOS looks for a batch file named AUTOEXEC.BAT, or waits for the next command from the user. That usually loads the first program. Some "smart" programs will check available memory when they begin to load and tell you if there isn't enough to continue.

Memory Types

Most PC memory is volatile RAM; it is useful as long as power is on. When the machine is turned off memory is erased. Static RAM, like ROM, keeps its contents current while the computer is turned off. The PC Convertible, IBM's laptop, uses Complimentary Metal Oxide Semiconductor (CMOS) memory, which is a form of static RAM. CMOS is sustained by a battery when normal AC power is turned off. This is nice if a thunderstorm knocks power out—you will not lose your data. It also allows you to turn your computer off without first saving the file you are working on. When you turn it back on later, you can pick up where you left off, without reloading the program or data.

MAKING THE BEST OF 640 KB

Early PC Programs

When the PC was unveiled in August 1981, a dozen or so of the then-popular programs like VisiCalc™, EasyWriter™, and Peachtree™ Accounting had already been converted from other systems to run under DOS. That is because IBM had been working with application developers, using prototype PC hardware and pre-release copies of DOS 1.0 and its language compilers. Most of the "first wave" of converted programs did not take advantage of more than 64 Kb of memory, since they were written on 8-bit systems and would have required significant changes to use more memory. The "64 Kb mentality" of the 1970s continued for awhile; 64 Kb machines and 64 Kb programs continued to sell, and users wondered if the 640 Kb limit would ever be challenged.

Over the next two or three years, competition among developers for the lucrative PC software market caused programs to grow in function, usability, appearance—and size. Program menus were added to guide the user. On-line help libraries lessened the need for large reference manuals. Data entry screens took on a "fill in the blanks" format, with immediate checking of entered information. "Memory is cheap," a phrase heard among some PC programmers, became a self-fulfilling prophecy as programs grew in size, demand for memory increased, and memory adapter cards dropped in price.

The Virtual Disk

Some PCs had memory capacity that was not fully used by DOS and its programs. DOS's Virtual Disk program (VDISK) put spare memory to work improving program performance. It did that by assigning a portion of memory as a virtual disk drive. What appears to the operating system as a second or third diskette drive (even down to its B: or C: label), is actually memory masquerading as a disk. A program can read and write data files to the virtual disk at very high memory-to-memory speeds (Figure 2–6).

VDISK is easy to use and gives an immediate performance boost to most programs. The danger of VDISK is its *volatility*: if you turn power off accidentally, all of memory is lost, including the contents of your virtual disk. If your active spreadsheet or database is in a virtual disk when a power loss occurs, you have to start all over. On an 8088 or 8086 system, the virtual disk is always somewhere below 640 Kb. On an 80286 machine it can use extended memory above 1 Mb.

In spite of larger memory systems, program overlays are still used in many PC applications. Some use overlays only when they have to, loading just enough program to get started, setting aside the rest as a program subroutine area. Then they load subroutines as needed. So, the program might start with a menu; selecting F2 (load data) would invoke one subroutine, F3 (Clear Memory) another, and F1 (Help) yet another. If sufficient memory is available, the program can keep all subroutines resident, instantly ready at the touch of a key—for maximum performance.

Many programmers would rather not use program overlays because they complicate program development, and the periodic disk activity reduces performance. On the other hand, the application can appeal to a wider range of users. Someone with a 256 Kb PC might purchase an overlay program to

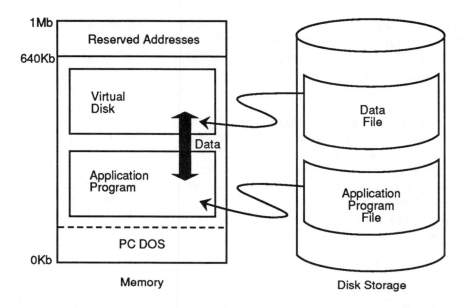

Figure 2–6   A virtual disk is a block of memory used as a substitute for disk storage. Program data access from a virtual disk is much faster than a real disk.

get features and function otherwise found only in much larger programs. If additional memory is added later, the program uses it and performance improves. A 512 or 640 Kb PC might run the same program at top speed, without overlays.

Expanded Memory

In spite of the 640 Kb limitation imposed by the 8088 and DOS, computer engineers sought ways to get around it. Special memory cards like AST's® RamPage™, Intel's Above Board™, and IBM's Expanded Memory Adapter (XMA) provide a partial solution. These cards contain *expanded* (not extended) *memory* with unassigned addresses. Special software, using circuitry on the card, maps, or *bank-switches* 16 Kb segments of expanded memory to real addresses below 1 Mb (Figure 2–7). A program or data segment can remain in expanded memory, while DOS reads or writes to it through the reusable register bank in low memory. No physical copying of segments from expanded to low memory is necessary, since the address-switching scheme lets a program use expanded memory directly. This special software interface has been developed by three PC software leaders: Lotus Corp., Intel, and Microsoft as the Expanded Memory Specification (EMS). EMS version 3.2 defines four 16 Kb memory registers with addresses ranging from 816 to 880 Kb. Up to 8 Mb of expanded memory is supported. The newer EMS version 4.0, which requires a new memory card design, supports up to 32 Mb.

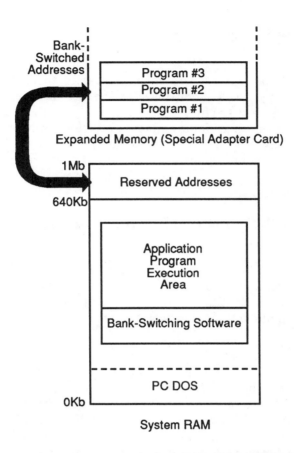

Figure 2–7 Expanded memory cards (such as IBM's XMA) support large memory work areas or multiple DOS programs. A bank of under-1 Mb addresses (which DOS recognizes) is switched, or mapped, to banks of expanded memory as needed.

Bank-switching lets the IBM 3270 Workstation Program , with the IBM Expanded Memory Adapter (XMA) card, support multiple host and PC DOS "sessions" in memory. This is a form of multi-application support that lets several DOS programs run together. The XMA card does not support program sizes of more than 512 Kb, however. We will have more to say about the 3270 Workstation Program/XMA solution in the next chapter.

Since bank-switching does not rely on the 80286's extended memory addressing, cards like the XMA can be built for 8088 and 8086 machines too. IBM offers Expanded Memory Adapters for most of its PC and Personal System/2 models. The PS/2 Models 50 and 60 use the 2 Mb Expanded Memory Adapter/A, a card redesigned for the Micro Channel bus form factor. No XMA card is required for the Model 80; the 3270 Workstation Program instead uses the 80386's virtual 8086 partitioning for its multiple program support.

THE 80286 MAKES ITS DEBUT

Although Intel Corp. makes several microprocessors, the 80286 has had the most impact on the young PC industry since the introduction of the 8088. Its designers looked far into the future, building in features that accommodated multi-user software such as Xenix and made possible the development of OS/2. While it has taken years to fully exploit the power of the 80286, the processor established a new hardware standard for future PC applications.

THE 80286: SOMETHING OLD, SOMETHING NEW

In this section we will review some of the built-in features of the 80286 that make extended memory possible. You will recognize some of these features as OS/2 features; the operating system is just taking advantage of what is already there, adding a few touches of its own.

The IBM PC AT

The IBM Personal Computer AT® was the first PC to use the Intel 80286 processor, with a 16-bit data bus and a 24-bit address register to support it. This gave the AT and subsequent 80286- and 80386-based machines the ability to use up to 16 Mb of memory. Just as the 8088's 20-bit address register supports 16 times as much memory as a 16-bit processor (1 Mb vs. 64 Kb), the 80286's 24-bit addressing (another 4-bit increment) supports 16 Mb. Until OS/2, however, very little software took advantage of the 80286's *extended memory*.

Extended Memory Support

The 80286's extended memory supports addressing between 0 and 16 Mb (or whatever physical amount up to 16 Mb is installed). Like the 8088, the programmer still must deal with memory in 64 Kb segments. PC DOS does not recognize extended memory, but one of its commands (VDISK) and some of its programs (such as the PS/2 Disk Cache program) do. They treat extended memory much like very fast disk storage: it is a good place to store programs and data, but programs must be loaded from extended memory into low memory to be executed. A DOS program may temporarily reside above 1 Mb, but normally cannot be run there. Two operating systems that manage both low *and* extended memory are OS/2 and PC Xenix. More about Xenix in Chapter 3.

When an 80286-based system is IPLed, the power-on self test (POST) finds and tests all addressable memory, first on the system board and then on memory cards. Memory addresses between 0 and 640 Kb are assigned first. The system reserved addresses between 640 Kb to 1 Mb are skipped. Then, addresses between 1 Mb and the maximum installed memory are assigned (Figure 2–8). Expanded memory type cards, described earlier, are not recognized by POST. They require special bank-switching software to be used by DOS programs, but OS/2 treats them as extended memory.

Real Mode

The 80286's natural, or default, condition is called Real Mode, and it is used by PC DOS and Operating System/2's DOS Mode. In Real Mode, the 80286

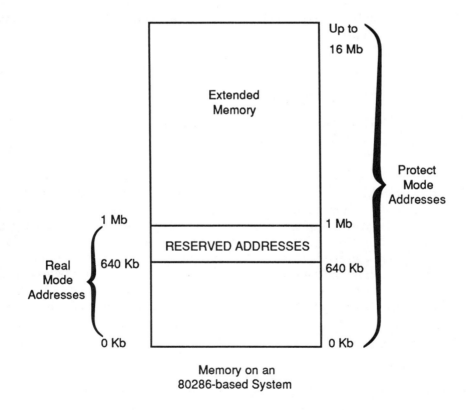

Memory on an
80286-based System

Figure 2–8   When an 80286 processor is in Real Mode, it acts like an 8086 or 8088, perfect for DOS but limited to 640 Kb memory addressing. The same processor in Protect Mode additionally recognizes addresses between 1 Mb and 16 Mb.

acts just like an 8086 or 8088 processor, using a subset of its full instruction set, and limiting memory addressing to 1 Mb. This mode was included for compatibility, allowing DOS and its application software to run in familiar surroundings. DOS programs will run faster on 80286 machines, but that is primarily due to their faster clock speeds. When DOS and its programs are running on an 80286 machine, they "think" the processor is an 8088 or 8086. Since DOS was not built to take advantage of the 80286's exclusive Protect Mode, it never switches it on.

Real Mode Enhancements

While 80286 Real Mode was designed for 8088/86 compatibility, a few additional features were added for performance. The 80286 Extended Instruction Set includes a few new commands that improve register usage. The processor includes new circuitry to speed up multiplications. It also has four dedicated units: Bus, Instruction, Execution, and Address Units, twice that of the 8086/88 (which has only Bus and Execution), expanding its own internal "multi-processing."

80286 LARGE MEMORY MANAGEMENT

Protect Mode

In order to address extended memory directly, the 80286 must first be switched to its Protect Mode. Both Xenix and Operating System/2 support Protect Mode, which carries with it the features needed to handle large programs and multi-tasking. Programs do not address memory directly as on the 8088, they use segment tables, which the operating system maintains. The segment register, instead of pointing to an actual memory address (as it does on an 8088 or in 80286 Real Mode), points to an entry in a table. 80286 tables isolate programs from each other, ensuring that a program cannot use a segment it does not own. This feature becomes especially important when multi-processing takes place.

Segments

The 80286, like the 8088, manages all of memory in segments of up to 64 Kb in size, but has additional built-in instructions, registers, and tables to improve efficiency and performance. All segments begin as disk files, and eventually end up in memory—although not always at the same time. Some segments are loaded initially, while others may be loaded and "linked" by the operating system later. Segments can also be shared between programs, not just using the same disk copy, but also sharing the same "live" segment in memory. When designing a family of related programs, segment-sharing can reduce overall disk and memory requirements.

There are two basic types of 80286 segments: program and data. An executing program segment cannot modify another program segment, even one of its own segments, so self-modifying programs are prohibited. A program can, of course, modify data in its work area, which is also managed as segments. A program can exclusively own its data segments, or share them with other programs.

Virtual Memory

The 80286 supports a memory-management scheme that is popular on large mainframe systems—virtual memory. A virtual program may be too large to fit entirely into real memory, or has been "squeezed out" by other programs. Or, it may have been designed so that only its key, performance-critical segments are loaded into memory, and the rest are kept on disk. By segmenting programs, the operating system can manage memory more efficiently. The first portion of a program is loaded and begins to run. Each time it attempts to read a segment that is not in memory, the operating system loads it. This goes on until all available memory is full of segments. As time goes on, new segments begin to overlay inactive ones so that memory always contains a set of relatively active segments (Figure 2–9). On systems with insufficient memory or several concurrent applications, frequent segment-loading can cause system performance to drop off. Installing additional memory on such a system will improve performance until all segments are resident.

Dynamic Linking

OS/2 uses 80286 segmentation to support a form of virtual memory called "dynamic linking." Some segments can be stored in a file that is separate from the main ".EXE" program file. If and when one of these segments is needed, it is loaded and linked to the program. Dynamically linked segments are not tied to a specific program, so they can be used by more than one. Since they are maintained in separate files (identified with a ".DLL" filename extension), dynamic linked segments can be replaced or upgraded without the need to modify or recompile the main program. As with any virtual memory scheme, dynamic linking should be used only when appropriate. Programs should be structured so that disk-resident portions are confined to less critical or infrequent sections like help text libraries, error handling, or file backup routines.

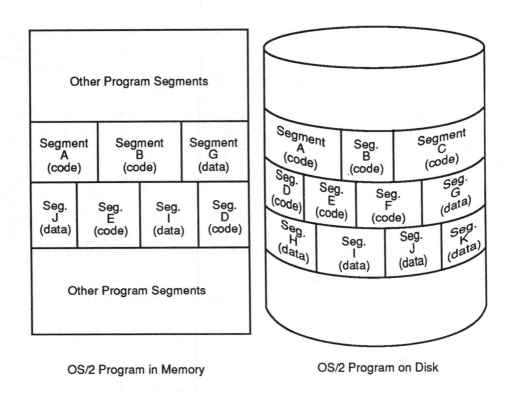

OS/2 Program in Memory   OS/2 Program on Disk

Figure 2–9 An OS/2 program may not be able to reside entirely in memory at once, especially if there are several programs running. OS/2 swaps and overlays both program and data segments to manage a limited memory space.

Memory Overcommit

Segmentation permits very large programs—even over 16 Mb—to be written and stored on disk. Like mainframe virtual programs, all of the segments can never fit entirely in memory at the same time, but OS/2 can still run the entire program, a segment at a time, making use of the memory available. Virtual addressing can handle segmented programs as large as 1 gigabyte, or 1024 Mb, much more than any existing disk drive can hold!

The Swap File

What does OS/2 do with segments that are overlayed? As new program and dynamic linked segments are loaded, old segments are either discarded or written to a temporary disk file named SWAPPER.DAT. This file, which is stored in the fixed disk's root directory, grows and shrinks in size as programs are started or stopped and data files are loaded, modified, and saved. You can observe the size of SWAPPER.DAT by selecting OS/2 Command Prompt and entering DIR SWAPPER.DAT. This file can sometimes become several hundred thousand bytes large, an indication that additional memory may be needed to improve performance.

Tasks

The 80286 manages tables of related program segments by tasks. A task can be a single application program, sometimes called a process, or a section of a program. Parallel processing can be achieved by starting multiple tasks at the same time, within a program. Tasks, processes, and threads will be described in the next chapter.

Descriptor Tables

The 80286 supports extended memory with a collection of built-in registers and tables. Segments are tracked in descriptor tables, where each entry describes one segment, containing its address, size, and access rights.

Each program has a Local Descriptor Table, (LDT). All of its segments, in memory and on disk, are recorded and tracked here. Each entry in the table contains a segment address, length, type (code, data, etc.), privilege level, and current location. In a multi-application environment, there are multiple LDTs. Shared program segments are cross-referenced in multiple LDTs. The operating system has its own table, called the Global Descriptor Table, (GDT), referencing all of the segments it uses. No application program can directly access another program's LDT, the GDT, or any other part of the operating system. Each table can hold up to 8,192 entries. If a program used the LDT and GDT to address 2 times 8,192 times 64 Kb per segment, a total of 1 billion bytes (1 gigabyte) of memory could be managed—theoretically.

Registers

The 80286 has two task registers: a GDT Register pointing to the location of the GDT, and an LDT Register pointing to the current task's LDT. Every time OS/2 changes tasks, the LDT register is changed to point to the new LDT. When a Real Mode (DOS) program is running, the segment register points to a real 64 Kb memory segment, somewhere between 0 and 640 Kb, just as it does when DOS is running alone. Whenever an OS/2 task resumes execution, the task register again points to its LDT, and a specific LDT program segment is resumed where it left off.

Physical Memory Limits

The original PC AT could support no more than 3 Mb (using IBM memory cards). The Personal System/2 Models 50 and 60 each come with 1 Mb on the system board. The Model 50 (Figure 2–10) can grow to 7 Mb (with the addition of three 2 Mb cards) and the Model 60 (Figure 2–11) to 15 Mb (with seven 2 Mb cards), but those limits are due to the physical packaging of the memory cards, not because of any 80286 limitation. With denser memory cards, 16 Mb could be used in any 80286/386-based OS/2 system. The Model 80, with 2 Mb on the system board and seven card slots, can be a full 16 Mb machine (Figure 2–12).

Fixed Disk Requirements

All of the IBM OS/2 systems, from the XT/286 to the PS/2 Model 80, have at least the minimum 20 Mb fixed disk that OS/2 requires. Depending on the

Figure 2–10 The desktop Personal System/2 Model 50, shown here, makes a good entry-level OS/2 system. OS/2 requires a mimimum memory of 2 Mb (when a DOS Mode session is run) and a 20 Mb fixed disk.

number and size of application programs and their data files, the disk
requirement could be much more. For that reason, the Model 50's 20 Mb disk
may be insufficient for some OS/2 installations. The Model 60 offers 44 or 70
Mb disks as standard, and a second drive of 44 to 115 Mb can be added. On
a Model 80, up to two 314 Mb drives can be installed.

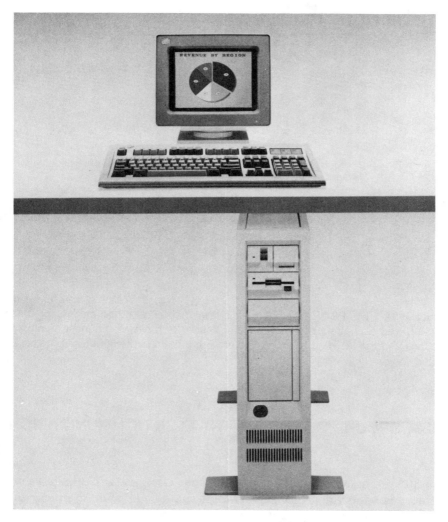

Figure 2–11   The floor-standing PS/2 Model 60, IBM's largest 80286-based system,
supports OS/2 with up to 15 Mb of memory and 185 Mb of fixed disk storage.

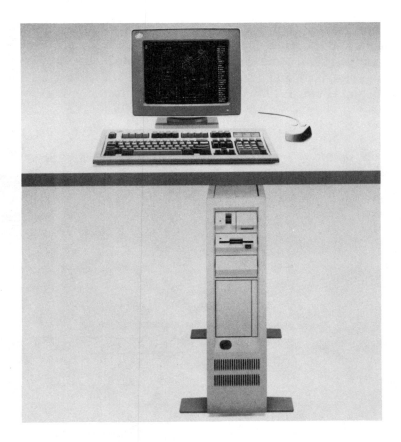

Figure 2–12   The PS/2 Model 80, here shown with an attached mouse, is IBM's first 80286-based computer. The floor-standing Model 80 provides the most memory, storage, and performance for Operating System/2. OS/2 drives the 80286 in its native 80286 Protect Mode.

80286 SECURITY AND TASK-TO-TASK COMMUNICATION

The 80286 has other built-in features that OS/2 uses. We have seen how memory is subdivided into segments; it can also be shared among several programs, and within a program, multiple tasks. The processor provides some important inter-task isolation or protection, which is why OS/2 Mode is also called Protect Mode. Protect Mode's descriptor tables effectively build a wall around each program, preventing it from accidentally (or intentionally) reading or writing into memory used by another program. In a multi-application environment it is very important to prevent a program from interfering with others or bringing down the entire system.

IOPL

The 80286 includes its own built-in security system, a series of rings, or layers, that further protect programs and operating systems from each other. Rings range from level 0 (most protected; the OS/2 kernel) to level 3 (application programs). Ring 2 is the Input Output Privileged Level (IOPL), which provides a "fast-path" to computer hardware, bypassing much of the operating system overhead. Each segment is assigned a ring level and normally cannot address a segment with a lower ring level (i.e., higher security).

Call Gates

There is, however, a proper way for a task to access another one in a lower ring. For example, OS/2 device drivers, which run in ring 2, need to be accessed by most application programs running in ring 3. This is done through an entry in the operating system's GDT. This entry is called a Gate, and it is used to pass a program CALL to a task that would be otherwise out of bounds. This provides a way for OS/2 to filter requests and pass them to a special system routine without giving an application direct control of a protected function.

Protect Mode Interrupts

The 8088/86 processors use interrupts for sending and receiving signals to and from various peripheral devices. Some interrupts, such as keystrokes, must be handled immediately. 8088 and 80286 Real Mode programs have to handle hardware interrupts themselves. Sometimes, while DOS is busy handling an interrupt, a second one arrives and is missed completely. This causes DOS to come to a complete stop—a system hang-up due to a "lost interrupt." The 80286 Protect Mode assists the operating system by translating interrupts to call gates through a table called the Interrupt Descriptor Table (IDT). The 80286 handles simultaneous interrupts through its Double Fault Exception, rather than simply shutting down. If the rare occurrence of a third interrupt happens while the Double Fault condition is being handled, OS/2 will then shutdown. This should significantly reduce the number and frequency of system "hangs."

PC DOS AND 80286 EXTENDED MEMORY .

The 1984 introduction of 80286-based PCs came at a time when OS/2 was still far off and DOS 3.0 offered little opportunity to exploit the 286's features. So some PC AT programmers invented a few "tricks" to get DOS (which remained a 640 Kb-limited operating system) to use 80286 extended memory in the 1 Mb—16 Mb range. Since DOS programs cannot address above 640 Kb, you have to somehow move a program and its data down below 640 Kb where DOS can get at it—or "trick" it with some programming magic. To be precise, normal DOS applications are limited to 640 Kb, but DOS addressing in the reserved range of 640 Kb—1 Mb is still possible.

Help from BIOS

One way to overcome DOS's addressing limitation on an 80286 machine is to store programs and data in extended memory and then copy them into low memory for execution. The PC AT's BIOS has a function that does precisely this, called a *transfer service*. Since memory-to-memory transfers are much faster than disk-to-memory loading, this kind of overlay technique can partially overcome the memory restriction without harming performance. IBM's Virtual Disk (VDISK) program uses this BIOS feature when running on a PC AT. On an 8088 machine VDISK reserves a portion of low memory as a simulated diskette drive, which you can read or write to just like the real thing, only much faster. When running on an 80286 computer, VDISK can use extended memory above 1 Mb, using the BIOS transfer routine to "page" segments into low memory as needed (Figure 2–13).

The Personal System/2 Disk Cache program, shipped with every Model 50, 60, and 80 on the PS/2 Reference Diskette, also uses extended memory. Since each of these machines comes with at least 1 Mb of memory, and PC DOS only uses 640 Kb, a minimum of 360 Kb is available for VDISK or disk caching. On a system with heavy file activity, the Disk Cache program can improve performance by using extended, otherwise unused memory as a disk buffer and a smaller amount of user memory for itself.

The PS/2 models 50, 60, and 80 also include a read only memory program called Advanced BIOS, or ABIOS, which provides the necessary software/hardware interface between OS/2 and the Micro Channel-based PS/2 hardware. The PS/2 architecture was designed with multi-tasking in mind. Multi-tasking will be discussed in more detail in the next chapter, but for now we will just call it a way to divide up the various resources used by a program—display, printer, calculations, etc.—into separate tasks that may be run concurrently. So, while you are typing a letter, a spell-checking task can be looking up each word and highlighting the ones that are misspelled. And another task can be printing the last letter you wrote.

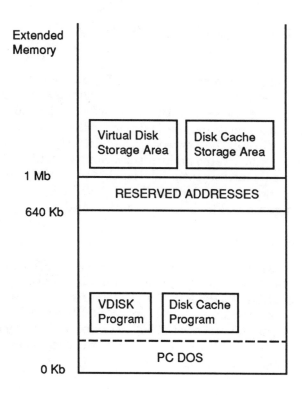

Figure 2–13 Some PC DOS programs use the 80286's 16 Mb extended memory despite DOS's inherent 640 Kb limitation. Here, the DOS Virtual Disk (VDISK) and PS/2 Disk Cache (IBMCACHE) programs have been loaded into low memory. Both use memory above 1 Mb as a data storage area, reducing disk activity to improve performance.

UNIX AND XENIX SYSTEMS ON THE 80286

On the day of its PC AT announcement in 1984, IBM unveiled PC Xenix with little fanfare. Yet this operating system, based on the original Unix® developed by AT&T® Bell Labs, resembles OS/2 more than DOS in many ways. It supports up to 16 Mb memory addressing, can run multiple applications at the same time, and even support multiple users—one at the PC AT and the others connected via "dumb" computer terminals. We will have more to say about Xenix at the end of the following chapter.

THE 80286 AND OPERATING SYSTEM/2

We have just seen the kind of potential the 80286 microprocessor offers for applications, and some ways PC DOS programmers have exploited its features. Now let's see how Operating System/2 handles 16 megabytes and how this additional capacity gets passed along to the user in the form of better applications. We will start by comparing the relatively simple approach of PC DOS with OS/2's sophisticated architecture. Next we will address the issue of performance, and its fundamental relationship to memory and disk storage. Then we will get down to the bottom line: OS/2's high-function, easy-to-use application programs and their large capacity for data.

80386 Machines

Up to now our focus has been on the 80286 processor. OS/2 also runs on 80386-based computers, such as the Personal System/2 Model 80. Since the 80386 has both a compatible "80286 Mode" and a "Real (8086) Mode," OS/2 and PC DOS run on a Model 80 just as they do on a Model 50 or 60, just faster. Unless stated otherwise, all functions of the 80286 can be assumed of the 80386, too. In the next chapter we will look into some of the exclusives of the 386 that promote multi-application support.

PC DOS'S MEMORY MANAGEMENT

DOS: A Collection of Files

PC DOS, like OS/2 and all other operating systems, "boots," or loads itself from disk into memory, when the computer is first turned on, and at least part of DOS is always present in memory. The remaining memory is where application programs are run, and their data is loaded or entered, calculated, sorted (and otherwise manipulated), before being printed or saved to disk.

Starting Up DOS

Whether you boot from a system diskette or a fixed disk, the initial program load (IPL) program in ROM BIOS reads the first track and then loads two "hidden" files named IBMBIO.COM and IBMDOS.COM. They are "hidden" because their names do not appear in the directory and cannot be erased without reformatting the whole diskette or disk. IBMBIO.COM is an extension of the ROM BIOS program that called it, and IBMDOS.COM is the DOS "nucleus," or operating system control program. Most of the time a third program is loaded: COMMAND.COM, the DOS command processor. COMMAND.COM is not a hidden file and can be found in the root directory of any fixed disk or bootable diskette. Its date corresponds with a specific release of DOS (3.1, 3.2, etc.).

PC DOS's User Interface

The command processor is PC DOS's only user interface. Its usual prompt: A> or C> (depending on whether it was booted from diskette or fixed disk), tells you it is waiting for a DOS command, batch file, or program name. Sometimes, when memory is scarce, COMMAND.COM will self-destruct by overlaying part of itself with an application program, and when the program terminates, DOS reloads COMMAND.COM and waits for the next instruction. The command processor also includes several internal DOS commands, like DIR, COPY, and ERASE. When you format a diskette as a *system diskette* (bootable, such as one that contains programs), DOS puts the IBMBIO.COM, IBMDOS.COM, and COMMAND.COM files on it. (The only one you will see in the directory is COMMAND.COM). OS/2 supports most of the same commands in its own command processor, named CMD.EXE.

User "shells" (such as the PC Convertible's Application Selector) add a user-friendly, front-end menu to DOS, simplifying the use of operating system commands and selection of programs. Several commercial programs such as IBM's TopView or Task Manager, are DOS shells. Multiple-application shells will be discussed in Chapter 3. OS/2's Presentation Manager user shell will be described in Chapter 4, which devotes itself to the OS/2 user interface.

Other DOS Commands

So, any system diskette contains at least three DOS files, but a copy of the original DOS diskette contains many more. These files, arranged in alphabetical order, include many DOS external commands like DISKCOPY, BACKUP, and FORMAT. They are called "external" because they are not part of the command processor, but are really just small programs that DOS loads and runs in memory, like an application. Some of these command files may be copied onto an application program diskette for convenience. For example, a copy of the DISKCOPY.COM file simplifies diskette duplication. PC DOS command files all end with a filename suffix of .COM or .EXE. OS/2's commands all end in .EXE.

IMPROVING PERFORMANCE

Memory and Performance

Memory has always had an indirect impact on application performance. That is because, on any computer, a large program that exceeds available memory must be divided into subroutines or segments that can be used and then overlaid to make room for the next one. This disk activity, although sometimes necessary, slows down performance. That is why many PC DOS applications will run faster when converted to OS/2, where time-consuming overlays are not required.

Memory can improve fixed disk data file performance even more dramatically. Earlier we saw how a portion of unused memory can be set aside as *cache memory*, a temporary storage area for disk file segments (Figure 2–

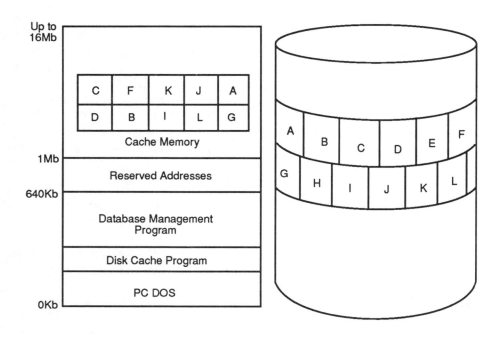

Figure 2–14 In this example, a DOS database management program uses a large inventory file. As each new sector of the file is accessed, the Disk Cache program places a copy of it in the extended memory above 1 Mb. The next time the program needs the same sector, it gets it directly from cache (extended) memory. Caching active disk sectors improves performance.

14). During disk file activity, each newly accessed 512-byte sector is saved in cache memory, and when a sector is accessed a second or third time, it is already in memory, so no disk activity is needed. PC DOS does not include a cache program but one with a filename of IBMCACHE.COM is provided on the Personal System/2 Model 50/60/80 Reference Diskette. This program is actually an installation program that copies the IBMCACHE.SYS device driver to the fixed disk root directory and either creates or modifies the CONFIG.SYS file to load the cache driver every time the system is used.

Cache memory improves fixed disk I/O activity, and the DOS 3.3 FASTOPEN command speeds up file access—the time it takes DOS to find a fixed disk file—which may be in a directory or subdirectory. When a file is first used, FASTOPEN adds its name and disk address to a list kept in memory. The next time DOS needs the file, it checks the FASTOPEN list first, and directory search time is eliminated. So, FASTOPEN helps DOS get to files faster, and IBMCACHE.SYS improves file reading and writing performance.

OS/2'S MEMORY MANAGEMENT

Larger Programs

So what are we going to do with all of this memory that OS/2 supports? Are *bigger* programs necessarily *better* programs? How will they be different from programs that run under PC DOS today? Big programs consume memory in two ways: they need space for themselves and they need space for a data work area. The two factors usually go hand in hand, but not always.

As the PC grew in popularity, competition between popular application packages accelerated. DisplayWrite™ and Writing Assistant™ replaced EasyWriter. MultiPlan and Lotus 1-2-3 replaced VisiCalc. Programs got better (and bigger) for two reasons: function and usability. A spreadsheet program with features like column-sorting and graph-drawing tended to be larger in size than a program that could not do either. A word processor with spell-checking took more memory and its dictionary required extra disk space. Programs also became easier to use, with pop-up and pull-down menus, mouse support, on-line help information, tutorial programs, and sample files for practice. All of this new function and usability translated into larger programs requiring more memory.

This trend has continued in today's high-function, easy-to-learn, easy-to-learn, software packages. A few years ago a fully loaded 640 Kb PC was rare, but today they are commonplace. The Personal System/2 Model 30 comes with 640 Kb, and the Models 50, 60, and 80 start with 1 or 2 Mb. The trends in software development that have brought us to this point have been temporarily put on hold or diverted to schemes like bank-switching to break the 640 Kb barrier. OS/2 has changed all of that, and the growth in functional, usable programs is taking off again, as never before.

More Data

Larger application programs alone are only half of the story. The object of a program is the information it handles. Sometimes that information is maintained outside of memory, such as a large database file. Only a fraction of a big file—a record, for example—is brought into memory at any point in time, so the work area is small. But many other programs will manage all of their active data in memory, where calculations and sorts can be performed, and disk activity is kept to a minimum. A large spreadsheet or document may require hundreds of kilobytes of memory for a work area.

The Personal System/2's four displays offer high-resolution and colors not possible on earlier PCs, and many application developers will exploit OS/2's Presentation Services graphics to mix text, charts, and images in their programs. High-resolution graphics require large files for storage, and a corresponding amount of memory to construct and manipulate the memory-hungry pictures. OS/2 Presentation Services also supports various character font styles and sizes, using dot graphics to draw the letters on the display. These also put a demand on memory.

Multi-Applications

Of course, OS/2's multi-application support (described in the next chapter) will increase memory requirements significantly beyond what is needed for a single application.

How much memory is enough? IBM recommends certain minimum machine memory sizes for Operating System/2, depending on a few variables. If you are running the OS/2 Standard Edition with no PC DOS Environment area, 1.5 Mb is suggested. Like DOS, OS/2 uses a portion of memory for itself and the rest is available for application programs. With the selection of the PC DOS Mode, 2.0 Mb is recommended. The OS/2 Extended Edition requires an estimated minimum system of 3.0 Mb. Remember, these are only minimum estimates, and actual memory requirements will vary widely, depending on the number and size of the application programs installed.

OS/2'S DISK AND MEMORY REQUIREMENTS

Fixed Disk Storage

OS/2 is not an operating system to be run from diskettes, so the 20 Mb fixed disk drive on the Personal System/2 Model 50 or Personal Computer AT is minimum storage for OS/2 and its entourage of commands, libraries, and other functions. Most files on the four 1.44 Mb, 3.5-inch (PS/2) diskettes or the four 1.2 Mb, 5.25-inch (PC AT) diskettes that OS/2 Standard Edition 1.0 is distributed on will be copied to the fixed disk. More than four diskettes will be used to distribute Standard Edition 1.1. About 5 Mb of disk space is used by OS/2 1.0 files, and additional space is used by swap and history files. Some users may erase optional files such as the familiarization program or help library to save fixed disk space.

The OS/2 Standard Edition 1.1 formats fixed disk space in a manner that is different from its predecessor. OS/2 1.0 formats disk partitions, or logical drives, of no more than 32 Mb each. This may require the allocation of program and data files across multiple partitions, addressed as drives C:, D:, E:, etc. OS/2 Standard Edition 1.1 formats the entire drive as a single, contiguous space, which is addressed only as drive C:.

OS/2 Memory Map

Figure 2–15 compares two OS/2 Standard Edition configurations through their memory maps. The first is an OS/2 installation with a maximum PC DOS Mode space of 640 Kb. The second example shows OS/2 with no PC DOS Mode, leaving more space for OS/2 programs.

The PC DOS Mode

During OS/2 installation, you have an option to provide a means for running unconverted DOS programs. DOS Mode consists of two things: reserved memory where PC DOS would normally run, and the use of the 80286's Real Mode, which gives DOS programs a friendly 8088-like environment. The result is a hardware-software simulation of a PC DOS machine (like a PC XT™ or AT), running what appears to a program as DOS 3.3. You do not need a copy of DOS 3.3 to do this; OS/2 has the function built in. To further enforce this realistic DOS simulation, DOS programs run in memory below 640 Kb, and the processor is switched to Real Mode whenever the DOS program receives a time-slice from OS/2.

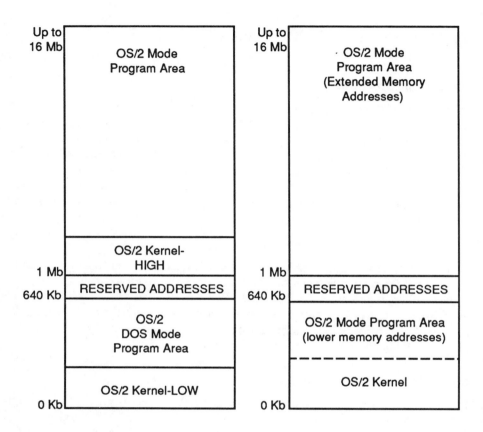

Figure 2–15 A memory map of OS/2 takes one of two forms: with or without DOS Mode. On the left, DOS Mode occupies memory up to 640 Kb, pushing OS/2 and its programs above 1 Mb. When DOS Mode isn't needed (right), OS/2 and its programs begin loading below 640 Kb, continuing above 1 Mb.

Whenever the processor is put in Real Mode it temporarily loses its unique 80286 characteristics, assuming an 8086 identity. No memory addressing above 1 Mb is possible, no multi-application support exists, and there is no multi-tasking or dynamic linking. When a PC DOS program is running in DOS Mode, OS/2 gives it time-slices in which to run, just as with any OS/2 program. Whenever the processor is in Protect Mode (when OS/2 takes a time-slice for itself or one of its programs), DOS Mode is shut off completely—the DOS program stays in memory, but it receives no attention or processor services. For these brief slices of time, a PC DOS program is *suspended* as a dormant background program.

Time-Dependent Applications

Some DOS programs are *timing-dependent*: they require continuous clock signals to perform their tasks. This includes programs that measure elapsed time or perform communications with other computers, on a network or connected to a host system. When a communications program is suspended (as all PC DOS Mode programs must be, sooner or later), it may drop the line and disconnect from the network or host. For this reason, many PC DOS communications programs are not supported under OS/2. Those programs would still run directly under PC DOS, whenever communications are needed, until they are converted to (or replaced by) OS/2 applications.

A few other PC DOS programs may encounter difficulty running in the OS/2 DOS Mode. Programs that perform real-time data collection and analysis are also time-dependent. DOS hardware-specific device drivers are incompatible with OS/2, and some programs may have to be adapted to use OS/2 drivers. In situations where unconverted DOS programs will not work correctly in OS/2's DOS Mode, a dual DOS-OS/2 system can be set up, with programs and data files from both operating systems resident on the same fixed disk. Dual systems will be explained in Chapter 6.

The OS/2 Mode

When the processor is not running in Real Mode (to service PC DOS programs), it is in what Intel calls Protect Mode and IBM calls the OS/2 Mode. This is what the 80286 and OS/2 were designed for: running large programs, multi-tasking, and using other advanced features. Both Family and Full-function applications can run in OS/2 Mode. Either a DOS or Family program can run in DOS Mode. If DOS Mode is not installed, the operating system stays in OS/2 Mode all the time.

	DOS MODE	OS/2 MODE
DOS Programs	X	
Family Programs	X	X
OS/2 Full-function Programs		X

No PC DOS Mode

Memory can be freed up for OS/2 by not installing the DOS Mode. This option can be taken at installation or by changing an option in the CONFIG.SYS configuration file (PROTECTONLY=YES) and rebooting. With the entire system used for OS/2 Protect Mode programs, the OS/2 nucleus, or kernel, will reside in low memory (0 to 640 Kb range) with its application programs occupying the remaining portion of low memory up to 640 Kb, skip the 640 Kb—1 Mb reserved memory addresses, and then continue with memory from 1 Mb upward.

OS/2: INITIALIZATION AND EXECUTION

When OS/2 boots, or performs an initial program load, it loads itself into memory, following a sequence prescribed in its own loader program, but a sequence that can be modified by the configuration file. CONFIG.SYS is placed in the fixed disk root directory during OS/2 installation. In that file are a series of commands and options that determine whether or not the DOS Mode will be used, how much memory it requires, and whether or not Input-Output Privilege Level programs can run. Like its PC DOS counterpart, the configuration file is also used to select country options and load device drivers.

Technically, the configuration file is optional, since OS/2 will set default options for many commands that do not appear there. However, the complexity of OS/2 will usually require that some options and drivers be listed in this file. Since CONFIG.SYS is an ordinary text file, the commands put there during installation can be examined and modified by a program or the user. This should be done only by someone familiar with the operating system and its various options. In Chapter 6 we will say more about this procedure.

OTHER OS/2 HARDWARE DEPENDENCIES

OS/2 on the Personal System/2

When Operating System/2 is running on a Personal System/2, it interfaces to a special program found in its read only memory (ROM), called Advanced BIOS, or ABIOS. Like the regular PC BIOS, which is also onboard the Personal System/2 for the sake of PC DOS compatibility, ABIOS supplies an important link between the operating system and the hardware it is running on. ABIOS provides functions missing from the old BIOS—including support for multi-tasking.

OS/2 on a PC AT

On the other hand, when OS/2 is loaded on an IBM Personal Computer AT or XT/286, it checks the machine type and "knows" that ABIOS is not there. So it provides its own RAM-resident drivers that serve essentially the same purpose as the Personal System/2 ABIOS: hardware interface and management.

Since there is no PC AT Micro Channel bus, each program's memory, disk, display, and printing activity must share the AT bus. All OS/2 programs should run on the AT without modification, although performance may be less than observed on the PS/2. This is partially due to slower AT clock speeds (between 4.77 and 8 Mhz, versus 10 to 20 Mhz on the Personal System/2), but also because of the hardware's inherent capacity for multi-tasking. This performance difference may become even more evident when advanced, multi-tasking applications are running.

OS/2 on Other Machines

OS/2 can run on many 80286- and 80386-based systems unchanged, once the necessary adaptation software layer is provided. This is the OS/2-machine "ABIOS" interface, and it has a strong dependency on a machine's specific bus and BIOS design. Microsoft, which shares a joint development and marketing agreement with IBM for the base operating system, will license their own version of OS/2 (called MS-OS/2)® to other computer manufacturers, providing adaptation software in many instances. Device drivers will be required to support a system's unique input and output devices. After all of the hardware/software interface differences have been accommodated, a machine's internal architecture (especially its bus) may restrict or enhance OS/2 performance.

OS/2 and the XMA Card

The IBM 80286 Expanded Memory Adapter/A, for the PS/2 Models 50 and 60, like the earlier version designed for the PC, XT, and AT, supports DOS programs written to the Expanded Memory Specification described previously. EMS, developed jointly by Lotus Corp., Intel Corp., and Microsoft Corp., uses special bank-switching circuits on the memory adapter to support additional memory for a large spreadsheet or to run multiple DOS programs. An example is IBM's 3270 Workstation Program, which uses the XMA card to multi-task four communication sessions and six DOS sessions. OS/2 does not need or use bank-switching for multi-application support, but it can use the 2 Mb of memory on the adapter as normal, above-1 Mb, extended memory.

APPLICATIONS, MEMORY, AND PERFORMANCE

Slices and Swapping

OS/2, like PC DOS, is affected by the traditional memory vs. performance tradeoff. A program that runs alone and does not have to swap memory segments to and from disk will always perform better than one that shares memory with other programs or is too big for available memory. An application sharing OS/2 with even a simple PC DOS program will get fewer time-slices and may experience segment-swapping to the fixed disk. As a result, performance suffers. Large programs designed for dynamic loading or Memory Overcommit may run in less memory, but segment-swapping to and from disk will slow them down. More than ever before, adding memory to a system may be the quickest, easiest way to speed it up.

Code segments are originally stored in a program file, one with a file name extension of .EXE. As the program runs, it loads additional segments from its .EXE file as needed. Other segments can be stored in separate files, to be dynamically linked with the main program when called. Dynamic linked files have a file extension of .DLL and can be used by more than one program. If there is not enough unused memory space for a new segment, one or more of the existing segments must be overlaid. This is done on a least-recently-used basis. If a data segment has not changed since it was loaded, it can be discarded. If it has changed, it must be first swapped to disk before it can be overlaid in memory. When swapping occurs, segments are temporarily written to a swap file named SWAPPER.DAT.

Memory Maintenance

With all of the programs, tasks, and segments that OS/2 must manage, some fragmentation, or pockets of unused memory, will appear over time (Figure 2–16). Since program segments can be of various sizes, small pockets of available memory are not large enough to hold larger segments. This can cause unnecessary swapping activity as OS/2 attempts to find room for them. The operating system recognizes this condition, and responds by doing some housekeeping, "unfragmenting" the pockets by moving active segments together, thus freeing up larger blocks of contiguous memory.

Message Handling

Memory can be saved and performance improved by keeping system messages in a separate file instead of within a program. This reduces program size, and an application can access a message from the message file quickly when needed. The OS/2 Toolkit provides assistance in creating message files.

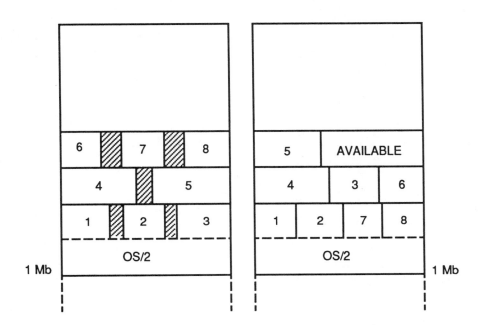

Figure 2–16 The OS/2 memory map on the left shows several pockets of unassigned memory (shaded areas) left behind during segment-swapping. After OS/2 performs memory compaction (right), segments are moved together, freeing up additional space.

Configuration File Options

In addition to the commands that establish the DOS Mode or IOPL option, the OS/2 configuration file contains other commands that affect memory and disk usage:

MEMMAN	Enables/disables segment swapping and segment motion. Default enables both.
SWAPPATH	Specifies subdirectory for SWAPPER.DAT. Default places it in the root directory (\SWAPPER.DAT).
RMSIZE	Sets aside memory for the DOS "compatibility box" reserved program area in the DOS Mode. Default is 640 Kb.
PROTECTONLY	Enables / disables DOS Mode.

3

OS/2's Multi-Tasking:
Computing in Parallel

Megabytes of memory are very convenient for running big programs and processing huge amounts of data, but there is a lot more to Operating System/2 than that. Personal computer owners have dreamed about doing what minicomputers and mainframes have been doing for years: running several programs, or tasks, at once. OS/2, like most operating systems, does not *really* run two applications simultaneously. It switches or *time-slices* processor time between programs to give the appearance of multi-processing. But by managing several input-output devices at once (printer, disk, communication link), parallel tasks can improve system throughput and still provide good response time.

In this chapter we will see how PC DOS supports limited multi-tasking through the PC's Math Coprocessor, "terminate and stay resident" programs, user "shells," and application bank-switching. We will contrast these simple PC DOS methods with hardware multi-tasking features that are built into each Intel 80286 microprocessor chip, and are now exploited by Operating System/2. We will examine OS/2 multi-tasking from the point of view of the end user and the application programmer, focusing on features that make it a good user shell and a base for new applications. We will look at the bottom line: how new OS/2 applications will improve the way we use computers. Finally, we will close the chapter by looking into our crystal ball to see what the 80386 processor and multi-user operating systems have for the future.

DEFINING SOME TERMS

With so many "multi" words in use today, it may be helpful to define some of the popular terms in light of their OS/2 usage.

Multi-Processing. A generic term that means doing several things at once on computers. On most PCs, this has required a user to add a new layer of software to DOS or a programmer to provide multi-processing support within a co-resident program. On mainframe and midrange computers, multi-processing often implies the use of additional processors to improve performance.

Multi-Tasking. As implemented on OS/2, it means that multiple tasks, or units of work (sometimes called *threads*) are executing at the same time. A task can be a single program or an activity within a program. A multi-tasking spreadsheet program, for example, could treat recalculation as one task and data entry as another, so that two activities could proceed in parallel. Application programmers can convert DOS serial task programs to OS/2 multi-tasking, often significantly improving application throughput.

Multiple Sessions. On OS/2 it usually means multiple application programs are running; up to 12 OS/2 sessions and one DOS Mode session are possible. A session can be active (currently executing, receiving processor time-slices), suspended (waiting for user interaction or another event before continuing), or it can be simply a DOS or OS/2 command prompt, with no program present. A communication "session" is a hook-up with a remote host computer or local area network (LAN). Multiple communication sessions can be initiated with the same host computer or with multiple computers. The DOS-based IBM PC 3270 Workstation Program, for example, supports up to six DOS program sessions, four host sessions, and two notepad sessions. Sessions can interact with each other, so that an electronic mail message can be "downloaded" from the host computer communication session for editing by a word processing program running in a DOS session. OS/2 Standard Edition 1.1 supports one screen group per session.

Multiple Segments. Multiple segments of memory, each no larger than 64 Kb, are used by OS/2 to manage application programs and their data. Segments can be loaded from disk to memory at program start-up or later, if and when they are needed. Infrequently used segments may be swapped to disk, freeing up memory space. Common segments can be shared among multiple programs. A program can be much larger than available memory, and OS/2 will manage its segments so that it can run in a smaller space.

Multiple Users.   Several users can share a personal computer through either of two common methods. A shared processor system allocates resources from a central system unit to multiple users. Its processor cycles, memory, and output devices are shared between users connected via "dumb" communication terminals or PCs. On a local area network, however, resource sharing (disks, printers, communications) is distributed across several interconnected personal computers, with each one doing its own processing (running programs).

Foreground Program.   On a multi-tasking system (such as OS/2) the foreground program currently has control of the user "console": the keyboard, display, and an optional mouse. Multiple programs may be "windowed" on the same screen, but only one can receive input. When the foreground program no longer requires user interaction, it may run unattended as a background program.

Background Program.   This program has no current user interaction via the keyboard, display, or mouse but can continue executing as long as no interaction is required. It may be observed via a screen window or run "hidden," out of sight. A background program can perform unattended tasks such as calculating, maintaining a communications line, or driving a printer. When it requires user interaction (such as selecting a menu option), it must be brought to the foreground or be suspended until the user can get back to it. Unattended background programs include "hotkey" calendar programs, print spoolers, and some features of network and communications programs.

TRADITIONAL MULTI-PROCESSING

Multi-processing is not new to large mainframe computers or even midrange, or minicomputer systems. Shared computers have proven to be a cost-effective solution for medium and large companies and for departments within a company. Large-capacity, high-speed computers with high-volume printers and inexpensive terminals can support hundreds of users, providing services not possible on stand alone PCs, such as electronic mail and data file sharing.

The Glass House

The traditional air-conditioned computer room or "glass house" (Figure 3–1) has long been the home of the corporate computer system. Many are serviced by a cadre of analysts, operators, and programmers, part of a company's Management Information Services, or MIS department. Big central computers originally ran multiple programs submitted "batch-style" on magnetic tapes or decks of cards, their printed output picked up later. Today their programs are often entered from remote terminals, stored on large-capacity disk drives, with output displayed on video screens. Interactive, "conversational" programs have replaced the old batch-style procedures.

In addition to running programs, users can share data and exchange messages with each other. Some of them use PCs or Personal Systems instead of "dumb" data terminals. These are often called intelligent workstations since they can be used to run local PC programs, or as host communication terminals, or both—a PC simultaneously providing local and host sessions. This enables a PC user to send an important data file to someone in another city via the company mainframe. It also lets PC programs in multiple branch offices "talk" with each other, processing transactions, coordinating complex projects, and updating time-critical information.

Figure 3–1 Large mainframe systems were the original multi-processing systems, often supporting hundreds of attached users. Today's mainframes are much smaller in size, such as the System/370 Model 3090 shown here.

The Departmental Computer

On a smaller scale, a department or group within a company might purchase a minicomputer for its own use (Figure 3–2). This may be done because the department has special needs that the glass house cannot provide, such as engineering design software, high-resolution displays, and plotters. Or the reason might be more political in nature: the department wants to get out from under the "control" of the MIS department.

Mid-range systems can be thought of as scaled-down versions of larger mainframe systems. They typically have less memory and storage, and support fewer terminals. They can be networked to the company MIS computer or other mid-range systems in order to provide electronic mail and data sharing. Some of these systems were not built to the same standards prevalent in the mainframe world, making them incompatible in such key areas

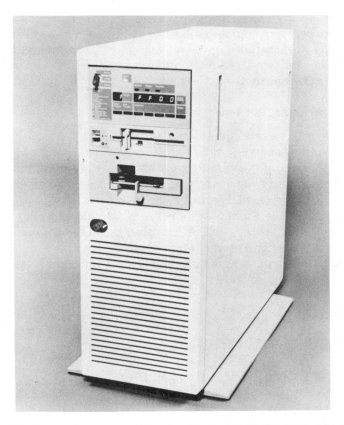

Figure 3–2   Mid-range systems, such as the System/36 Model 5363 shown here, place the power of a small mainframe system in a PC-size package.

as communications, programming languages, data file formats, and operating systems. The Unix operating system, for example, which was created for multi-application, multi-user minicomputers many years before DOS, was not compatible with mainframe operating systems or PC DOS. In recent years, the growth in speed and capacity of microcomputers and local area networks (LAN), and the ability of the super-PC to take on specialized jobs, has caused the popularity of the minicomputer to decline.

Distributed Processing

Computer manufacturers and users have long sought true *distributed processing*: the interconnection of mainframe, mid-range, and microcomputer systems to balance computing power and resources throughout a company. An ideal distributed system would "know" where shared data or under-utilized computing power resided. An overloaded central mainframe computer on a distributed system might assign some of its work, or tasks, to remote mini or micro systems, and assemble the results when they are done. Or, a query to a PC workstation's database manager might merge up-to-date information from its own fixed disk, a shared network server, and a remote host, all done transparently to the user.

Real-Time Applications

Business programs certainly are not the only form of multi-tasking software. Many manufacturing and laboratory applications require an operating system that can process multiple input and output signals, measuring data, calculating and range-checking, and returning control signals back to the process. A computerized security system can monitor badge readers and open doors. An office cooling system reads thermostats and switches air conditioning units on and off. A robotic assembly line uses a PC programmed to monitor and control every step. Each component of a real-time process—input, calculate, and output—can be a separate task communicating with others as necessary.

PC DOS MULTI-PROCESSING

Hardware-Assisted Multi-Processing

The speed of any computer system is dependent on many things such as the processor clock speed, bus design, installed memory capacity, and disk access and transfer rates. But even when a system's single processor becomes a bottleneck, performance can sometimes be improved by adding additional horsepower in the form of optional chips or cards.

Math Co-Processors

The original PC performance-booster is the co-processor. An empty socket on the PC's system board is reserved for the 8087 Math Co-processor, or simply, the 8087. This chip, designed as a companion to the PC's 8088 processor, is a high-speed floating-point arithmetic "machine," capable of performing addition, subtraction, multiplication, and division in a fraction of the time that the 8088 takes. It also handles longer numbers, to provide greater numerical accuracy. Since the 8087 works in parallel with the main processor, performing calculations that are returned to it, it was a key component in the original PC multi-processing system. In most applications, the program must still wait for the results of a calculation before continuing, so any noticeable performance improvement is usually due to the co-processor's faster speed, not because of any significant parallel activity.

Just as the 8087 goes with the 8088 (or 8086), the 80287 co-processor is a companion for the 80286, and can be installed on PC ATs and PS/2 Models 50 and 60. The 80387 and 80386 are another matched set found on PS/2 Model 80s.

To use an 8087, software must be written with it in mind. The 8087 responds to floating-point math instructions, which are ignored by the 8088. So, you might run a "non-8087" number-cruncher program on your PC and find that adding a math co-processor does nothing for it at all. Or, you might run an 8087-based program on a PC without the co-processor, and discover that it does not work.

After the PC had been around a few years, some application programmers learned to design programs that could run compatibly on PCs *with or without* an 8087. These "smart" programs sense the presence of the co-processor when they are started. If the 8087 is installed, the program passes it math routines in the form of 8087 instructions. If the co-processor is not installed, the program performs arithmetic with its own math routines, using regular 8088 instructions—which take longer to perform. An advantage of this type of program is that you can run it on a PC without the 8087 and later install the co-processor for an immediate boost in speed. Some PC DOS language compilers (such as FORTRAN or PASCAL) build this flexibility into programs, relieving the programmer of including "either-or" math routines.

Computers On a Card

Several companies make PC adapter cards that contain their own processors. Microsoft manufactured one of the first, a Z-80 card for the Apple II™, which supported the CP/M® operating system. 80286 and 80386 add-on cards boost performance on PCs (and could be used to run OS/2). These additional processors may share system memory and other resources or provide their own. Another kind of add-on processor card is used for a specific task, which can be as simple as a memory printer buffer or spooler, or as sophisticated as a network server. On the Personal System/2, the Micro Channel bus can support multiple, concurrently executing adapter cards, each with its own onboard processor.

BANK-SWITCHING

Expanded memory or bank-switching, introduced in the last chapter, assigns memory on a special adapter card to low-memory addresses that DOS recognizes. It "tricks" a program into using this memory by dynamically assigning blocks of expanded memory addresses to it. A variation of this technique can be used to support multiple programs.

The IBM Expanded Memory Adapter (XMA)

The IBM XMA card, introduced in the last chapter, contains 2 Mb of memory and the special electronics needed to bank-switch blocks of its memory into a reserved bank of under-1 Mb addresses. The memory-switching is done by a multi-tasking control program, the IBM 3270 Workstation Program.

This means that up to six DOS sessions, each containing a single DOS program no larger than 512 Kb, can be resident in the XMA's memory. As the control program brings each expanded memory application into the DOS address space, it receives a "slice," or interval of processing time. This technique does not break the DOS 640 Kb memory barrier, but it does provide a limited form of multi-tasking, and most DOS programs will require little or no modification.

Later we will see how the 80286 processor provides multi-tasking support without the need for special memory cards.

SOFTWARE MULTI-TASKING

PC DOS was designed as a single-program, single-task, serial-processing operating system. Although DOS has been improved over time and many companion software products have been added, it was never intended to manage multiple programs or tasks within a program. Yet thousands, perhaps millions, of PC users perform multi-tasking every day, many without realizing it. That is because application developers, using clever programming techniques, have figured out ways to let multiple programs share the processor, memory, display, and printer. These programs fall into two main categories: first are the special programs that are designed to run in the background while a regular PC program runs in the foreground. They must manage their own sharing of the processor and memory. Then there are the multi-processing extensions to DOS: programs written to enable multiple non-sharing programs to co-exist on the same system.

DOS BACKGROUND PROGRAMS

Terminate and Stay Resident Programs

Some popular PC programs are designed to "terminate and stay resident" (T&SR), residing in memory, out of sight until needed. In the meantime, an ordinary DOS program like a spreadsheet or word processor can run normally in the foreground. Examples of background programs are the "pop up" calendar that is called to the screen with a special key combination, or the notepad that attaches little reminders to your spreadsheet. Such "background" programs do not require frequent user interaction, sharing memory with the main "foreground" program, the operating system, and sometimes with each other. Like all good multi-tasking applications, T&SR programs do not require you to stop everything and return to DOS when you need the background program. A T&SR program is usually loaded by the DOS AUTOEXEC.BAT batch file at power-up time, and waits out of sight until invoked with a special key combination.

Cross-Program Interference

DOS T&SR programs, due to their unorthodox background status, break the DOS rules. The operating system does not support multi-tasking, so each program must provide its own, carefully sharing memory and other system resources with the main application, trying to keep out of the way. Since they are written with unofficial, unpublished DOS and BIOS program interfaces, conflicts can occur. Each background program operates with a set of rules established by its programmer, and sometimes those rules clash with those of other programs. In order to avoid such conflicts, some programs often come with installation or usage rules, such as "load me first" or "load me last."

Device Management

Another factor that makes T&SR programs difficult to write and risky to use is the way DOS manages system devices. Since DOS is a single-program operating system, each program is written as if it "owns" all of available memory, the entire display screen, and access to the printer. Co-resident programs attempt to share memory and the screen, and sometimes use the printer. This may lead to problems.

Imagine this hypothetical situation: Three T&SR programs are loaded on a PC AT every day with DOS when it is powered up. One is a print buffer that spools documents to the printer while the user does other things. The second program is a character font generator that lets the user print documents in any of several different type styles. It captures characters on the way to the printer, substituting its own. The third background program provides the user with a communications session to a host computer providing electronic mail. Each of these programs apparently "thinks" it has sole control of the printer. Occasionally when the user tries to do too much at once, such as trying to print from the communication program while the word processor is sending output through the print buffer and font generator, the system freezes up and everything stops. The only solution then is to reboot and start over. It is likely the people who wrote those three programs never had a conference to discuss how they would avoid such conflicts; they probably were not aware of each others' programs. If PC DOS had been designed for multi-tasking the way OS/2 is, it would be the arbitrator of possible conflicts.

The demand for PC multi-tasking has created a market for special programs like these, in spite of the occasional glitches that occur. A review of some popular DOS background program types will also provide an introduction to OS/2's multi-application environment. Later we will see how OS/2 solves DOS problems by properly managing multi-tasking.

Spooling

One of the original forms of PC multi-tasking is print spooling. Spooling intercepts text destined for the printer and diverts it first to a reserved area in memory, called a "buffer." Since the printer is a relatively slow device, the program can fill the memory buffer much faster than it takes to print it (Figure 3–3).

The printer can start printing from the spool buffer before it is filled. Each time the spooler program receives a "ready" interrupt from the printer, it borrows the processor just long enough to send the printer another line of buffered text, a pause that is barely noticeable. The spooler does not need the processor again until the printer is ready for the next line. There is plenty of time between the lines to do other work, such as filling the memory

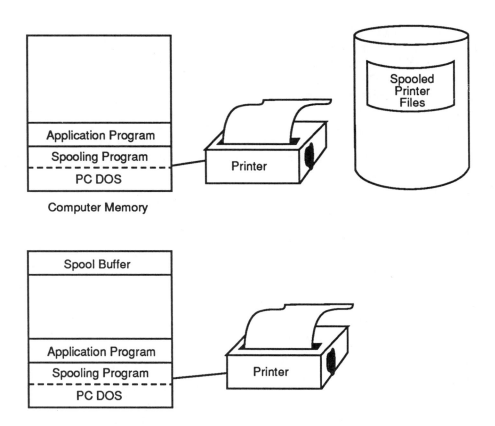

Figure 3–3 Printer spooling was one of the first forms of PC multi-tasking. There are two basic spooling techniques: files can be first spooled to disk to await printing (top), or they can be buffered, or queued, to a reserved memory area (bottom). In both cases, the processor can do other work while managing the relatively slow printer.

buffer with the rest of a document or letting the operator work on something else. From the user's point of view, printing appears to proceed completely in parallel with other work.

There are two types of spooling. The PRINT command that comes with PC DOS is one type. It establishes a printer buffer and a *queue*. The queue is a list of DOS disk files that are waiting to print. PRINT feeds the printer with text from a file, one line at a time, until the file is finished, at which point it goes on to the next file in the queue. This continues until the queue is empty. During this time a regular DOS program can run virtually uninterrupted. You can look at the queue of waiting documents from time to time, delete files from the list, or add files to the list.

There is a disadvantage to this kind of spooling: before a document can be printed, it must be saved in a "print image" file. This is created from the "Print to Disk" option on many word processing programs. The entire document is "written" to disk, complete with margins, headings, page numbers, and other formatting options, exactly as it appears on the printed page. Later, when the print image file is spooled to the printer, it will look as if it had been printed directly by the word processor. Print image files temporarily take up space on the disk, but they can be deleted after printing.

The other category of print spooler is the memory buffer type described earlier. It includes products like IBM's Print Buffer Online. PBO doesn't require files to be saved to disk first; it buffers printer output as soon as it leaves the program and usually requires no user intervention. Once a document is "printed" to the buffer, another one can be started, and so on until the buffer is full. No queue of file names is maintained by the program; it buffers all printer output in the order received. When the buffer is filled, you can go on with other work. Once this kind of spooler is loaded you can almost forget that it is there—it is automatic and does not require any intervention from you. It "borrows" some memory that might have been used for other purposes, but that is all. With more memory allocated for the buffer, more text can be handled at once.

Virtual Disks

As we saw in the last chapter, a little spare memory can be used to enhance system performance, and memory-sharing background programs are a good example of this. PC DOS's VDISK program reserves a block of memory as a virtual, or RAM "disk." The operating system treats this memory as if it were a very fast diskette drive: you can read and write data, run programs, and list the virtual disk directory with the DIR command. When an application program has frequent disk access, such as when several graphic images are displayed in succession, the VDISK program can speed things up. This is because a memory-to-memory operation is much faster than disk-to-memory. VDISK is easy to use; once started, it uses an unassigned drive letter (like D: or E:) for its virtual disk. Performance-sensitive program and data files can be copied there (using a batch file) and run as they always do—only faster. When a program is finished, a batch file must copy any modified VDISK files back to the real disk again.

Cache Memory

The IBMCACHE.SYS program distributed with the Personal System/2 Models 50, 60, and 80 sets aside a memory buffer for active 512-byte file sectors. When a new file sector is accessed, the cache program, which runs in the background, adds it to the buffer. If the sector is still in memory when a program needs it again, there is no need to read the disk. Adding cache memory improves performance: more at first, and then it levels off as the buffer becomes saturated. Actually, most programs, depending on the number, size, and access characteristics of their files, will demonstrate nearly optimum performance at a cache memory size of 128 or 256 Kb. Memory increments beyond the saturation point will produce little gain. The IBM PC LAN Program version 1.2 comes with its own disk cache program, which can greatly assist the performance of a network file server (a PC that provides shared files for network users). It works in the same way as the Personal System/2 disk cache program.

Session Managers

Another popular type of DOS multi-tasking program supports multiple "sessions" for DOS programs and communications with a host computer. The IBM PC 3270 Emulation Program Entry Level is an example of this, emulating a 3270 communications terminal to establish a remote host system session. You can then "hotkey" (by pressing <Alt + Esc>) to a DOS session where most PC programs can be run. Whenever you need to talk to the host (such as to check your incoming mail), you can hotkey back to the host session. Session management is important in communications for a couple of reasons: First, a suspended, or shut-off communications program cannot maintain its connection with a host. It must remain active while in the background. Second, communication sessions are often characterized by long inactive periods (when no incoming mail or data files are waiting) and you could use that time to do something else, like working on a financial report.

Some simple asynchronous communications programs, used to communicate with data services like CompuServe®, The Source®, and MCI Mail®, do a little multi-tasking of their own. For example, ProComm™ lets you switch to your favorite word processing program while it maintains the connection with the remote system, so you can review or edit a downloaded file. That way you can be certain that the long stock report or news summary that you just copied to disk arrived okay, or make a last-minute change to the sales report you are about to send to headquarters.

The DOS FASTOPEN command is another background program that sets aside memory to improve performance—in this case, the "seek time" to locate a disk file. It reserves a small area in memory as a directory of recently accessed disk files. When a file is opened a second time, the directory points to its disk location, thus saving DOS unnecessary search time. You can establish the size of this directory, depending on the amount of disk activity anticipated.

DOS MULTI-PROCESSING EXTENSIONS

In the previous examples, each program provided its own built-in multi-processing capability. Another approach is to add a DOS companion program, or layer, which permits memory-sharing and multi-application support for programs that do not coexist naturally.

THREE KINDS OF DOS SHELLS

The demand for multi-tasking has led developers to invent several innovative ways of supporting a multiple program environment. All use a DOS shell to improve the user interface, but they vary on how application programs are loaded and run.

The first technique is a simple "program-selector" approach: a program is selected from a menu and loaded into memory until another one is selected to replace it. No co-residency or multi-tasking is supported. The second type is the "session-selector," where multiple DOS programs are loaded into memory and can be switched, or toggled between. A background program is always suspended. The third kind is the "multi-tasking" shell that allows background programs to continue running while a foreground program is being used. Sometimes multiple applications can be windowed to the same screen.

Application Selectors

The IBM PC Convertible uses a simple approach to multi-application support, basically a program-selector with a limited dual-session capability. The Convertible's Application Selector is a menu front end for the Convertible's built-in SystemApps and user-installed application programs. A Convertible program started from the Application Selector can be temporarily suspended to the background (by pressing the <Fn + Esc> hotkey combination) while you use one of the four System Applications: a simple word processor, calendar, telephone dialer, or calculator. When you have finished checking your schedule or jotting down a note, you resume the suspended program where you left off. Programs are suspended while in the background. The Application Selector is smart enough to know that a communications program cannot be suspended, so the <Fn + Esc> command is disabled while communicating. To learn more about the PC Convertible, the author's book, *Power Portable Computing* published by John Wiley & Sons is suggested.

A simple session-selector is DoubleDOS™, by SoftLogic. It manages two DOS sessions (sharing memory below 640 Kb), which the user can toggle between. Background programs are suspended, although background printing is supported. A minimum 256 Kb PC is needed to run DoubleDOS, which uses 30 Kb for itself, and divides the rest between DOS and the two application programs. The sizes of the two segments are set by the user.

DoubleDOS's big brother is a program named Software Carousel™, also by SoftLogic. It supports up to 10 DOS applications, and uses under-640 Kb memory, up to 8 Mb of expanded (EMS) memory, or up to 16 Mb of extended (80286) memory. A RAM disk is also available. Each Carousel program can be up to 512 Kb. Multiple copies of the same program can be started, so that each session can work on a different file. An example of this would be using multiple word processing sessions to work on several chapters of a book. If insufficient memory is available for all programs, idle sessions can be swapped out to fixed disk. Like other session-selector shells, background programs are always suspended.

Some other program-selector and session-selector products are GEM Desktop™, Resident™, and DOSamatic™.

MULTI-TASKING DOS SHELLS

The most advanced DOS shells add a sophisticated user interface and multi-tasking support, approaching OS/2's Presentation Manager. IBM's 3270 Workstation Program and TopView® products, Microsoft's Windows™, and Quarterdeck's DESQview™ are examples of multi-tasking shells. In addition to providing a mouse-driven, windowing interface, they support the concurrent use of many existing, unmodified DOS applications. Background programs can run unattended. A current user of any of these programs will find similarities between them and the OS/2 Presentation Manager interface incorporated in OS/2 Standard Edition release 1.1.

3270 Workstation Program

The IBM 3270 Workstation Program is probably the most sophisticated of the DOS multiple-session products. It manages up to six concurrent DOS sessions and four host sessions, so you can switch between your choice of remote mainframe computers and favorite PC DOS programs (Figure 3–4). You can also "cut and paste" information between sessions, so you could extract regional sales summaries from several remote sales offices, and insert the results in a corporate report you are preparing—all without retyping anything.

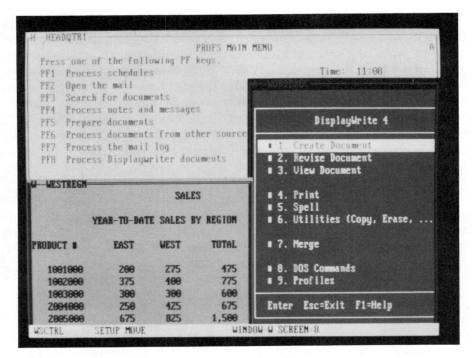

Figure 3–4   IBM's 3270 Workstation Program, shown here, supports up to six concurrent DOS and four host sessions. In this example, screen windows show a PROFS™ electronic mail menu from corporate headquarters, sales data from a regional office, and a local DisplayWrite 4 word processing session.

The 3270 Workstation Program uses the IBM Expanded Memory Adapter card (described in the previous chapter), which provides 2 Mb of memory above DOS's 640 Kb upper limit. There are two versions of the XMA: one for the PC and PS/2 Models 25 and 30, using the old PC adapter card type and bus interface. Another version is designed for the PS/2 Models 50 and 60. The 3270 Workstation Program does not require the XMA card on the Model 80; it uses the Virtual 8086 feature of the 80386 processor for large memory, multi-tasking support. This is one of the few DOS programs to take advantage of an 80386-exclusive feature.

A DOS application program can be written to communicate with a host system through the 3270 Workstation Program's application program interface, (API). Much of this API is compatible with the Operating System/2 Extended Edition. This means that some program development and conversion activity can be done without OS/2, using the 3270 Workstation Program. Later, when the Extended Edition is available, the final program conversion steps should be minimal.

IBM'S TOPVIEW

TopView is an IBM DOS shell product. It was developed as a response to requests for a better user interface for DOS and a standard application interface for a DOS multi-application environment. While TopView was never intended to replace DOS or to serve as a new operating system, it does provide several improvements to DOS. TopView has been updated for DOS 3.3 and the Personal System/2, but OS/2 is clearly IBM's strategy for an advanced multi-application, large memory, windowing system.

Easy Installation

Applications are "installed" on TopView's program menu, and can be loaded and run concurrently, up to PC DOS's traditional 640 Kb limit. Program Information Files (PIFs) contains essential information about an application and its operating characteristics that TopView uses to set program options at load time. If the application does not already provide a PIF file, the user can create one.

Windowing

Each TopView application program can send display output through a screen window, which can be any size up to the dimensions of the display, fully controlled by the user. This includes moving, hiding, unhiding, adjusting, and scrolling information, or overlaying one window with another. Programmers can use the TopView application interface to improve usability, such as by adding "pop up" menus or help text panels.

Pointing Devices

In addition to keyboard and mouse control, TopView supports a light pen, graphics tablet, touch-sensitive display, joystick, track ball, or touch pad. Pointing devices can be used for things like menu-selection and windowing, but a keyboard is always required for data entry and other functions. Device drivers are provided for the most popular input and output attachments, and the TopView Toolkit provides help for the programmer in writing special device drivers for new products.

Data Transfer Between Applications

TopView supports cut-and-paste of text from one window to another. Using a mouse or the four cursor-control keys, a box is drawn around the text to be transferred. The cursor is then moved to the receiving application, at the point where the copied text is to be inserted. Pressing a key or mouse button finishes the job.

Foreground/Background Applications

A TopView foreground program has the immediate attention of the user, via the screen and the keyboard or mouse device. As long as the program is well-behaved (i.e., it does not write directly to the screen, bypassing DOS), it may be restricted to a single screen window. A TopView foreground window has a double line border around it and may be thought of as the top piece of paper on your "desk" (not partially covered by other windows). Other programs, if any, continue to run in the background, as long as they have something to do. Background programs awaiting user interaction are suspended, and will resume running when brought to the foreground again. Well-behaved background programs can be assigned windows, and be partially overlaid by other programs.

Limited Memory and Performance

DOS and TopView reside in memory, and the remainder becomes the application area—around 400 Kb on a 640 Kb system. Some programs may have to be loaded from disk when needed, rather than residing in memory. On a PC AT, PC/XT 286, Personal System/2 Model 50/60/80, and other 80286 systems, TopView supports the temporary storage of inactive programs in extended memory above 1 Mb, using DOS's VDISK program. Transfer of programs between the virtual disk and TopView's active address space takes place much faster than from the fixed disk.

Programs that need to stay in the DOS address space because of performance requirements or to avoid interruption (such as communication programs) may be so designated. When a non-resident program is selected from TopView's list, it first checks to see if enough unused memory is available. If not, it swaps out to a virtual or real disk one of its currently resident, swappable programs. Swapped-out programs are then marked as such on the program switch list.

Program Groups

All programs that a user plans to run in a session can be listed in a *program group*. When a group is selected from the program list, all of its applications are loaded into the system. One such group can be designated for autostart, so that it will automatically load when the system is first started.

Restrictions

TopView, like other DOS shells, places restrictions on many "ill-behaved" programs—those that are not written to the official, supported DOS interface. For example, a program that sends its output directly to the display, bypassing DOS, cannot be windowed by TopView. Such a program would have to take over, or "own," the entire screen while it is running, and turn control back to TopView when finished. TopView cannot mix text and graphics output on the screen, so graphics programs must also use the full screen (thus prohibiting windowing) while they are running as foreground programs. Many normally ill-behaved programs will work under TopView, by indicating their peculiarities in their PIF file. That way, TopView will accommodate them as much as possible.

DOS Services

There is no need to exit the TopView shell to perform many DOS commands. Copying, renaming, listing, printing, and erasing of files can be done from the DOS Services menu. Program output can be re-directed to an alternate device, such as when printer output is sent to a local area network print server. You can spool up to 32 files (which must first be stored in print-image format) for background printing. A Scratchpad feature lets you customize up to ten frequently used DOS commands, and you can always exit to the DOS command line for just about anything else.

Toolkit

The TopView Programmer's Toolkit is intended to ease the installation of programs under TopView and create compatible new applications. The Windows Design Aid can be used to create a variety of input and output screen formats for use in programs.

Personal System/2 Version

Recent versions of TopView are fully compatible with other IBM DOS companion products such as the PC Network program, 3270 Emulation, and graphics (VDI) support. TopView version 1.12 has been released for PC DOS 3.3, supporting the new Personal System/2 models, including their high-resolution graphics displays.

MICROSOFT WINDOWS

Microsoft Windows is another popular PC DOS multi-application shell. In addition to multi-application windowing, Windows includes a built-in word processor, graphics, communications, notepad, calculator, calendar, and printer spooler. Like TopView, Windows comes with device drivers for popular PC printers and other I/O devices. Unlike TopView, Windows lets you mix text and graphics output on the same screen. Its Clipboard feature lets you cut and paste information between screen windows.

A Peek into the Future

Since Microsoft is a co-developer of OS/2 with IBM, the OS/2 Presentation Manager (described in more detail in the next chapter) will have many of the characteristics of Microsoft Windows version 2.0. OS/2 version 1.1 screens will closely resemble Windows 2.0 screens, with common features such as caption bars (names of program and associated data files), pull-down menus, mouse support, and interactive dialog boxes.

Built-In Programs

Windows 2.0 comes with a useful set of built-in programs. Notepad is a handy full-screen editor that can be used to modify system files such as CONFIG.SYS and AUTOEXEC.BAT. Cardfile is a mini-database. Write™ is a word processor, Paint™ is a graphics drawing program, Reversi is a game, and Terminal is a communications program. Clock, Calendar, and Calculator are self-descriptive.

Making DOS Easy to Use

The MS-DOS Executive is a shell for common DOS commands like LOAD, COPY, DELETE, and RENAME. A print spooler and Control Panel (for changing Windows options) are provided. Windows' user interface has several interesting innovations. An application window can be reduced in size down to a small icon, or symbol representing the application. When an inactive background program has a message for the user, it beeps and then flashes the menu title bar or icon for the application. An application can be started by selecting one of its data files from a list of files. Windows loads the application that created the file.

Virtual Disk

Windows includes a virtual disk program named SMARTDrive. It uses expanded memory on a bank-switching card like the Intel Above Board, AST RAMPage, or IBM's Expanded Memory Adapter. It also uses extended memory above 1 Mb on an 80286 system.

Many applications have already been written to the Windows interface, including Microsoft's Excel spreadsheet and Micrografx's In*a*Vision™. In order to run a "standard" application not written for Windows, the user must create a program information file using the PIF editor. The PIF file provides Windows with certain information, such as the minimum memory it needs to run in. All Windows applications will require some conversion before they are recompiled for OS/2.

Windows needs at least 512 Kb, although 640 Kb is recommended. 1.5 Mb of fixed disk space is also required.

OTHER DOS SHELL PRODUCTS

GEM Desktop

Digital Research, Inc. offers several multi-tasking and multi-user operating systems and DOS shells for 8086, 80286, and 80386 microprocessors, including DOS Plus™, Concurrent PC DOS™ Expanded Memory (XM), Concurrent DOS 386, Flex OS™, and GEM Desktop. Desktop is a DOS graphics shell that comes with each of several GEM products for presentation graphics and publications (Figure 3–5).

MultiLink Advanced®, a product of The Software Link, is a multi-tasking, multi-user extension to DOS. It supports the Software Link's AT Gizmo card™ for the PC AT, letting up to 17 applications (and users) share the

Figure 3–5 Several PC DOS shells, or application selector programs, act as an umbrella for multiple programs. The GEM Desktop series, by Digital Research, is a family of programs for creating text and graphics output.

processor and providing up to 8 Mb of extended memory. Multi-Link also supports Intel's Above Board 286™ card, which provides up to 1 Mb of expanded memory for large spreadsheets and databases. MultiLink Advanced can be purchased with or without terminal support, which supports up to 16 attached users via serial ports.

DESQview, by Quarterdeck Office Systems, is a multi-tasking DOS shell product that supports the PC's CGA and EGA graphics modes, as well as the PS/2's VGA (Figure 3–6). Like Microsoft Windows, DESQview supports foreground and background programs, windowing, use of keyboard and mouse, extended memory, and expanded memory on 8086/8088, 80286, and 80386 systems. The application program interface is compatible with IBM's TopView.

80286/386 MULTI-TASKING

We saw in the last chapter how the architecture of the 80286 microprocessor—particularly its larger address bus—supports higher memory ad-

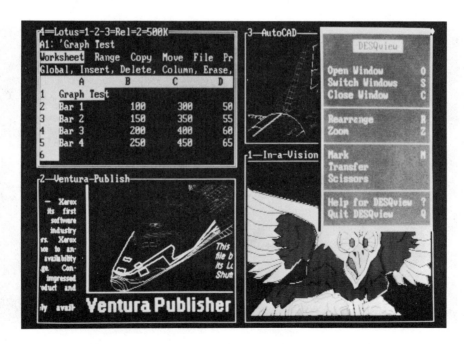

Figure 3–6   DESQview, by Quarterdeck Office Systems, is a windowing, multi-tasking DOS shell. DESQview supports expanded memory on 8086/8088 systems and extended memory on 80286/386 systems.

dressability. You certainly need more memory if you want to run several programs at once, but that is just the beginning. The operating system will need to manage those programs and their use of computer resources such as the processor, display, and printer. If the processor has some built-in circuitry to manage multi-tasking, so much the better. The 80286 was designed for this dynamic environment, and although PC DOS does not take advantage of 80286 exclusives, OS/2 does. In this section we will first look at multi-tasking from the view of the processor and its associated hardware; then we will see how OS/2 exploits and enhances these capabilities.

If we were to summarize the main features of a multi-tasking operating system, we could group them into four system areas: (1) the processor itself, (2) other built-in hardware (such as the bus architecture and system ROM), (3) the operating system, and (4) optional add-on hardware (such as the Math Co-processor). The following table lists those features and shows which components provide them:

Multi-Processing Needs	80286 Processor	Computer Circuitry	Operator System	Add-on Hardware
DOS Compatibility	X		X	
Program Protection	X		X	
Program Sharing	X		X	
Multi-tasking	X	X	X	X
Program Security	X		X	
Co-processing		X	X	X
Program Switching	X		X	
Screen Windowing			X	
Program Interface			X	
Multiple Users		X	X	X

TWO OPERATING MODES

Real Mode

We have already seen that the 80286 supports two main "modes," or "environments." What IBM calls the DOS Mode is what Intel refers to as the 80286 Real Mode. When in Real Mode, the 80286 mimics its 8088 and 8086 predecessors: same instructions, same addressing limits, etc. This provides a built-in environment for DOS programs. As soon as the operating system switches the 80286 to its Protect Mode (IBM's OS/2 Mode), the processor assumes its true identity, which enables OS/2 to run larger programs, support multiple applications, etc. In OS/2, the Real, or DOS Mode becomes active each time you select DOS Command Prompt from the Program Selector. Whenever the user switches out of DOS Mode by selecting an OS/2 session, the DOS program is suspended. This helps prevent an "ill-behaved" DOS program from interfering with the rest of the system.

Protect Mode

The term *Protect Mode* refers to the 80286's ability to "protect" its programs. It does this by carefully managing a collection of memory segments used by each OS/2 application program and its associated data. If a program attempts to address a segment currently assigned to another program (or more important, the operating system), the 80286 prohibits it. That is because each segment is listed in a Local Descriptor Table (LDT) (Figure 3–7). This is more than just a security scheme: it prevents system-crashing program collisions or "clobbering," intentional or accidental. There are two kinds of segments: program (code) segments and data segments. A program segment can never write to another program segment, even within the same program. Program segments are always "execute only," unlike data segments, which are classified "read/write." In a moment we will see how the 80286 Protect Mode makes multi-tasking possible.

The 80386 processor features the 80286 Protect Mode and the 8066 Real Mode. This lets it run the same DOS and OS/2 software that the 80286 supports. The 80386 also features an exclusive Virtual 8086 Mode. This mode supports multiple Real Mode program sessions, allowing several unconverted DOS programs to share memory and processor cycles. Current versions of OS/2 do not support the 80386's Virtual 8086 Mode, but it is found in some DOS shells, such as the IBM 3270 Workstation Program and Microsoft Windows 386™. The 3270 Workstation program utilizes Virtual 8086 Mode only when an 80386 is present, and requires an XMA card on other systems. Microsoft Windows 386 runs only on a 80386-based system such as the PS/2 Model 80. The Quarterdeck Expanded Memory Manager–386™ (QEMM) product also exploits the 80386.

SEGMENTATION MANAGEMENT

LDTs support very large programs—even larger than the Personal System/2's physical 16 Mb memory capacity. Multiple tables keep track of segments used by multiple programs. Segments can also be shared. If two or more

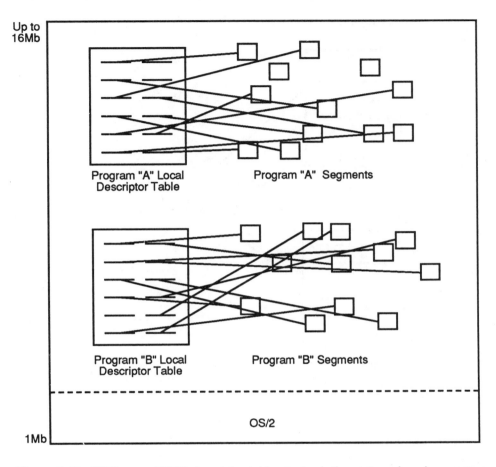

Figure 3–7 OS/2 uses 80286 descriptor tables to track the status of each program memory segment. Here, two OS/2 programs, A and B, have Local Descriptor Tables (LDTs) pointing to the specific location of each segment. Some are currently in memory, as shown here; the rest are on the fixed disk. LDTs help OS/2 manage program switching and a limited memory work area.

programs require an identical function (such as a file manager common to a family of programs), one copy can be shared among them, thus saving memory (Figure 3–8). Or, if two sessions of a word processing program are started, OS/2 does not have to load the same program segments twice. For example, device drivers are shared re-entrant tasks that all programs can use to communicate with attached devices. Data segments can also be intentionally shared, providing a way for two concurrent programs to communicate with each other.

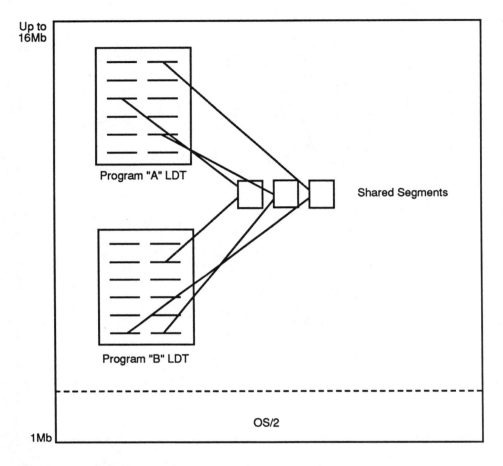

Figure 3–8   Two or more programs can share common memory segments as a means of communicating between them. Segment sharing also lets multiple copies of the same program reside in memory without unnecessary duplication of segments.

Segmentation provides other benefits. Infrequently used program routines or data, such as a help facility or "on-line" reference library, can be segregated from the rest of the program as dynamic-linked segments. These are loaded when needed, freeing memory for active segments of other applications. Segmentation also enables a form of virtual storage called memory overcommit. This lets a 10 Mb program run in 5 Mb of memory, swapping inactive segments between disk and memory as needed. Memory overcommitt should be used with care, since segment-swapping greatly impacts the performance of the system.

Multi-Processing Within a Program

Application programs contain one or more processes, and each process "owns" a set of system resources: the memory used by its segments, all or part of the screen, access to the printer, disk, etc. Within a process a programmer can create several threads, or tasks, where each task, using the same resources owned by its parent process, can run in parallel with other tasks. The use of tasks can significantly improve performance, since calculations, printing, and disk activity can take place concurrently within a program.

Multi-tasking, in order to improve performance, must be done selectively. For example, if a spreadsheet program performs two long calculations as parallel tasks, no overall improvement in performance is detected. That is because the processor has to alternate time-slices between the two tasks, but the total elapsed time would be about the same. On the other hand, if calculations can proceed while other work is done, the total elapsed time is less (Figure 3–9). In OS/2, overlapped operations, such as when an interactive program is started while printing and disk I/O continue, are the most efficient utilization of a multi-tasking system. Sometimes overlapped operations are managed internally by a "smart" program; at other times the user may overlap work between several unrelated application programs. Either way, user wait time is reduced and system throughput is improved.

Task Management

As we saw in the last chapter, each program has its own LDT to manage its use of processor cycles and memory. But more than LDTs are needed to manage multiple applications. To do this, the processor keeps a table in memory called the Task State Segment (TSS), and uses a special register, called the Task Register. Each entry in the TSS points to the LDT of a different process. It also temporarily stores certain important information about each program that is not currently executing: register contents, flags, and instruction pointers that must be restored to the processor when the program gets its next time-slice.

The TSS entry for the current program (the one executing at any point in time) is always found in the Task Register. The 80286 performs task-switching very quickly, and the operating system only has to time the interval, or slice of time that each task receives, and signal to the processor when the next one can begin. The Task Register is then updated with information from the next entry in the TSS table. Then the new program, using memory segments listed in its own LDT, picks up where it left off.

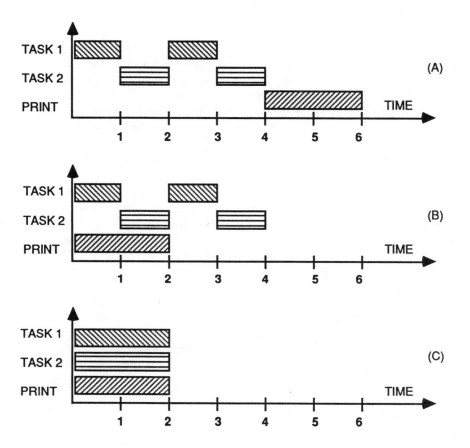

Figure 3–9   Multi-tasking can improve program throughput. In (A), two calculation tasks are time-sliced before printing begins; total elapsed time is six units. In (B), the printing task proceeds concurrently, but the two calculations must share the same processor, so they still take four units to complete. In (C), an additional processor is added, allowing two calculations to take place concurrently in two units of time.

MULTI-TASKING SECURITY

We have already seen how OS/2 protects programs from each other by keeping track of their memory segments in separate tables, called LDTs. OS/2 also segregates program code segments, that can be executed but not changed, from code segments that can be modified.

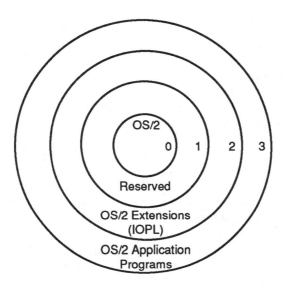

Figure 3–10 OS/2 uses the 80286's four protection rings, or security levels, to protect itself from accidential or intentional interference from applications. Programs may not access other programs or OS/2 components running at lower levels. Applications run at outer level 3, OS/2 extensions at level 2, and the OS/2 kernel or nucleus at level 0. Level 1 is reserved for future use.

Protection Rings and IOPL

The 80286 has another feature that, like inter-program protection, improves program security and helps prevent system crashes. Each program task runs in one of four security levels, which can be thought of as concentric rings (Figure 3–10). The center ring, at level zero, has the highest, or most privileged access, and can cross boundaries to access outer rings. Level zero tasks can execute privileged instructions that are not available in outer levels. The reverse is not true: a task running in security level 2 or 3 cannot access a more privileged task in an inner ring.

OS/2 reserves the inner ring (level 0) for itself, saving it for important functions such as memory management and device drivers. Level 1 is reserved for future use. Level 2 is used for operating system extensions like the Input/Output Privilege Level and special user application tasks, such as password protection, database management, and network file-sharing. All application programs run in level 3.

The Input/Output Privilege Level (IOPL), which runs in level 2, is used by some programs as a "fast path" to the system hardware. This way, an application program can be temporarily granted direct access to a system device, such as the display, bypassing operating system overhead to gain speed. For example, a graphics program might use IOPL to create a high-speed animated sequence. This special privileged status comes with penalties, however. Other programs would be suspended during the sequence, and the application would be given the entire screen for its output. Once the IOPL task is finished, OS/2 regains control of the system, and multi-tasking, dynamic linking, windowing, and other functions are restored.

IOPL is an accommodation to application developers who previously wrote "ill-behaved" DOS programs, bypassing normal operating system interfaces (and overhead) to achieve a boost in performance. Those programs achieved speed at the cost of compatibility, since unpublished DOS addresses and interrupts sometimes changed between versions. IOPL, which is enabled by the 80286 processor, lets performance-sensitive applications run optimally in a multi-tasking environment. An OS/2 user should be aware of programs that use IOPL, and their impact on other applications. IOPL can be disallowed by setting a parameter (IOPL=NO) in the CONFIG.SYS configuration file. This will prevent an IOPL program from running and slowing down or suspending other programs.

PERSONAL SYSTEM/2 MULTI-TASKING SUPPORT

The multi-tasking-enabling features discussed so far in this section are conveniently built into the 80286 processor chip—available to hardware and software designers for exploitation, and used by OS/2. But there is a lot of "glue," or processor-supporting circuitry in a personal computer, and it can make the difference between a restrictive bottleneck and a powerful, efficient computer system. Some of these features are as old as the PC itself, and others are as new as the Personal System/2.

SUPPORTING HARDWARE

Expanded Bus

The Personal System/2 takes multi-processing a big step further. Its Micro Channel architecture supports several tasks running in parallel, using system resources like memory, display, or main processor time-slices. System resources can be used for special tasks such as local area network management. The Micro Channel bus supports several tasks in application or multiple background programs that run without user attention. Up to eight concurrent master processors (like 80286s or 80386s) can share the bus, in addition to direct memory access (DMA) device controllers. This bus enables the design of redundant, fault-tolerant adapter cards that use parallel circuits to improve reliability.

Co-Processing

Earlier in this chapter we saw how the 8087 Math Co-processor off-loaded arithmetic and thus boosted performance over an 8088 running alone. The Personal System/2 Models 50 and 60 support the 80287 co-processor, a companion to the 80286 processor. The 80287 is analogous to the 8087, but supports the 16-bit bus and runs at a faster speed. The Model 80 uses an 80387 to accompany its 32-bit 80386, but OS/2 supports it while running as an 80287. This is multi-processing: the 80287 monitors the bus for instructions that only it can recognize: addition, subtraction, multiplication, and division. When it gets something to do, it proceeds to do it at high speed, while the main processor can do something else. The 80287 signals the 80286 when it is finished, ready with the answer. Only programs compiled for co-processor support will take advantage of an installed 80287 or 80387. Some may check for the presence of a co-processor, and substitute software math routines if it is not there.

Advanced BIOS

The Personal System/2 includes a standard PC Basic Input Output System (BIOS) in ROM, which provides a compatible, PC-like hardware interface for PC DOS 3.3 and OS/2's PC DOS Mode. But Models 50, 60, and 80 also have a BIOS extension called Advanced BIOS, or ABIOS. ABIOS provides some machine-specific routines for the Personal System/2, including multi-tasking on the Micro Channel. Unlike BIOS, ABIOS supports memory addresses above 1 Mb. ABIOS exploits the unique multi-tasking features of the 80286 and surrounding PS/2 hardware, providing a stable base for OS/2 and a platform for future application development (Figure 3–11).

The ABIOS also provides an interface for OS/2 device drivers, supporting both DOS and OS/2 Mode programs. OS/2 initializes the ABIOS at IPL, building a table of installed input/output devices and matching device drivers.

When OS/2 is run on a Personal Computer AT or XT/286, it senses the machine type of the system unit, and "knows" that the ABIOS ROM is not there. So it provides the missing interface through special device drivers. But the AT and XT/286 are based on the old PC architecture, which supports limited multi-tasking, its narrow bus becoming a bottleneck when the sys-

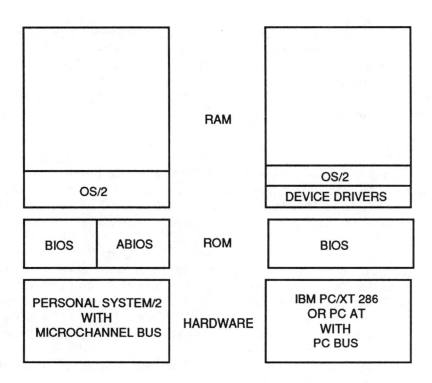

Figure 3–11   When running on a Personal System/2 (left), OS/2 uses the standard BIOS interface for DOS programs and the PS/2's ABIOS for OS/2 programs. ABIOS is designed as an interface between OS/2's multi-tasking environment and the PS/2's Micro Channel hardware. When running on a PC AT or XT/286, OS/2 provides its own substitution for the missing ABIOS interface, in the form of device drivers.

tem gets busy. So, while OS/2 and its multi-tasking programs will run on either old or new architecture machines, the difference in performance may be dramatic.

OS/2 MULTI-TASKING

Up to now we have discussed some features of the 80286 and Personal System/2 that enable multiple applications and tasks, features that the operating system exploits to its advantage. But OS/2 also must do many things itself, providing function that was impractical to build into hardware. In this section we will review the main aspects of OS/2 multi-tasking. Subsequent chapters will address the OS/2 user and programming interfaces in more detail.

OS/2 MULTI-TASKING: USER INTERFACE

Using OS/2 in a Multi-Application Environment

The new OS/2 user should find the multi-application environment easy to adapt to. The user interface supports program selection and windowing from the keyboard or a mouse, and the tutorial program and on-line help are available to get you started or answer questions. A Personal System/2 user who has learned how to interact with the OS/2 display and keyboard will be ready to use all Systems Application Architecture programs, running under OS/2 or other SAA-compatible systems such as the System/36 or System/370.

Tuning the System

Managing many programs, tasks, and segments, OS/2 must distribute units of valuable processor time fairly. An application program has some control over its own priority, or time-slice interval (as long as every program does not try to "take over" the system), and the user does too. Depending on the relative importance of a program's performance, you can control its time-slice allocation. OS/2's default, or natural condition, is to give the current foreground program the highest priority. This gives the user acceptable response time with interactive programs. All OS/2 background programs share the remaining processor cycles.

Controlling OS/2 Multi-Tasking

Internally, OS/2 manages several concurrent programs and tasks. The main OS/2 user interface is through the display and keyboard/mouse, but the configuration file can be also used to modify the system or select options. Here are four multi-tasking options:

MAXWAIT	Limits the amount of time a process or thread has to wait for a time-slice.
PRIORITY	Determines the priority method used.
THREADS	The maximum number of threads supported.
TIMESLICE	Minimum and maximum time increment used for a process.

OS/2 multi-tasking on versions 1.0 and 1.1 is essentially the same, except for 1.1's windowing interface. Up to 12 OS/2 Mode and one DOS Mode programs can be run at once, and the user can "hotkey" or switch between them. OS/2 maintains the changing contents of each program's screen in memory, whether you are viewing it or not. In release 1.1 the handling of screen groups changes significantly. Instead of allocating one full-screen "window" to each application, OS/2 can divide the screen among several applications. The term *screen group* refers to "a group of related windows," since a program can build multiple menus or dialog boxes on the same screen, a form of windowing within an application. Some programs, such as OS/2 IOPL or DOS Mode programs, continue to be restricted to a full, non-windowed screen. Release 1.1 also includes OS/2 graphics support.

Resource Management

The OS/2 user interface is also improved—indirectly—by the way the operating system manages system resources, particularly output devices. Many PC DOS programs required changes when a new higher-resolution display or letter quality printer was added to a system. OS/2 keeps track of attached devices, their names, and their device drivers. Installation changes do not impact application programs.

What Is Coming

The terminate and stay resident background programs of PC DOS were the first PC multi-tasking programs. OS/2, with the help of the Personal System/2's multi-tasking hardware, is capable of much more. The actual improvement to throughput and user productivity will depend on the skill and imagination of application programmers. We can expect to see multi-function programs that combine features of traditional spreadsheet, word processing and database programs. There should be more applications with SAA-standard user, program, and data compatibility between them. Multi-tasking programs will be smarter, more user-friendly, and faster than their DOS predecessors. Background tasks will perform non-user-dependent work while foreground tasks handle response-time sensitive user interaction.

The OS/2 Extended Edition Database and Communication Managers will replace complicated data file access and query procedures with simple Structured Query Language commands. The collection of terminals in the stockbroker's office will be replaced by a single Personal System/2 display with multiple, adjustable windows for data readouts. Multi-tasking data collection programs will continuously analyze, update, and chart information. Networked multi-tasking systems will automate the office, coordinating information from data sources on local PCs, network file servers, and remote host systems. More will be said about the OS/2 user interface in Chapter 4.

OS/2 MULTI-TASKING: PROGRAMMING INTERFACE

Programming a Multi-Tasking Application

OS/2 has three interfaces with the "outside world": one to hardware (the ABIOS in ROM), one to the end user (screen groups), and another to the application program interface (API). Since the new operating system's success is only as good as its applications, the API plays a key role.

Each OS/2 program can be written or converted from DOS using any of six IBM language compilers: COBOL, FORTRAN, C, PASCAL, BASIC, or Macro Assembler. It interacts with the operating system and system I/O devices through the CALL command instead of interrupts, as on PC DOS. The OS/2 Programmer's Toolkit puts the finishing touches on a program, simplifying difficult programming jobs such as window design and user dialog sessions. Toolkit-created programs can be SAA-compatible.

Inter-program and intra-program tasks communicate with each other in several ways. Shared program segments are one way. Semaphores are "flags" of information set aside by one task that another task can read. Pipes are software interconnections between two concurrent tasks that enable the sending and receiving of data between them (Figure 3–12). These features enable a program to react dynamically to events in the multi-tasking environment.

For example, let's say a spreadsheet program starts a task that recalculates the entire sheet, row by row, column by column. While the recalculation is proceeding, the user can start another task, such as printing. Since printing is relatively slow, there isn't much danger of it getting ahead of the recalculation and printing outdated numbers. But what if the user then decided to change a key cell affecting one of the spreadsheet's formulas? That would void the recalculation. If the "cell update" task communicates with the "recalculate" task, it can restart the calculations and printing. Or, a clock-watching function could start an automatic file backup routine or a late-night communication session to transmit data to a mainframe computer.

OS/2 full-function applications are free to use any of the operating system's features. OS/2 Family applications, in order to run under either PC

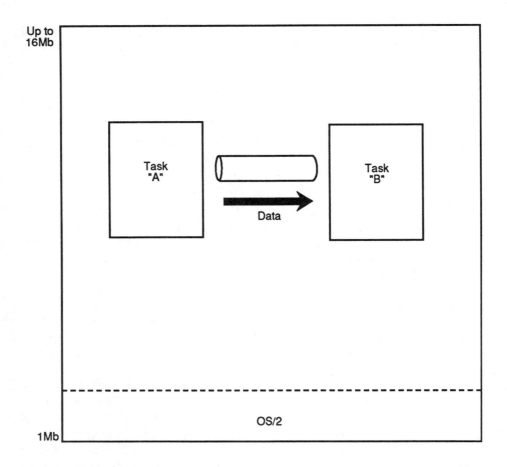

Figure 3–12 OS/2 supports pipes, a technique for passing data between concurrent tasks. Other methods of inter-program communication include segment-sharing, queues, semaphores, and flags.

DOS or OS/2, must restrict themselves to a subset of OS/2 features. This still includes sharing memory above 1 Mb with other OS/2 Mode programs, although a Family program cannot do internal multi-tasking. The OS/2 Programmer's Toolkit assists the application developer in converting PC DOS programs or writing new ones.

OS/2 MULTI-TASKING: HARDWARE INTERFACE

OS/2 is very dependent on the hardware it is running on. The personal computer must use an 80286, 80386, or compatible processor. On a Personal System/2, OS/2 uses the ABIOS built into read only memory. The Microsoft version of OS/2, called MS-OS/2, will be produced under contract for manufacturers of 80286- and 80386-based systems. While the kernel, or base portion of MS-OS/2, will remain essentially the same as IBM's OS/2 Standard Edition, each machine-specific adaptation will require a customized layer of adaptation software. This code, often in the form of device drivers, will take advantage of a system's BIOS, bus architecture, and other unique features.

PC MULTI-USER SOLUTIONS

When many new PC owners think of a "multi-user" system, a central computer with attached terminals comes to mind. This is the traditional shared processor system, which is still relatively rare among personal computer installations. In many companies, remote PCs communicate with a larger, multi-user computer with shared program libraries, file upload/download, and electronic mail facilities.

The local area network (LAN), or interconnected PC-to-PC hookup, is the most popular type of PC multi-user system. Yet the only form of "network" in many multi-PC companies is still the "sneaker-net," where PC users hand-carry data diskettes from one computer to another to exchange information. The OS/2 Extended Edition, with its built-in LAN and host communications, brings multi-tasking and multi-user support to the office.

LOCAL AREA NETWORKS (LANs)

The IBM PC local area network (LAN) was introduced just three years after the PC itself. On the same day, IBM PC Xenix, a shared-processor operating system, was also announced. Both are examples of using PCs in a multi-user environment. A LAN interconnects, or daisy-chains PCs together to communicate and share disks and printers. Xenix, which today runs on several popular PC systems, supports multiple terminals connected to a central computer. The PC performs the processing and shares its own disk and printer with its attached users. Both LANs and shared processors are designed to bring computing power to multiple users, reducing overall costs and improving information-sharing (Figure 3–13). Both methods let those users share programs, data, disk space, and printers, and exchange messages with each other.

But there are many differences. A LAN interconnects PCs to each other, but "nobody's in charge." Each PC has equal weight on a network, sharing a common high-speed cable link. If one system fails, it does not shut down the rest of the network. Some PCs also act as servers, providing a shared fixed disk or printer.

In a shared processor system, the central computer is the "brains" of the operation, and can support one user at its own console, or keyboard/display. Other users, at low-cost communication terminals, are connected via serial (asynchronous) ports. A PC running a communications program may also be used as a terminal or (to use a popular buzzword) intelligent workstation. But PC Xenix is quite different from DOS or OS/2, and it does not support their programs.

LAN Hardware

The cost of a LAN depends on the number of PCs and the cost of network adapter cards, cabling, and software. Network accessories can cost between $500 and $1500 per PC. Adapter and cabling costs are decreasing (some LANs, like the IBM Baseband Network, use low-cost telephone twisted-pair), and newer fixed disks and printers provide greater capability at lower prices, further justifying the cost of a LAN.

LAN Servers

Network disk-sharing requires careful planning. Server directories provide access to files shared by multiple users. Some shared files may be restricted to certain users, requiring password protection for access. If more than one user has update access to a shared file, file-locking is needed to prevent two programs from trying to modify it at the same time. A high-speed, high-capacity PC (such as a Personal System/2 Model 80 with one or two 314 Mb fixed disks) can provide program and data storage for many network users.

Shared devices, such as expensive laser printers, further reduce the per-user installation cost and improve the quality of its services. Multiple print jobs originating from several PCs are spooled to a shared printer by OS/2. Users can periodically check on the status of work in the print queue, and pick it up when finished.

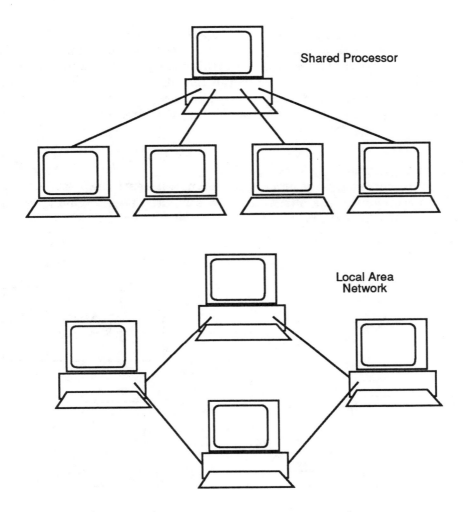

Figure 3–13   Most multi-user PC systems fall under one of two categories. Shared processor systems (top) use a personal computer, running a multi-user operating system, to support users connected via "dumb" terminals. In a network system (bottom), each user has a "smart" PC "daisy-chained" with others for the purpose of file and printer-sharing and message-handling.

LAN Software

Each PC or PS/2 on a network must run a copy of the LAN program as a background task. The latest IBM PC Network program, for PC DOS, supports all forms of IBM networks: broadband, baseband, and the faster, mainframe-compatible Token Ring network.

Like the operating system/BIOS relationship, network software must interface to network hardware through its own BIOS, or Net BIOS. Early network adapter cards included Net BIOS in their own onboard, read only memory. The latest PC Network program includes the Net BIOS software in RAM–loadable form. When selecting network components, it is important to use compatible adapter cards and supporting software.

Gateways

Like disk and printer servers, a network gateway system can share an important resource among several concurrent users. A gateway program maintains a communications link with a host computer, allowing multiple network PCs to access the host as if each had a direct line to it (Figure 3–14).

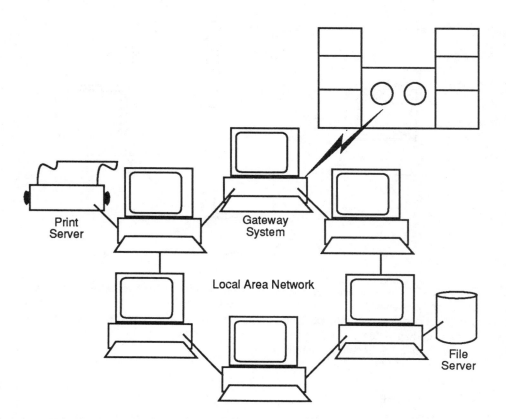

Figure 3–14 A local area network can provide host communication services for several users through a single gateway system. The gateway PC maintains a shared communication line with a remote host system.

Applications

Network software includes its own application program interface, or API, enabling the development of special network applications. Such programs can "hide" network commands from the user, and provide PC-to-PC and program-to-program interaction. For example, a customized network installation could include programs that run programs or access data on other network stations as needed, without the user ever being aware of where a program was running or where the data is coming from.

IBM is building OS/2 network support into the Extended Edition's Communication Manager. By making communications part of the operating system, OS/2 applications can share a common API and the user can run several sessions at once. Software vendors writing communicating applications have two choices. They can develop programs for the Extended Edition's API, or they can write their own communications packages from scratch. Stand-alone packages, like Microsoft's OS/2 LAN Manager™, can also run on the OS/2 Standard Edition.

SHARED PROCESSOR SYSTEMS

A local area network interconnects personal computers so they can share files and printers and communicate with each other. Each computer is an equal member of the network; no one is in charge, but that's okay. The network program, adapter cards, and interconnecting cable are designed for the peaceful coexistence of multiple systems. A traditional multi-user installation shares a central computer among several people at terminals. This is a *shared processor* system, and it differs from a network in several ways.

All of the work—computing, memory management, disk storage, and printing—is performed at the central shared processor system. Its software must not only support multiple application programs, as OS/2 does, but multiple users too. Each user, working at an attached terminal (or at a PC running a terminal emulation program), appears to have sole control of the computer, running programs as if no one else was connected. This puts quite a burden on the shared processor, which requires significant "horsepower"—primarily processor speed—to keep up. A PC or Personal System/2 can serve as a limited shared processor, with an appropriate time-sharing operating system. While OS/2 Extended Edition supports a local area network-type multi-user scheme, Unix-based systems have provided central, shared-processor support on minicomputers and PCs for several years.

Unix, Xenix

Long before the PC and DOS, the Unix operating system was developed at AT&T's Bell Laboratories for programmers working together on large projects. Its designers were looking for a way to build a large application as several smaller pieces, and combine them later. Its popularity spread from the lab to the college campus, and then with graduates to various businesses. Since Unix did not require a large mainframe computer, and ran on several of the popular mini-computers of the sixties, it was adapted for word processing, accounting, engineering, and other work. This helped drive down the per-user cost of computing, long before personal computers came along. A central system with attached terminals is often less expensive than network PCs.

Unix itself was written in a new language called C, and C was also the language supported for Unix application development. Small C programs were written, compiled, and executed to produce results equivalent to much larger programs. Inter-program communication was accomplished with pipes and filters, concepts that were later carried over to DOS and then to OS/2.

Initially, Unix was not known especially for its ease of use, responding only to abbreviated commands like CD (change directory), LS (list directory), or PWD (print working directory). But programmers have never been especially fussy about fancy menus or command prompting, as long as the operating system provides the commands and application interface they need. Later, as Unix grew in popularity and became a base for multi-user applications, *shells*, or interface programs, were written to isolate the user from the technical side of the system. Shell *scripts*, much like DOS or OS/2 batch files, automated command and program sequences.

PC XENIX

AT&T licensed some companies to adapt Unix to other computers. Microsoft Corporation called their version *Xenix*, and it was adapted to run on 80286-based systems. IBM introduced PC Xenix in 1984 with the PC AT model, one of the first 80286 machines. PC Xenix was sold in three parts: a base operating system, a text processing package, and a software development toolkit.

Exploiting the 286

Xenix exploited the 80286's multi-tasking and large memory capability more than three years before OS/2. Xenix addressed up to 16 megabytes, and supported up to 16 users—if you (1) installed enough high-density memory cards, and (2) added additional serial ports to the AT. The PC AT's BIOS supported two serial ports (addressed as COM1 and COM2) for attached terminals, and the keyboard/display "console" became the third user. Additional users could be attached by adding (1) additional multi-port serial adapter cards, and (2) software device drivers so Xenix could use more than the three standard ports. The attached terminals could be either low-cost asynchronous devices or personal computers running simple asynch communications programs.

PC Xenix had modest memory requirements for a multi-user, multitasking operating system: 256 Kb for a single-user installation, and 512 Kb for multiple users. Like OS/2, Xenix could share the same fixed disk with PC DOS, but unlike OS/2, a separate Xenix partition had to be assigned. Through a utility program, Xenix and DOS could exchange data files. DOS programs could not run under Xenix, however, and this single factor probably hurt Xenix's success more than any other. PC DOS had a three-year head start on PC Xenix, and thousands of popular DOS application programs demanded compatibility in future operating systems. Xenix and DOS were simply too different to suggest a merging of the two.

Easy to Install

PC Xenix is shipped on four 1.2 Mb, PC AT diskettes. First, any PC DOS files are backed up from the fixed disk to diskette—temporarily. They are returned to the disk following the Xenix installation. PC Xenix becomes the operating system that boots up each time you power on, so it uses the first two tracks for its boot record, and reserves a special disk partition for its files.

Next, the Xenix installation diskette is booted. The fixed disk is reformatted, and a Xenix partition is created. Disk storage space not needed for Xenix and its programs can be used to create a DOS partition later. Xenix prompts you to insert each of the other three diskettes in sequence, as all of its files are copied over to the various directories. The last step asks for the superuser's password. The superuser is the Xenix system administrator, the person who can add and remove users, access public and private libraries, etc. This is a good time to add the other user passwords.

Using Xenix

Each user logs onto Xenix, much as you would to a remote multi-user system. One person can use the PC AT's console, or keyboard/display, and the others are attached via the system's serial ports. A PC running an asynchronous communications program (even the DOS diskette's COMM program will do the trick) makes a good Xenix terminal, and doubles as an ordinary DOS-based PC the rest of the time.

Microsoft added several usability extras to Xenix that were not part of most Unix systems: the Bourne, C, and Visual shells, the VI full-screen editor, file and record-locking, function key, and color support. Performance, as on all multi-tasking systems, was dependent on the number of users and the set of concurrent application programs. The performance experienced by someone on a three-user PC AT system should be roughly the same as a single-user PC/XT. The additional processor and bus speed of the AT would compensate for much of the overhead and time-sharing impact.

A Common Heritage

Microsoft has drawn on its Xenix development experience in building new operating systems. A programmer familiar with a Unix or Xenix system will recognize many of the commands and features in PC DOS and OS/2. Pipes and filters were mentioned earlier. Tree-structured directories are the same, except that Xenix uses the "front slash" character as a separator: /NFL/AFC/DOLPHINS. Many commands, such as CD (change directory) and RD (remove directory) remain the same. Shared memory, semaphores, and protection rings are found on both Xenix and OS/2. The configuration file is named CONFIG.SYS on both systems.

There are many other differences. Xenix can provide detailed accounting statistics on each user of a system. A rich collection of commands, many of them added through several generations of Unix, are included. (Some users complain about the "excess baggage" of rarely used functions that characterize a Unix or Xenix system, whereas others argue that such commands are important for program and user compatibility.) Xenix recognizes many special key combinations, like <Ctrl + D> that are now better provided by function and cursor-control keys that didn't exist when Unix was developed. Disk directories include, in addition to file names, dates, times, etc., several security options. A file can be set for Read, Write, or Execute, or any combination of the three. A file can be accessed by a single user, a group of users, or everyone.

Xenix communication support provides a little of host connectivity, "networking," and PC-to-PC communications. Dial-in and dial-out lines can be configured to provide an electronic mail and file-exchange capability between remote Xenix installations. The MicNet network feature strings Xenix machines together as an elementary (serial to serial) local area network.

SCO Xenix

The Santa Cruz Operation, a company that has shared several joint ventures with Microsoft, further adapted Xenix for personal computers. Two recent releases are Personal System/2 adaptations, SCO Xenix 286 for the

Models 50 and 60, and Xenix 386 for the Model 80. Using multi-port adapter cards, up to 30 users can share a Model 80. A variety of application programs are running with SCO Xenix, including point of sale (cash registers as "terminals"), accounting, finance, and office management. SCO's MultView™ provides a windowing interface.

DOS Under Xenix

A frustrating characteristic of Xenix is that it does not support DOS programs in its native form. The SCO VP/ix product, developed by Phoenix Technologies Ltd. and Interactive Systems Corp., runs with SCO Xenix 386 to support multiple DOS programs. Both Xenix and DOS programs can share the same system. DOS text-based programs can be run from any attached terminal, but DOS graphics programs can only be run from the keyboard/display console of the system unit.

IBM AIX

IBM is offering a Unix-based Advanced Interactive Executive (AIX)™ system for the Personal System/2 Model 80. It supports programs written for the latest Unix System V level, and is compatible with the AIX system for the RT PC.

Other Unix Derivatives

PC/IX™, by Interactive Systems Corporation, and Venix™, by Unisource, are Unix-derivatives for the XT. All are single-user, under-640 Kb implementations, due to the 8088's limited architecture.

The Winner: OS/2 or Unix?

Many people continue to speculate about the outcome of the Unix-vs.-DOS or Unix-vs.-OS/2 "race." Who will capture the market? Will Unix's shared processor implementation win out over OS/2's local area network solution for the multi-user market? In spite of several Unix-type operating systems on the XT and AT, DOS has not only held on to its sizable majority of dedicated users, but it has continued to grow. Unix and Xenix versions have attracted a much smaller percentage of PC users, and many of them also use PC DOS. Unix systems appeal primarily to programming, education, engineering, and scientific users, but programs can be found in many business applications as well.

Application programmers and computer dealers also have a lot to say about the popularity of PC operating systems. Unix programs, in their compiled, or executable form, exist in a binary format that DOS, and OS/2 do not recognize. If applications are written in the C language, they can be ported from OS/2 to Unix/Xenix systems (or vice-versa), modified, and then recompiled. The DOS and Unix application program interfaces are different, although conceptually a single-user program will require few changes. Multiuser applications, with program-to-program communication or access security, may require a major conversion effort. Neither IBM nor Microsoft have expressed any intention to merge Xenix function with OS/2. Products such as VP/ix appear to be the best way to run DOS and Xenix programs on the same system.

Software houses and computer dealers prefer to deal with as few program versions as possible. Because of reprogramming, maintenance, store shelf space, and customer support, many specialize in one operating system. Applications that require different operating systems (e.g., Xenix) or processors (e.g., the 80386) require multiple versions. The PC software development and retail distribution industries carry a lot of weight, and popular, mass-market packages often precipitate a shakeout of less popular products.

Whether Unix and its relatives will be replaced by OS/2 installations or continue to serve a market "niche" depends ultimately on the popularity of two multiple user PC solutions. Some PC users prefer a shared processor, Xenix-like system to a local area network, but neither IBM nor Microsoft has committed multi-user support for future OS/2 versions. The 80386 has several built-in features, such as virtual 8086 "machine" support, that make it more useful to a shared-processor operating system. OS/2's developers saw the 80286 chip as a popular, "lowest common denominator" base for OS/2. While this decision ruled out an OS/2 version for 8088 or 8086 machines, in no way did it restrict adaptations for future processors. For the time being, 80386-OS/2 systems will have to run in "286 mode." Still, the 80386 is gaining in popularity, and an 80486 is on the horizon.

THE FUTURE

Powerful processors like the 80386 and its successors will have a lot to say about the way future personal systems are used, but their support of higher clock speeds and wider buses are only part of the story. Add-on co-processor boards may do much more for performance than a faster main processor. The Personal System/2 Micro Channel bus, with multiple "master" processors, promises to push PC performance to new levels. Yet the successors to the 80286 offer more than speed enhancement, and the 80386 promises to be the next base for PC hardware and software development.

THE 80386 SUPER-CHIP

Up to now, everything we have covered pertains to the first two generations of Intel PC processors—the 8088/8086 first generation and the 80286 second generation. But already the third generation is upon us in the form of the 80386 and the IBM Personal System/2 Model 80. Operating System/2, at least in its current versions, runs on the 80386 in its compatible 80286 Mode, while taking advantage of the processor's faster clock speed, 32-bit bus, and 32-bit memory.

THE PERSONAL SYSTEM/2 MODEL 80

80386 Performance

The IBM Personal System/2 Model 80 is the first 80386-based IBM personal computer. Models 80-041 and 80-071 run at a clock speed of 16 Mhz, and the Models 80-111 and 80-311 run at 20 Mhz, significantly faster than the 10 Mhz Models 50 and 60. The Model 80 supports the 32-bit 80387 Math Co-processor, which runs faster than the 80287 for those programs written to use a math co-processor. Further, there is a 20 MHz version of the 80387 for the Models 80-111 and 80-311. Future 32-bit devices, in the form of adapter cards or attached I/O, may further extend the 80's performance advantage.

80386 Compatibility: 80286 Modes

The 8086 and 8088 are one-mode processors. The 80286 has two modes: an 8086 Real Mode for compatibility with its predecessors, and a Protect Mode of its own for large memory, multi-tasking support. The 80386 is a three-mode processor, with an 8086 Real, 80286 Protect, and its own Virtual 8086 Mode.

Much of the time OS/2 keeps the 80386 in 80286 Protect Mode, which is virtually identical to the way the operating system runs on an 80286. When DOS programs are running, the processor is switched to Real Mode, just as OS/2 does on the 80286. In DOS Mode memory addressing is limited to 1 Mb as if the processor was an 8088 or 8086, executing only 8086 instructions and using 16 bits of the 32-bit 80386 registers. Programs that have timing dependencies, such as repetitive loops used to measure an interval of time, may require modification.

80386 Virtual 8086 Mode

One unique feature of the 80386 was designed to support multi-tasking in the form of multiple DOS memory partitions. OS/2 does not use this mode, since it provides its own 80286 Protect Mode multi-tasking scheme. Virtual 8086 Mode, used by DOS shells such as Microsoft's Windows 386 and IBM's 3270 Workstation Program, allocates blocks of memory, each up to 1 Mb in size, for PC DOS programs. In each partition, a copy of DOS and an application program can run. Software that supports this feature switches control from one partition to the next, time-slicing processor cycles among the concurrent programs. Each partition is protected from accidental or intentional "clobbering" by other programs. It is possible for an 80386 to concurrently run all three modes at the same time: 8086 Real, 80286 Protect, and 8086 Virtual Mode—*if* an operating system supports them.

80386 Large Memory

The 80386 is designed for the large memory personal computer of the future. Going beyond the 16 Mb physical memory limit of the 80286, the 80386's 32-bit address register and bus can directly address up to 4 gigabytes (billions of bytes), or 2 to the power of 32 bytes of memory. Virtual memory programs can theoretically address up to the mind-boggling 64 terabytes (trillions of bytes), or 2 to the power of 46! An onboard 80386 paging unit swaps 4 Kb memory segments (pages) between RAM and disk, much like a mainframe virtual memory system. OS/2 does not support this 80386 feature, and few personal computers have disk storage devices with the capacity and speed that virtual memory requires.

80386-EXCLUSIVE SOFTWARE

Some programs, like IBM's 3270 Workstation Program, are smart enough to know when they are running on an 80386 system, and take advantage of the Virtual 8086 Mode to run multiple DOS programs. Others, like the IBM AIX operating system and Microsoft Windows 386, are designed only for the 386, and will not run on 80286-based systems.

Quarterdeck's DESQview multi-tasking shell, used with the Quarterdeck Expanded Memory Manager 386, takes advantage of the 386's Virtual 8086 mode, improving DESQview's windowing and background processing support, and reducing its overhead. The Software Link's PC-MOS/386™ replaces DOS on an 80386-based system, supporting many DOS applications for up to 25 users.

4

OS/2's User Interface: Windows on the World

$\mathbf{C}$hapters 2 and 3 described two of the three most important OS/2 improvements: large memory support and multi-tasking. Their impact on application software can be seen in terms of greater function and efficiency. The third major OS/2 enhancement will be discussed in this chapter: the new user interface to the operating system. The manner in which the PC user communicates with application programs, the computer hardware, and the operating system itself depends on the OS/2 user interface. The goal of every personal computer hardware and software engineer—to produce a computer that is easy for everyone to use—starts here.

DEFINING SOME TERMS

As in previous chapters, a few terms will be used frequently. Let's take a moment to define them.

Command Processor. The command processors of both DOS and OS/2 provide a simple user interface for executing commands, batch files, and application programs. The OS/2 command processor, named CMD.EXE, is very similar to DOS's COMMAND.COM.

Internal Commands. The command processor has several built-in commands, such as DIR, COPY, and ERASE. No external command files are required to use them.

External Commands. An external command is one that is not part of the command processor, and exists as a separate file, such as DISKCOPY.COM and FORMAT.COM.

Batch File. A batch file is a list of commands, program names, and other batch file names that can be used to automate the flow of an application. DOS batch files have a file name extension of .BAT, and OS/2's batch files end with .CMD.

Console. A computer's user interface is its console, or keyboard/display, combination. A mouse may also be part of the console.

Mouse. A mouse is a hand-held input device that can be moved across a flat surface. It controls the position of a display pointer or cursor, and has two or three buttons that let the user input application options such as selecting a program from a list of names.

Windowing. A display screen can be subdivided into smaller areas called windows. Each window can provide a view of a larger screen from one of several concurrent programs, or it may be one of several windows created by a single program.

Program Selector. A program selector is a front-end menu, or shell to an operating system, used to start or switch to an application program.

Active Session. An active session is an executing program that can be viewed and controlled by the user (foreground) or execute out of sight (background).

Inactive Session. An inactive session is a suspended program that occupies memory space, is listed on the Program Selector screen, but is not currently executing.

Detached Program. A detached program is one that runs in the background with only occasional user interaction. Like the DOS terminate and stay resident programs, a detached program may be hotkeyed to the foreground when needed. A "pop-up" calendar is an example of a detached program.

Presentation Manager. The OS/2 Presentation Manager introduces an improved user interface and graphics program support to OS/2 Release 1.1.

Editor. An editor is a program that can be used to modify a simple ASCII-format DOS file. A line editor, like DOS's EDLIN, modifies, adds, or deletes a line of text at a time. A full-screen editor, like IBM's Personal Editor, works much like a word processing program.

Code Page. OS/2 has five code pages or character sets of 256 characters each, containing letters, numbers, and special symbols. An application can change the code page in order to display text in a foreign language.

PC DOS USER INTERFACE

The PC DOS command processor was modeled on the old CP/M operating system interface. DOS's "front end," COMMAND.COM, is automatically loaded when a diskette or fixed disk is booted. It receives its input, mostly DOS commands and program names, directly from the user or from a stored sequence called a batch file. The command processor provides no menu; instead a simple screen prompt, such as C>, lets you know it is awaiting your next command.

The COMMAND.COM file is one of three DOS files that must be resident on any bootable program diskette or fixed disk. You cannot see the other two in a directory listing—they are hidden files that make up the PC DOS nucleus, or kernel. Once they are successfully booted into memory, the command processor takes over.

AUTOEXEC.BAT

The saving grace of the DOS command processor is the batch file, particularly a special auto-startup batch file named AUTOEXEC.BAT. Since DOS does not have a program selector or shell of its own (other than COMMAND.COM), the batch file isolates the user from the necessity of entering command or program names to get things going. On a diskette, AUTOEXEC usually calls the resident application program. Before hardware clock/calendar chips and cards became popular, the DOS DATE and TIME commands often appeared just before the program name. Today (at least on the Personal System/2) this is not necessary.

User Shells

On many fixed disk systems, AUTOEXEC loads a shell program that provides a menu from which other applications can be selected. TopView and Windows, their multi-programming support discussed in the last chapter, also provide a good user interface for a DOS fixed disk system. There are other, simpler shell programs for PC DOS, such as the PC Convertible's built-in Application Selector. With a menu or shell, the inexperienced PC user can be isolated from the command processor, its commands, and even batch file and program names. Microsoft Windows version 2.0, described in the last chapter, provides an interface to PC DOS that is similar to OS/2's Presentation Manager.

The International User Interface

While the messages, menus, and publications of OS/2 are currently available only in English, OS/2 is nonetheless a multi-lingual operating system. It supports five code pages, or character sets of 256 characters each. Many of the characters in the four new code pages (such as the standard 26 lowercase and 26 uppercase letters) are the same as the original PC code page 437. Other changes (like replacing some line graphic symbols with accented vowels) accommodate non-English languages. The new code pages, plus foreign keyboard, currency, and other international options support the following 13 languages in OS/2 Standard Edition 1.0:

Canadian French
Danish
Dutch
US English
UK English
French
German
Italian
Finnish
Norwegian
Portugese
Spanish
Swedish

USER INTERFACE HARDWARE

Keyboard

The keyboard is an important element of the user interface, in spite of the growing use of mouse devices for input. The PC Enhanced Keyboard on PC ATs, XTs, and the Personal System/2 is the result of an evolution that began with the original 1981 PC keyboard. The PC keyboard still serves people with a wide range of experience and preferences, including the word processing typist, computer terminal operator, and programmer.

The *typist* is already accustomed to the layout of the "typing area": four familiar rows of letter and number keys. A few typewriter characters such as the cent-sign (¢) have been dropped to make way for characters like \ and ~, part of the ASCII-standard 96-character set and used by DOS, OS/2, and some application programs. Ctrl and Alt are used in combination with other keys to create characters not on existing keys or to issue program commands. Editing keys (DEL, INS, ESC, etc.) are the same, including the command processor "template," which temporarily stores the previous command for possible modification and re-entry. <Ctrl + Alt + Del> is still used to reboot the system.

The four direction keys and the Enter key can be used in place of a mouse to position the pointer and make a choice, such as when selecting a program from a menu. Some OS/2 screens also contain references to frequently used function keys, such as [F1 = Help]. These selections can be made by either pressing the keyboard function key or by a "point and click" with the mouse. But even an accomplished mouse user still needs a keyboard to do what no mouse can do: enter text and numbers.

The Mouse

The mouse has become a popular PC attachment in recent years, replacing joysticks and light pens for business applications. This hand-held device is moved across a flat surface (usually a desk), causing an arrow or other indicator to follow its movement on the screen. A mouse can have up to three buttons, although most of the time OS/2 uses only one. The Personal System/2 makes it easy to use a mouse, providing a special connector on every system. Many other systems attach a mouse via their serial port.

Display

A PC's display is the other key element in the hardware user interface. The original PC Monochrome Display set new standards for text quality but did not support graphics. Today's Personal System/2 Displays are equally adept at showing crisp text and detailed, colorful pictures and computer-generated graphics. The OS/2 user interface depends on high-speed, high-resolution graphics for windowing and cut-and-paste operations.

The Personal System/2's Video Graphic Array (VGA) controller generates text characters in a 9 x 16 character box to the 8503 (Figure 4–1), 8512, and 8513 (Figure 4–2) displays, and up to a 12 x 20 character box for the 8514 (Figure 4–3) display, using the optional 8514/A Display Adapter. DOS and OS/2 text-based programs require no modification to produce VGA text quality, since the controller does the work. The same DOS or OS/2 text programs running on an XT or AT with a Color/Graphics Adapter (CGA) produce a lower-resolution, 8 x 8 character box.

Figure 4–1   The IBM Personal System/2 8503 Monochrome Display is a 12-inch, black and white display that can be used with OS/2 on a PS/2 Model 50, 60, or 80. Colors are automatically converted into 64 unique shades of gray. OS/2's 640-by-480 graphics mode is supported.

Graphics programs are another matter, since the individual dots, or pels, that make up an image or graph are controlled directly by the program. They are more likely to require conversion to fully exploit VGA's resolution and color selection. OS/2 Standard Edition 1.1, which includes graphics support, can also produce optional character fonts, or styles, by replacing the VGA's built-in font with its own.

Other Output Devices

A wide range of printers and plotters can be driven by OS/2's flexible device management. User installation of new hardware and accompanying device drivers is simple, and output device selection or re-direction can be done by the user. OS/2 Standard Edition 1.1 will include alternate character font styles for printers to match those it provides for displays.

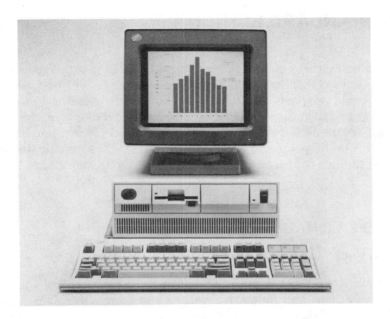

Figure 4–2   The IBM Personal System/2 8513 Color Display is a 12-inch, 640-by-480 display supporting OS/2 on a PS/2 Model 50, 60, or 80.

Figure 4–3   The IBM Personal System/2 8514 Color Display is a 14-inch, high resolution display supporting OS/2 on a PS/2 Model 50, 60, or 80. In addition to the PS/2's 640-by-480 graphics mode, the 8514 supports a 1024-by-768 mode with the addition of the PS/2 Display Adapter 8514/A.

OS/2 STANDARD EDITION 1.0

The various features comprising the new OS/2 user interface are not all available in the OS/2 Standard Edition's first release. The program selector shell supports program installation, loading, and switching in version 1.0. OS/2 program output is restricted to full-screen text displays. Existing DOS graphics programs can run in the full-screen DOS Mode. Mouse support is limited to simple "point and click" operations. OS/2's sophisticated windowing and graphics support appears in version 1.1's Presentation Manager.

THE OS/2 1.0 HARDWARE INTERFACE

Version 1.0 Keyboard and Mouse Support.

Most of the time, OS/2 responds to non-character keys (control and alternate key combinations, and function keys) the same way DOS does. Because of the unique multi-tasking environment of OS/2, there are some differences. For example, an OS/2 "cursor" does not always refer to the blinking underline character familiar to DOS users, but is instead a reverse image bar used to highlight a list entry. Here is a brief summary of some OS/2 1.0 additions to the traditional DOS keyboard commands:

Key Combination	Function
REQUEST KEY <Ctrl + Esc>	Returns to the Program Selector screen, where you can start a new program, a DOS or OS/2 Command Prompt session, or switches to an already-running program.
HOT KEY <Alt + Esc>	Rotates through currently running programs in the order originally selected, displaying the current screen of each one in turn. This command works only *after* a Program Selector selection has been made.
ENTER	Selects item under cursor.
ESCAPE (Esc)	Escapes, or backs up to previous display screen, or cancels command currently displayed.
F1	Displays on-line help information.

Some OS/2 commands, like F1 = Help, are listed on the screen. They can be selected by pressing the appropriate function key or moving the cursor to the command and pressing Enter.

STARTING AND SWITCHING OS/2 PROGRAMS

Booting Up

In this chapter we will assume that OS/2 has been installed on the fixed disk of a Personal System/2 Model 50, 60, or 80, or a Personal Computer AT, or a PC/XT Model 286. This means that the system can be booted up by simply turning it on or pressing <Ctrl + Alt + Del>. It is possible to boot OS/2 from its Installation Diskette, but this is not the way most users will run on a regular basis. We will also assume that the DOS Mode option was taken during installation. In the next chapter we will discuss the installation steps in more detail.

OS/2 Program Selector

The Program Selector screen (Figure 4–4) is the first thing an OS/2 1.0 user sees each day, unless the system has been set up to load and start a program automatically. In that case, the program's first screen appears. The OS/2 Release 1.0 Program Selector is a basic program selection menu, much simpler in appearance and usage than OS/2 1.1's Presentation Services windowing and graphics interface.

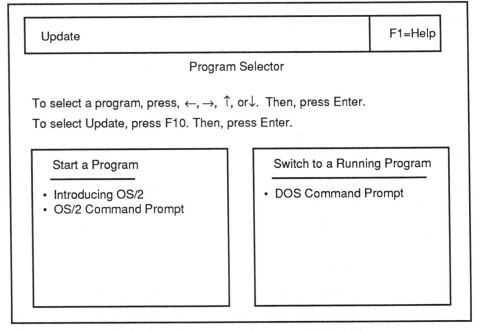

Figure 4–4   OS/2 Standard Edition 1.1 replaces the Program Selector shown here with the Presentation Manager's windowing interface.

Program Selector options are listed on the screen, and selected by keyboard or mouse. The reverse image "bar" is moved to the desired menu item, which is highlighted. To select it, you can either press the Enter key or the first mouse button.

DISK ON THE LEFT; MEMORY ON THE RIGHT

Starting DOS Mode

The right-hand box is labelled "Switch to a Running Program." If no OS/2 programs were pre-loaded, this box contains a single entry: "DOS Command Prompt." This is another name for OS/2's DOS Mode. Why is it listed as a running program? In many ways, the DOS command processor is a special application under OS/2. Since the DOS Mode option was taken during installation, each time you boot up the system, the DOS Mode memory is set aside and the DOS command processor is loaded. DOS Mode is not actually started until you select DOS Command Prompt for the first time. That is when the DOS AUTOEXEC.BAT file (if one exists in the root directory) is run, loading a DOS program. Otherwise, DOS Mode asks for the date and time, just as PC DOS itself does. The command processor behaves just as it does on a pure DOS system. With it you can load a DOS program or use a DOS command. DOS Mode remains under control of OS/2, and is suspended (it and its program are stopped cold) whenever the operating system or one of its programs takes control.

The "Start a Program" box, on the left, is *not* for DOS programs; it is used to start installed OS/2 (Protect Mode) programs only. We will get to it in a moment.

PC DOS MODE USER INTERFACE

Starting DOS Mode

In order to install or run a DOS program, you must first enter DOS Mode. From the Program Selector screen, select the DOS Command Prompt entry in the right-hand box and press Enter. Next you will see a screen with the standard DOS prompt C:\>.

Running DOS Programs

Since the DOS command processor is essentially identical to its DOS 3.3 counterpart, it will act the same. You can use DOS commands like DIR, DISKCOPY, and BACKUP, and run most DOS programs—one at a time. To start a program, you must know its batch file or program name, including the directory path name, if appropriate. For example, \DIR2\PAYROLL might be used to start a payroll program. DOS Mode programs cannot be listed on the Program Selector menu.

Ending a DOS Program

PC DOS programs should be allowed to finish "gracefully" prior to exiting a DOS Mode session, especially those with active data files. Since a DOS Mode program is suspended when an OS/2 program is on the screen, and its files, memory, and output devices are not managed by OS/2, there is a danger of losing data. Until the program is ended normally, some data may still be in memory, and possibly lost if the session is ended abruptly. Or, you may have sent a document to the printer. Let it finish printing before you end the DOS Mode. Always make sure that every DOS program reaches a normal conclusion before you run another one or end OS/2. If you cannot wait, or the program is "hung up," and you do not care about saving data or finishing output, you may be able to "break" the program by pressing the Escape key or the <Ctrl + Break> key combination. That should bring you back to the DOS prompt.

You cannot use the EXIT command to end a DOS Command Prompt session, as you can with an OS/2 session. The most you can do is return to the command processor's C: \ prompt. You can leave DOS Mode by pressing Request, <Ctrl + Esc>, to return to the Program selector, or Hotkey, <Alt + Esc>, to switch to an OS/2 session. DOS Mode does not go away, nor does the memory allocated to it. To remove it entirely, you must modify the CONFIG.SYS file and reboot the system. We will describe those steps in the next chapter.

DOS Command Changes

The DOS Mode includes most of the DOS 3.3 commands. The following commands work *only* in DOS Mode because they are not needed by OS/2: APPEND, ASSIGN, BREAK, SUBST, GRAFTABL, and JOIN. Some old DOS commands have been removed since they are no longer needed: CTTY, EXE2BIN, NLSFUNC, SELECT, and SHARE. (Three commands work *only* in the OS/2 Mode: ANSI, DETACH, and DPATH. More on them later.)

Customizing DOS Mode

Since you will be dealing with both DOS and OS/2 Modes, you may wish to customize the DOS prompt with the PROMPT command. For example, let's assume that you have a directory named \WRITE where all the DOS Writing Assistant application has been stored. To remind you when you are in this directory, you could change the prompt like this: PROMPT $P:. Now, when you finish using Writing Assistant, the prompt \WRITE: will appear.

An AUTOEXEC.BAT batch file in the root directory is run automatically, not when you boot the system, but only when the DOS Command Prompt is first selected. Since there can be only one AUTOEXEC.BAT file, it can be used to automatically run only one program. If you will be using several DOS programs, you may prefer to load each one "manually" by name when needed or use a DOS menu-selector shell.

OS/2 MODE USER INTERFACE

Starting OS/2 Programs

The left-hand box on the Program Selector screen is labelled "Start a Program." This box contains the names of OS/2 programs, both Family and Full-function types. The names are provided during program installation, and new ones can be added at any time. If there are more names than the box can hold, you can use the up or down directional keys (or mouse) to scroll through the list. Once the desired program has been selected, press Enter to run it. A new OS /2 session will be created for the program, and it will be added to the right-hand Switch to a Running Program list.

The Start a Program list is maintained in alphabetical order. One item in the list is always "OS/2 Command Prompt." You select it every time you want to go to the OS/2 command processor to use a command or "manually" run an OS/2 application program not on the list. An "uninstalled" OS/2 program can be run from the fixed disk or a diskette by entering its name, just as you would with DOS. Multiple OS/2 Command Prompt sessions can be started; they are numbered 1, 2, 3, etc.

Switching Programs

You can start additional OS/2 programs (up to 12 at a time, memory permitting) by returning to the Program Selector. This can be done anytime by pressing <Ctrl + Esc>. Now, in the *Switch to a Running Program* box on the right, you will see the names of all currently running OS/2 programs. If an uninstalled program is running (started from the OS/2 command prompt), it will not have a name, just "OS/2 Command Prompt," followed by a number (1, 2, 3, etc.). If you move left to the Start a Program box again, you can start additional programs from the list or manually from the OS/2 prompt. Or, on the right, you can return to any of the current set of running programs. The right-hand Program Selector list is analogous to selecting a TV program by pressing a channel number on a TV remote control unit. Then, to "rotate" through your set of running programs, just press the <Alt + Esc> key combination as many times as you need to, until you see the screen of the one you want to work with next. This is like pressing the "next channel" button on the TV remote control.

Foreground Session

When you select or rotate into a new program session, that becomes the active, or foreground, session. You can now interact with this program just as you would if it were running alone. If the program had been working on a big calculation or print job, you may find that it is still working on it, or it may be finished, waiting for further instructions or data. You will also discover that a program runs faster when in the foreground. By default, OS/2 gives the current foreground program a higher priority. This improves user response time and the performance of the program currently getting most of the attention. Background programs may run slower as a result.

One Program, Multiple Sessions

The same program can be started in several sessions. Why would anyone want to do that? Let's say most of your work involves writing computer books. You could have three sessions of your OS/2 word processing program running at the same time, one printing a chapter, another being spell-checked, and a third chapter in final editing stages. You can hotkey between them easily, and with the Presentation Manager, clipboard (cut-and-paste) paragraphs between them. If your program was designed to share segments, OS/2 will not waste memory by maintaining three duplicate copies. The three word processing sessions will share common segments.

Background Sessions

While you are interacting with one program (the active session), all others are inactive, or background, programs, out of sight from the user. Background sessions continue to run, performing calculations or other work, until user interaction is required or they finish running. Then they become inactive, or suspended, still on the Running Program list, but performing no work until the user brings them to the foreground again. DOS Mode programs are *always* suspended, regardless of what they were doing, while in the background. OS/2 maintains the unseen screens of background programs, called logical displays, in memory until they are returned to the foreground.

Detachable Programs

Some OS/2 programs can run in the background by themselves, and require no user interaction until needed. These are like the terminate and stay resident, or hotkey programs that run under DOS. When you start such a program, it is done with the OS/2 DETACH command, and a process identification number (PID) is returned to you. When the detached program ends, OS/2 confirms its termination by displaying another message.

Cancelled Sessions

When an installed OS/2 Mode program has finished, it will automatically return you to the Program Selector screen. When a command prompt-started program is ended, it returns you to the command prompt. The OS/2 EXIT command terminates the session and returns to the Program Selector. Unterminated sessions (those that have finished, but not EXITed) appear on the Running Program list as "OS/2 Command Prompt 1" (or 2 or 3, etc.).

OS/2 COMMANDS AND OPTIONS

OS/2 Command Processor

The OS/2 command processor (or prompt) is a file named CMD.EXE, which works very much like DOS's COMMAND.COM. Its prompt looks a little different from PC DOS's prompt, surrounded in brackets: [C:\]. Most of the DOS commands are also in OS/2, but there are differences. The following commands work only in the OS/2 Mode:

Command	Function
DETACH	Starts a special process as a background session. Example: DETACH SPOOL would be used to start the OS/2 SPOOL program, which is a non-interactive, background program.
ANSI	Installs the ANSI escape sequence in OS/2 Mode.
DPATH	Works like PATH command to search directories for data files (those without .EXE, .COM, .BAT, or .CMD file name extensions). Similar to DOS APPEND.
SPOOL	More than a command, SPOOL is an OS/2 background program that is started with DETACH (above). It intercepts multiple output files destined for the printer and stores them as temporary files until they are printed. The spooler is usually started in the CONFIG.SYS file with the RUN command.
HELP	Provides additional information relating to a warning or error message.
CMD	Starts a secondary OS/2 command processor.

Internal Commands

The following OS/2 commands (which include the new DETACH and DPATH) are built into the CMD.EXE command processor, and do not exist as separate OS/2 files. Most have the same function as their PC DOS counterparts.

BREAK	ECHO	REN
CHCP	EXIT	RMDIR
CHDIR	FOR	SET
CLS	GOTO	SHIFT
COPY	IF	TIME
DATE	MKDIR	TYPE
DEL	PATH	VER
DETACH	PAUSE	VERIFY
DIR	PROMPT	VOL
DPATH	REM	

External Commands

The following commands are not part of the CMD.EXE command processor, and can be found as OS/2 command files, each with the file name extension of .EXE. The OS/2 Install program puts them in a fixed disk directory named \OS2. OS/2 includes a built-in PATH command to that directory. If you move any of these command files to a different directory, you should use PATH to indicate the change.

ANSI	FDISK	PATCH
APPEND	FIND	PRINT
ASSIGN	FORMAT	RECOVER
ATTRIB	GRAFTABL	REPLACE
BACKUP	HELPMSG	RESTORE
CHKDSK	JOIN	SORT
CMD	KEYB_	SUBST
COMMAND	LABEL	SYS
COMP	MODE	TREE
DISKCOMP	MORE	XCOPY
DISKCOPY		

USING SOME COMMON OS/2 COMMANDS

As with PC DOS, there are still many occasions when the OS/2 user will need to use operating system commands. OS/2 Release 1.1, with its improved user interface, will simplify some OS/2 operations, but a few commands are always good to know. For more information, consult the On-line Help Library, the OS/2 User's Guide, or the OS/2 User's Reference.

File names   File names and formats are identical to those created by PC DOS programs. File names consist of up to eight characters followed optionally by an extension of not more than three characters. An example: SPY-FILE.CIA. The period can be used as a separator between the two portions of a name, but not in the name itself. The following symbols cannot be used in OS/2 file names:

. " / \ [ ] : ? * | <> + = ; , ( ) & ^

Conditional Use of Commands   OS/2 commands can be "stacked" together so that the outcome of one command determines if the next one will be used. The And (&&) and Or (| |) operators are used for conditional command execution. For example, DIR \WRITE\TEST && DEL \WRITE\TEST means "if the file TEST appears in the \WRITE directory, delete it."

MKDIR or MD   The Make Directory command is used to create directories and subdirectories on a fixed disk, usually to store application programs and their related data files.

Example: MD\SPREAD creates a directory named SPREAD, which will later be used for a spreadsheet program.

COPY   COPY is one of the most frequently used DOS commands, and will probably remain so for OS/2. It can copy files from and to diskettes, fixed disk, display, and printer. A typical use is to copy a group of files from diskette to fixed disk.

Example: COPY A:*.* C:\SPREAD copies all files on the diskette in drive A: to the directory named SPREAD on the fixed disk drive C:.

XCOPY   An improved version of COPY is particularly useful for backing up files from fixed disk to diskette, since it can selectively copy only files that have changed after a given date or since the last XCOPY.

Example: XCOPY C:\SPREAD*.* A: /M copies all files that have been created or modified since the last time XCOPY was used. (A bit in each file's directory is set on whenever the file is changed and off when XCOPYed.)

RENAME or REN   This command is used to change file names.

Example: RENAME C:\SPREAD\THISYEAR LASTYEAR

PRINT   The PRINT command sends a "print image" file to the printer. A print image file is in ASCII (text) format, which is used by some word processing programs to store documents. Better yet, it is a file that was produced as output from a word processor (a "print to disk" option). Note: OS/2 has a SPOOL program that can be used to send a queue of several files to the printer as a background session.

Example: PRINT C:\TEXT\REPORT.PRT prints a file named REPORT.PRT, which was created by a word processing program earlier.

TYPE   TYPE gives you a display listing of a text file.

Example: TYPE C:\CONFIG.SYS

ERASE   This command erases files you no longer need.

Example: ERASE C: \SPREAD\JUNK

CHDIR or CD   This command changes the directory you are currently in. (Sometimes in order to run a program, you may need to use CD first to enter the program's directory. This may be required in order to store program data files in the same directory.)

Example: CD C: \SPREAD

DIR   Directory listings are important to the maintenance of any personal computer system, especially in directories where program data files are stored. A directory listing will provide an indication of the size and age of files.

Example: DIR C: \SPREAD lists the file directory for directory SPREAD.

RMDIR or RD   The Remove Directory command is needed to erase directories that are no longer needed. Before removing a directory, use ERASE to remove any files from the directory.

Example: RD C: \SPREAD

DISKCOPY This command copies diskettes of the same capacity, if they are not copy-protected by the manufacturer. If the system has only one diskette drive, OS/2 (or DOS) will prompt you to swap between the Source and Target diskettes during the duplication process.

Example: DISKCOPY A: B:

FORMAT.   FORMAT is used to prepare a diskette or fixed disk for use by erasing and checking the entire disk. If you FORMAT an old diskette, you erase any files it may have had on it.

GETTING HELP

OS/2 provides two sources of on-line assistance: Help Messages and the On-line Help Library.

Help Messages

When OS/2 detects an error, it returns a brief, one-line message, such as:

    SYS0002: THE SYSTEM CANNOT FIND THE FILE SPECIFIED

If you wanted a better description of the problem, you could go to the OS/2 command line and type:

    HELP 2

OS/2 would then return an expanded version of the same message, something like:

    THE FILE NAMED IN THE COMMAND DOES NOT EXIST IN THE DIRECTORY
    OR THE DRIVE SPECIFIED. YOU MAY HAVE TYPED THE FILENAME INCOR-
    RECTLY, OR YOU MAY HAVE USED AN UNACCEPTABLE CHARACTER. RETRY
    THE COMMAND USING A CORRECT FILENAME.

The HELP command is a quick way to get additional information without looking it up in the book. It can also be used to display a list of frequently needed function keys at the top of the screen, as a reminder.

OS/2's On-line Help Information

OS/2 reference information can be accessed from OS/2 screens by pressing the F1 key (Figure 4–5). This displays one or more screens of text explaining OS/2 features and functions. The Help Library is context-sensitive, so it attempts to assist you by noticing just where you were when you pressed F1. If you were attempting a disk copy, you would first get help with the DISKCOPY command. You can still page through the library for other information.

Since F1 (for Help) is defined as part of IBM's Systems Application Architecture, you can expect to find it used in many OS/2 programs. In most cases, a Help library is maintained as a separate text file in order to save program and work area space.

OS/2 System Editor

OS/2 1.1 provides a full-screen text editor that can be used to create or modify any ASCII-format file, including the system configuration file (CONFIG. SYS), the OS/2 Startup file (STARTUP.CMD), and the DOS Mode AUTOEXEC.BAT file.

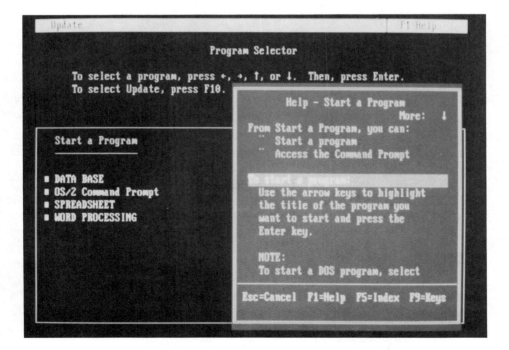

Figure 4–5 The first Help screen (a window invoked by pressing the F1 key from the Program Selector) is the first level of OS/2's On-line Help Library.

OS/2 BATCH FILES

Batch files store commands and program names that the operating system recognizes. Instead of manually entering a program name, you can have it called from a batch file instead. PC DOS batch files all have a filename extension of .BAT and will not run in an OS/2 Mode session. On the other hand, OS/2 batch files end in .CMD and will not run under the DOS Mode. Otherwise, they are very much alike. PC DOS looks for a standard batch file named AUTOEXEC.BAT every time it starts; this is how programs are set up to run automatically when a system is turned on. In OS/2, the startup batch file is named STARTUP.CMD. Both AUTOEXEC.BAT and STARTUP.CMD are created during the OS/2 installation process, and may be modified by the user to change the way the system is started.

Batch files indirectly affect the user interface, "invisibly" executing commands and calling programs in sequence. We mention them here because in the course of running any PC system, regardless of operating system, it sometimes becomes necessary to examine, modify, or create a batch file. Most of the time you will be running applications under the control of batch files, and you will never realize it (or care). But if you are called on to create one in a hurry, it does not hurt to know a few pointers.

Make Your Own Batch File

If necessary, you can create a batch file yourself. In the OS/2 1.1 versions, this can be done by using the OS/2 System Editor. There is an even quicker way to create a short file, using a shortcut familiar to many DOS veterans. The COPY command (which is the same in either DOS or OS/2 Modes) can be used to "copy" a short file from the screen to disk. Here's how:

Let's say that you want to create a simple batch file named PAY.CMD that runs the PAYROLL program in the DIR2 directory, and then exits the OS/2 Mode session when finished. First, select an OS/2 session with Start a Program. Next, enter: COPY CON PAY.CMD. On the next line, enter: \DIR2\PAYROLL. On the third line, enter: EXIT. (The first line names the file and the last two lines comprise the contents of the file.) Now, to close the file, on the last line you need to enter an "end of file" character, by pressing either <Ctrl + Z> or function key F6. To verify your work, enter: TYPE PAY.CMD. If you made an error, start over. You will find more in the OS/2 Reference.

New Batch Commands

OS/2 has added some new commands for use within batch files. These are in addition to those found in previous DOS versions.

Command	Function
CALL	Calls one batch file from another. New for PC DOS 3.3, DOS Mode, and the OS/2 Mode.
ENDLOCAL	Restores the drive, directory, and environment settings in effect before the SETLOCAL command was used.
EXTPROC	Defines an external batch file processor. This gives developers the option of using their own batch file processors instead of the OS/2 version.
SETLOCAL	Lets you define drive, directory, and environment variables for the current batch file.
START	Start OS/2 sessions and programs in those sessions; issued from STARTUP.CMD or any batch file.

STARTUP.CMD Batch File

When OS/2 is first loaded into a system, it looks for a special file named STARTUP.CMD in the root directory. If found, the Program Selector screen is bypassed and the first OS/2 session and program are started. The program name is provided inside the STARTUP.CMD batch file. Additional programs can be started at the same time from START commands in the same file. Each START command initiates another OS/2 Mode session, loading the program specified (Example: START FINANCE). A descriptive name can also be given to each program, so that a description (instead of a filename) appears on the Program Selector.

OS/2 STANDARD EDITION 1.1

One major difference between OS/2 Standard Edition release 1.0 and 1.1 is obvious. The relatively simple text-based, single-screen, hotkey-switching user interface of OS/2 1.0 has been replaced by the graphics-based, windowing interface of version 1.1. This is the OS/2 Presentation Manager, an improved operating system shell that conforms with the Common User Access portion of IBM's Systems Application Architecture.

SYSTEMS APPLICATION ARCHITECTURE

SAA was introduced to simplify the transfer of application programs between large and small IBM systems, promoting multi-system usability and connectivity. This new programming architecture encompasses much more than language compilers; it defines application interfaces for communications, graphics, databases, and the user interface. Many people can benefit from Systems Application Architecture: the programmer can be less concerned about differences between various systems, and users can benefit from a familiar, consistent program interface. The appearance and behavior of screens and keyboards will often be the same. Less retraining is needed, and office efficiency benefits.

In this section we will examine SAA's impact on the user, through the OS/2 Presentation Manager. In later chapters we will see how it affects the OS/2 application programming, communications, and database interfaces.

SAA Common User Access

The Common User Access portion of Systems Application Architecture deals with how people use a program. It establishes how information can be displayed on a screen, and how the user responds to it. It covers things like screen formats, mouse movement, and function key assignments.

SAA Dialog Interface

Part of Common User Access defines how the computer talks to the user. This includes the various ways programs display information: menus, messages, selections, window formats, etc. Another part focuses on how the user responds to a program: using mouse buttons, standard function key assignments, and the meaning and use of commands (like SAVE, GET, etc.).

An operating system's Dialog Manager can greatly simplify the programmer's task in writing consistent, usable programs. SAA defines an interface specification based on the existing IBM Personal Computer EZ-VU™ Run Time Facility. Users who are already using EZ-VU based applications will find the SAA definition familiar. Dialog Manager services include program commands such as "display a panel," "get panel input," "write a message," and "get a variable."

SAA Graphics Interface

Graphics play an important role in both the SAA Common User Access and OS/2's Presentation Manager. The graphics interface is based largely on the existing System/370 Graphical Data Display Manager (GDDM) and its set of graphics primitives, or program commands. This includes a compatible set of language elements for drawing lines, setting colors, choosing and using character fonts, and creating windows and menus. Graphics primitives in a program should produce the same results on different systems, with operating system device drivers providing the necessary hardware interface. SAA support for images (such as pictures captured with a scanner) will be limited, since image compatibility is often restricted to a family of high-resolution displays, such as the PS/2 display.

SAA Query Interface

The Query portion of the user interface deals with relational databases and creating reports based on them. It will be discussed in Chapter 7, OS/2 Extended Edition.

OS/2 is the first IBM software product to participate in SAA (its April 1987 announcement followed SAA's by a few weeks). Not all of SAA will appear in the first release of OS/2; the architecture and the operating system will evolve over a period of time. OS/2 Standard Edition 1.0 has very little SAA content. Standard Edition 1.1 will be the first version to encompass much of the SAA programming and user interface. The Extended Edition will include much of the Common Communications and Database architecture of SAA.

The OS/2 Programmer's Toolkit 1.1 assists the application developer in creating Presentation Manager programs and assures high SAA content. IBM has stated its intent to develop SAA-conforming applications, and we can expect to see many of these running under OS/2.

PRESENTATION MANAGER

The OS/2 Presentation Manager performs three primary functions. First, it provides an improved user interface to the operating system and its application programs. Second, it can display, or window, multiple programs on the screen at the same time (Figure 4–6). Third, it gives the programmer an application program interface (API) for writing programs that output text and graphics to a variety of devices, support windowing within a program, and are consistent and compatible across a variety of programs and systems. Most applications written for the OS/2 Standard Edition version 1.0 will run under the Presentation Manager without change; further modifications are needed to utilize the API.

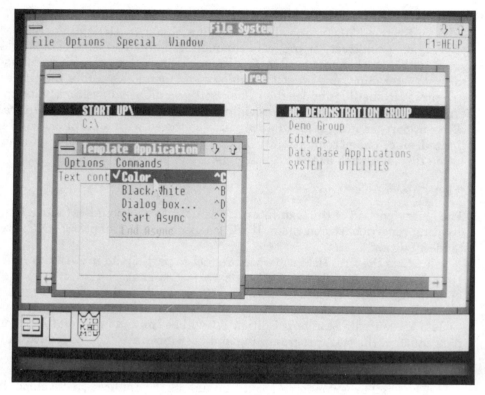

Figure 4–6   OS/2 Standard Edition 1.1 replaces the Program Selector with the Presentation Manager's windowing interface.

PROGRAM SELECTION

User Shell

The user interface of the Presentation Manager is based on the Common User Access portion of Systems Application Architecture, beginning with an improved OS/2 Program Selector. In addition to starting programs from a list, a command line can be used for entering commands or program names directly. Or, the user can switch to another active program in the running programs list, rotate between them in round-robin fashion, or window them all on a single display. The size and position of each application window can be adjusted.

Other User Shell Functions

A special menu is provided to interface with the OS/2 file system: listing directories, copying, erasing or renaming files, etc. Various options, such as screen colors and window borders can also be set. Another menu is available to control printing, including selecting the current output device and building a queue of print jobs. The print spooler can be controlled by the user to change fonts, reorder, or flush jobs from the queue.

Version 1.1 Keyboard Commands

The same two key combinations that were used on version 1.0 to return to the Program Selector or switch to another program perform essentially the same function on version 1.1, within the Presentation Manager's windowing interface.

<Ctrl + Esc>   Drop-Down Menu listing current application programs.

<Alt + Esc>   Select application screen group.

Non-Presentation Manager Programs

PC DOS programs, as in release 1.0, always take over the entire screen while in use. When not being used, a DOS program is suspended, receiving no processor time or system resources. Some OS/2 programs written for version 1.0 cannot be windowed on the same screen with others. This includes programs written to directly access the screen. Like DOS programs, they "take over" the screen while in foreground use. They disappear when other programs, or the Program Selector, return to the screen.

MULTI-APPLICATION WINDOWING

Screen Appearance

As other programs are started, they appear as overlapping screen windows. Each application window shows a portion of a full, 80-column by 25-row screen. Its contents are not reduced proportionately in size, but trimmed to fit the window's space. The first screen containing the Program Selector always remains visible until removed by the user. As additional programs are started, each one overlays the others so that the last one is on top, but portions of the others can still be seen underneath. The top-level window is always the active, or foreground, window, ready for user interaction. The entire screen is known as the Presentation Manager *screen group*, or collection of windows.

Screen Groups

Some programs are designed as screen groups, meaning they create their own overlapping windows. Some DOS applications, such as IBM's Assistant

Series, do this. For example, Writing Assistant can be interrupted by pressing the Escape key to display a program menu. Pressing the "4" key brings up an overlapping menu for loading a file, followed by a file directory menu, and so forth. When the new file has been loaded, the user can back out of the overlapping windows, and begin working on the document. Application windows are generated in a parent-child relationship. The first window is the parent, and it creates child windows, which are fully contained within the parent. A user can interact with a child window of an active parent.

The user can change a background, or inactive window, to a foreground, or active one by either pressing <Alt + Esc> to rotate through the active selections, or by moving the pointer to a spot inside the desired window and selecting it with a mouse button or Enter. There are several ways a user can interact with a program.

PROGRAM INTERACTION

The Pointer

The pointer is a small figure such as an arrow that can be moved around the screen with a mouse or by using the four directional keys. Sometimes the appearance of the pointer, or selection cursor, when it is moved inside an application window, changes to a reverse-image bar or a blinking underline. The pointer's appearance may also vary as it moves from selectable to non-selectable list items.

The point of the arrow can be used to highlight an item that is then selected by pressing Enter or a mouse button.

Window Format

A Presentation Manager window is more than a simple rectangular box. It contains certain fixed and optional information that helps the user in identifying it from other windows, changing its size, and scrolling information inside it. Each window can contain a frame, border, title bar, scroll bar, menu bar, min/max bar, and icons.

The border is optional, and it can be of different widths. By moving the mouse pointer to the border and "dragging" it (holding a button down), the window's size can be changed. Dragging the title bar moves the entire window. The title bar is the program name that is highlighted when the window is currently active. One or two optional scroll bars may appear. A Vertical Scroll Bar, on the right, and a Horizontal Scroll Bar, on the bottom, can be used by the mouse to move information around within the window. The keyboard page up and page down keys may also be used. The Menu Bar is a horizontal list of application commands or options, and may be used to select another menu. Icons are little figures that can be selected to activate the system menu, or to change the size of the window.

When a "parent" application program creates "child" windows of its own, it can control various window options, such as information that appears inside the window, and give the user control of its size and position. A child window or dialog box is always drawn within the parent window. An underlying window can be brought to the top by pointing to it and pressing a mouse button or Enter.

Menus

When a secondary menu is selected from a window's menu bar, it usually appears as a pull-down menu, directly under the bar. That menu contains additional options, and when one is selected, the menu may disappear or be partially overlaid while the option is performed.

Dialog Boxes

Not all of the user interface to an application program can be satisfied by menus. A program dialog box is used to send messages and other information to the user and also to receive input back from the user. The dialog box offers the programmer the flexibility of choosing from among several input techniques. Push buttons, check boxes, and list boxes are used to select from listed items when more than one selection is permitted. Radio buttons are used to choose from a mutually exclusive list of options, such as when selecting a printer for program output.

An Input Field is simply an area into which text can be typed. It may already contain sample or default information, which can be overwritten. Scroll bars can be used to view more text than will fit in a dialog box, similar to the ones used to move information in menu lists.

Clipboarding

When an OS/2 program uses the Presentation Manager interface, you can cut and paste data between windows within an application or between two applications. Clipboarding is a handy means of moving information from a spreadsheet to a document file or moving data within a file, without relying on special application features.

TEXT OUTPUT

Mixing Graphics and Text

Most PC DOS programs run either in text or graphics mode. A DOS text program can display no graphics, and most graphics programs have very limited text capability, primarily due to limitations of the original PC Color/ Graphics Adapter. A 320 x 200, 4-color graphics chart has only a double-wide, 40-column text font for titles and labels, and 80-column text is restricted to the 640 x 200, black and white mode. The OS/2 Presentation Manager supports graphics and text mixing, with a variety of optional character fonts.

Text Enhancements

OS/2 supports both the built-in text characters of a graphics adapter (EGA or VGA) and an improved set of its own. In its alternative text format, up to four OS/2 or application-loaded character sets can be used to provide italics, bold, and other font styles and sizes. Underscoring is supported, so that an underlined passage in a document will appear on the screen as it will in printed form. Character strike-through is also supported, so that characters can be superimposed in the same space.

Typographic Text

High-quality text can be sent to both displays and printers. An application can select (or let the user choose) from among the built-in fonts of a particular printer, use one of the OS/2 fonts, or it can define its own. Proportional font styles, where characters have different widths, can help produce "book-quality" output.

Vector Fonts

In addition to a set of letter-quality, "image" fonts, the Presentation Manager also provides vector, or outline, fonts, commonly used to label charts and engineering drawings. While vector fonts do not have the quality of image fonts, they are often easier to read in the smaller sizes, particularly on lower-resolution displays. They are generally faster to produce and, most important, they, like graphics primitives, allow a program to be migrated to other systems.

GRAPHICS OUTPUT

Two Kinds of Graphics

There are two ways that an OS/2 program can display graphics information on the screen. One method uses graphics primitives, or program instructions to draw lines, circles, paint, and move objects. These primitives can be used by the same program running on another computer system with a different display type, and are compatible with Systems Application Architecture. The other form of graphics output deals with images, or pictures that were captured with a device such as a scanner or digitizer, and then displayed in snapshot form, much like a slide viewer. Such pictures, or bitmaps, are often specific for a particular graphics controller, such as the Personal System/2's MCGA or VGA. They may not be SAA-compatible, and may not map-over to another computer system without a compatible graphics interface.

Graphics Primitives

A graphics program draws its charts, graphs, or schematics on a "virtual screen," a standard set of coordinates that the operating system later maps over to the actual dimensions (640 x 480, etc.) of a real display. OS/2 device drivers also map text and graphics output to printers and plotters.

The simplest primitive is the line between two points. Some electrical and engineering drawings are comprised almost entirely of lines. Circles, arcs, fillets, splines, and pies all use curved lines. The pie primitive, for example, would be used in a program displaying data in the form of pie charts. An enclosed area can be filled with a solid color or a pattern. Some programs draw bar charts using both colors and patterns to identify different information. This way, a black and white photocopy of a color bar chart still provides meaningful information.

Graphics Attributes

Each picture can be modified by changing one or more attributes. The screen background color, and the colors of each line or object can be set. Linestyles and area patterns can be changed. Markers, or symbols used to mark points on a graph, can be used. Text character style, size, and angle can be selected. Transformations can scale, rotate, or move previously drawn objects around the screen. Clipping is used to restrict an object to a particular region, or window of the screen.

Images can be created the hard way: by defining a rectangular array of pixels, or colored dots in the form of an icon or other small picture. Unlike captured pictures, images created with primitives can be migrated between various systems. Text, lines, and other information can always be added to an image, such as when the description of a house is superimposed over its picture.

Retained Images

Any portion of a drawing can be saved and redisplayed elsewhere on the same screen or on another drawing. For example, a small picture of a PC could be reproduced many times in a drawing of a local area network.

Bitmaps

Not all of the features of the OS/2 Presentation Manager are part of Systems Application Architecture. One feature is designed to support high-resolution graphics. It is called bitmaps: a tool for graphics programs that optimizes their performance. Bitmaps contain text or graphics information that can be copied and displayed very quickly, such as to restore a menu to the screen or generate an animated sequence. An application using bitmaps may be written for Personal System/2 computers and displays, but may not be compatible with other SAA systems.

Command Line

The command line provides direct access to the OS/2 command processor, CMD.EXE, giving an experienced user an alternate to the menu interface. Most OS/2 commands are the same as DOS 3.3.

USER INTERFACE HARDWARE

Device Independence

A program's printer output can be modified to support various devices and character fonts. Each program is written against a general output interface in the OS/2 application program interface. Through device drivers, the Presentation Manager directs program output to a specific printer or plotter, without requiring any modification to the program itself. New drivers can be written by a hardware manufacturer to match a new device, and then easily installed by the OS/2 user. An escape function is provided so a programmer can exploit unique features of a device, such as special plotter commands not found on printers.

Displays

Operating System/2 is supported on the Personal Computer AT and XT/286 and Personal System/2 Models 50, 60, and 80. The OS/2 Presentation Manager supports attached displays on each system as follows:

PC AT and XT/286

The IBM Color/Graphics Display Adapter supports the lowest-resolution OS/2 output. Presentation Manager uses the CGA's 640 x 200 mode, which displays only in black and white. The 320 x 200, 4-color mode, with its 40-column text limitation, is insufficient for the detailed OS/2 screens. The IBM Enhanced Graphics Adapter and Display are recommended, with a 640 x 350, 16-color resolution. The VGA graphics support of the Personal System/2 can be added to an AT or XT/286 by installing a Personal System/2 Display Adapter.

Personal System/2

The Video Graphics Array support (built into the PS/2 model 50/60/80 system unit) provides a 640 x 480, 16-color mode for OS/2, supported on all Personal System/2 displays: the 8503, 8512, 8513, and 8514. If the optional Personal System/2 Display Adapter 8514/A is added, additional modes are available. The 8514/A card supports the 640 x 480, 256-color mode on all PS/2 displays. The 8514/A card and 8514 display together support two higher-resolution modes: 1024 x 768, 16-color, or 1024 x 768, 256-color.

OS/2 1.1 support of fixed disks is improved, abolishing the 32 Mb partition requirement of the earlier release. A filing system provides a menu-controlled environment for everyday tasks such as creating directories, copying files, etc.

Printing

IBM has announced OS/2 support for the IBM Proprinter™ Model 1, Proprinter II, XL Model 1, X24, and XL24. Other supported printers are the IBM 5152 Graphics Printer Model 2; 5182 Color Printer Model 1; Quietwriter® Model 1, 2, and III; Wheelprinter Model 1; and Wheelprinter E, Model 1. A menu of various output devices is provided, and it can be modified as new drivers are installed. The print spooler lets you add and delete files from the print queue, select the number of copies, pause and resume printing, etc.

Plotters

Several IBM plotters can be used for OS/2 output: the IBM models 6180, 6184, 6186, 7371, 7372, 7374, and 7375 are supported.

Several Mouse Devices are supported as input devices. The IBM Personal System/2 Mouse is supported for the PS/2 only. The Microsoft Mouse for IBM Personal Computers (100 or 200 pels per inch models), PC Mouse™, and Visi On Mouse™ serial port devices are supported on all IBM OS/2 systems. The Inport Microsoft Mouse for IBM Personal Computer AT and XT/286, and the parallel port versions of the Microsoft Mouse support the AT and XT/286 only.

OS/2 User Interface: The Future

The output device driver interface of Presentation Manager is flexible enough to support a wide range of present and future devices. As personal computing hardware improves in video and print quality, new device drivers can be added to support new output devices. A new device driver may have to be written by the hardware manufacturer (or application developer), using the documented interface to OS/2. Once the user installs (copies) the new device driver to OS/2, no further changes are required to either the operating system or its applications.

Generally, there are three types of OS/2 application that work with OS/2 1.1's Presentation Manager. DOS Mode programs and some OS/2 programs will require a full screen and cannot be windowed. Programs with a Program Information File (PIF) can be windowed (by the user) on the screen with other OS/2 programs. The third category includes programs written to take advantage of the full OS/2 API. Such programs may create their own screen groups and can be windowed with others.

OS/2 Integrated Applications

The OS/2 Presentation Manager gives the application developer a powerful tool for creating new, easy-to-use, migratable programs. Some PC DOS software vendors created their own families of programs, using their own consistent, windowing interface. Since DOS does not have the facilities of a Presentation Manager, programmers had to invent their own tricks and create their own programming tools. Programs often cost more and were larger in size. In OS/2, development of application families has been simplified through the use of built-in OS/2 features. The programmer does not have to spend as much time on cosmetic features, since OS/2 makes them available to all programs. The user benefits from programs with a consistent interface, built-in features like clipboarding for data exchange, selectable character fonts, etc. In many cases, the OS/2 program, unburdened by unnecessary overhead, is smaller in size than its DOS counterpart.

Toolkit 1.1

The OS/2 Programmer's Toolkit is upgraded for release 1.1 and the Presentation Manager. New editors are provided to simplify and streamline some of the more difficult aspects of writing programs. A Dialog Editor lets the programmer create interactive dialog boxes, placing text and user controls (buttons, check boxes, etc.) within them. A Bitmap/Cursor Editor assists with the creation of pointers, icons, and other small images. The Font Editor enables the design of new text fonts and other special characters.

Dialog boxes, icons, pointers, fonts, and other output from these three editors can be made into an application resource file through the use of the Resource Compiler. A set of sample programs are provided to illustrate the use of these editors and other Toolkit features. More will be said about the Toolkit and OS/2 application development in Chapter 8.

5

OS/2 Conversion: Making the Big Switch

If you or your company are considering a conversion from DOS to OS/2, there are several things you should look at before starting. In this chapter we will examine the various steps involved in planning for an OS/2 installation.

We will assume that you have had some experience with DOS and use it as the starting point for a conversion to OS/2. We will consider the changes to PC DOS version 3.3, which are also found in OS/2's DOS Mode. In a few cases, DOS 3.3 may still have to be run (by itself, without OS/2) to support communications programs and others that will not run under DOS Mode. We will also look at some DOS companion products, which can serve as a "bridge" to OS/2. You will see that most of the function that these programs provided optionally under DOS is now built into OS/2.

Then we will review some other conversion-related items: special hardware for diskette compatibility, IBM publications you will be using, and a look at software. But first, here are a few terms you should be familiar with.

DEFINING SOME TERMS

Logical Drives (DOS 3.3, OS/2 1.0). A fixed disk larger than 32 Mb can be supported by creating multiple disk partitions or logical drives. Each logical drive may be no larger than 32 Mb. Logical drives are unnecessary in OS/2 1.1.

Batch File Calls (DOS 3.3, OS/2).   A batch file may call another batch file. When the called file is finished, control returns to the calling file at its next instruction.

Nesting (DOS 3.3, OS/2).   A batch file may call a second batch file, which may call a third, which in turn can call a fourth, up to ten nesting levels deep.

Disk Cache.   Memory can be used to temporarily store file segments as they are read or written to a fixed disk. The segments stay in cache memory and are immediately available, without fixed disk access, when needed again. This improves fixed disk performance by speeding up the handling of file data.

FASTOPEN (DOS 3.3).   This new DOS command creates a temporary table in memory that records precisely where files are located on a fixed disk. On a fixed disk with several directories and subdirectories, or one that is especially busy (such as a network server), FASTOPEN can improve performance by locating files faster. It can be used with the Cache program.

Multi-Track I/O (DOS 3.3).   This speeds up fixed disk I/O by reading or writing all tracks of a file cylinder simultaneously. A cylinder consists of two or more concentric tracks on parallel disk surfaces. This feature is built into DOS 3.3, and requires no command to use it. Performance improvement may be observed on larger files.

Code Pages (DOS 3.3, OS/2).   The IBM PC has always used a standard code page or character set of 256 letters, numbers, and symbols. Now four additional code pages are provided for Canadian French, Portuguese, and other languages.

Companion Products (DOS).   PC DOS has never provided many functions that will be standard on OS/2, such as a windowing interface, graphics support, network and host communications, and a database manager. These have been and continue to be provided by optional programs known sometimes as DOS companion products.

HLLAPIs (DOS, OS/2).   High-Level Language Application Program Interfaces are standard instructions in COBOL, FORTRAN, C, and other languages that are used to control operating system and companion product functions. Some DOS companion product HLLAPIs are highly compatible with those on OS/2, and can be used as a bridge for program conversion.

VDI (DOS, OS/2). The Virtual Device Interface is a graphics standard for some DOS application programs. Programs written to the VDI do not require modifications when new displays or other output devices are added. A new device driver is all that is needed.

Command Diagrams (OS/2). IBM's OS/2 publications use new diagrams to illustrate the various permitted options and defaults for its commands.

Startup Diskette (DOS 3.3). When DOS and OS/2 share a system's fixed disk, a DOS startup diskette may be used to initiate DOS. Without one, OS/2 always boots from the fixed disk.

Data Migration (DOS 3.3, OS/2). When a PC user converts to a Personal System/2, program and data files must be migrated to 3.5-inch diskettes. This can be done via a cable connection between two computers, by installing an external diskette drive, or by uploading and downloading files through a local area network or host system.

Copy-Protection (DOS). Many software manufacturers create program diskettes that defy standard diskette-copying techniques such as DOS's DISKCOPY program. Copy-protected 5.25-inch diskettes may have to be exchanged for 3.5-inch versions, or run from a Personal System/2 external 5.25-inch drive.

Null-Modem Adapter. Two computers can exchange files over a standard serial cable that has been modified with a null-modem, or modem-eliminator adapter. This crosses the send and receive wires so that one computer's send becomes the other machine's receive.

WHO NEEDS OS/2?

The OS/2 Candidate

Many PC and Personal System/2 users will want to convert to OS/2 as soon as possible. This includes people who are already running several applications, switching back and forth between them as work demands. They may have a need to move data between programs or send the final results to one or more high-resolution printers or plotters. There may be a need to migrate software between personal, mid-range, and mainframe systems. The personal computers used in many large companies stopped being "PCs" a long time ago; they are *intelligent workstations* capable of maintaining network or host communications while running local applications. For them, the change to OS/2 cannot happen soon enough.

Wait and See

Not everyone will be in a hurry to switch to OS/2. Some people, even those with a Personal System/2 Model 50 or greater, may be perfectly happy with PC DOS, at least for the time being. They have a need for the capabilities of OS/2, but perhaps the right software is not yet available. They will keep an eye on the growing OS/2 software market, and make the switch at a later time.

When the switch is made, the new OS/2 user will find much that is familiar. DOS data files require no conversion, and disk directories are created and managed in the same way. The DOS command processor is present in DOS Mode, maintaining the same interface, command set, and program compatibility.

Traditional PC Users

Then there are many traditional PC DOS users, whose needs are satisfied by a 640 Kb single-application environment, with no need to run large, multiple applications. This might be someone who usually works on a single application such as spreadsheets or word processing and rarely needs anything else. Or, it could be the owner of a PS/2 Model 25 or 30, which cannot run OS/2 (Figure 5–1).

Even a "vanilla" DOS user should at least migrate to PC DOS 3.3, which offers several enhancements over previous versions, provides software compatibility for old programs running on all IBM PCs, and supports the new Personal System/2 hardware. An upgrade offer from IBM lets the purchaser of an earlier DOS release buy version 3.3 at a reduced price.

CONVERSION CASE STUDIES

The magnitude of the DOS to OS/2 conversion depends on the size of a business, the application mix, the number and size of installed systems, and anticipated future growth. A look at each of three typical PC users will be useful in illustrating the scope of three unique migration scenarios.

The Small User

User "A" owns a single PC AT and uses four application programs: a word processor, database manager, spreadsheet, and communication program. He obtains upgrades to OS/2 for the spreadsheet and word processing pro-

IBM Personal System/2™

	Model 25	Model 30	Model 50	Model 60	Model 80
Microprocessor	8086	8086	80286	80286	80386
Potential system throughput[1]	More than 2 times Personal Computer	More than 2 times PC XT™	Up to 2 times Personal Computer AT*	Up to 2 times Personal Computer AT	Up to 3½ times Personal Computer AT
Standard memory	512, 640KB	640KB	1MB	1MB	Up to 2MB
Expandable to	640KB		7MB	15MB	16MB
Diskette size and capacity	3.5-inch 720KB	3.5-inch 720KB	3.5-inch 1.44MB	3.5-inch 1.44MB	3.5-inch 1.44MB
Fixed disk[2]		20MB	20MB	44, 70MB	44, 70, 115, 314MB
Additional options	3.5-inch 720KB drive			44, 70, 115MB	44, 70, 115, 314MB
Maximum configuration[3]		20MB	20MB	185MB	628MB
Expansion slots[4]	2[5]	3	3	7	7
Operating system(s)	PC DOS 3.3	PC DOS 3.3	PC DOS 3.3 and Operating System/2™	PC DOS 3.3 and Operating System/2	PC DOS 3.3 and Operating System/2

1. Based on the testing described in the IBM Personal System 2 Performance Guide. Your results may vary. 2. Model 30 also comes in a diskette-based configuration. 3. Models with 44MB fixed disk expandable to 88MB. 4. Model 30 accepts most IBM PC and IBM PC XT option cards. Models 50, 60, and 80 accept new IBM Micro Channel™ option cards. 5. One slot is 8 inches.

Personal System/2, PC XT, Operating System/2 and Micro Channel are trademarks of IBM Corporation.
Personal Computer AT is a registered trademark of IBM Corporation.

Figure 5–1   This table compares five models of the IBM Personal System/2. All can run PC DOS, but only the 80286-based Models 50 and 60 and 80386-based Model 80 support OS/2.

grams, to support larger files. No upgrade is available for the database program, and the communication program must be run under DOS until an upgrade becomes available.

User "A" installs OS/2 on his DOS-based PC AT, so that they share the same fixed disk, and the system memory is increased to 3 Mb. The new OS/2 word processor and spreadsheet are auto-started at OS/2 boot time, and the DOS database program is called by the DOS Mode AUTOEXEC.BAT file. When user "A" needs to communicate, he boots from a DOS diskette and runs the communications program. He has no plans to upgrade to the OS/2 Extended Edition.

The Intermediate User

User "B" has two PC XTs, two ATs, and three Personal System/2s—a Model 30, a Model 50, and a Model 60, interconnected over a PC Network. She adds external drives to some machines to facilitate file copying, and installs OS/2 on the Model 50 and 60. Her company has several in-house programs, written in BASIC. They will be converted to OS/2 and recompiled to OS/2 Family format so they can run on all systems, DOS or OS/2. The two OS/2 systems will be upgraded to Extended Edition later.

The Large User

User "C" is the MIS Director for a large corporation with hundreds of installed PCs and PS/2s. They are in the process of upgrading many of their systems to PS/2 Models 60 and 80, and all will run OS/2. The PC Support Center has some machines interconnected with the Data Migration Facility to facilitate diskette copying.

About half of the installed systems communicate with the corporate mainframe system, mostly for electronic mail, file-routing between PC users, and running host-resident programs. User "C" has several in-house programs written against the 3270 application program interface, and these will be migrated to run under the OS/2 Extended Edition. The systems in each department are being networked together, and a distributed corporate database is in the design stage. The OS/2 Database Manager and Structured Query Language will play an important role.

Regardless of immediate need, all personal computer users would be wise to learn about OS/2 and then track the periodic announcements of new OS/2 application products. Eventually, many of today's 80286 and 80386-based PC owners will switch to OS/2 in order to take advantage of its increased function and advanced applications.

PC DOS 3.3: BRIDGE TO OS/2

The basic architecture of PC DOS has not changed much since 1981. The DOS restrictions that motivated the need for OS/2—memory, single-tasking, etc.—still exist. Its upward-compatibility has been maintained, so that programs and data from earlier versions work with DOS 3.3, and will be supported by future releases as well.

PC DOS 3.3 is installed and used in the same manner as previous releases. Since it will be used as an interim operating system to OS/2 for many users, and the same function is part of OS/2's DOS Mode, we will look at some of its recent changes.

DOS PERSONAL SYSTEM/2 HARDWARE SUPPORT

1.44 Mb Diskette Drives

One reason for DOS 3.3 is the need for Personal System/2 hardware support. The Personal System/2 has several new features that were not recognized by DOS 3.1 or 3.2. First, 3.3 is the first DOS to support (that means read, write, and format) the 1.44 Mb, 3.5-inch diskette. In true DOS tradition, 3.3 will also read, write and format the lower-capacity, 720 Kb, 3.5-inch diskettes (in any 3.5-inch drive), and the variety of 5.25-inch diskettes (160 Kb, 180 Kb, 320 Kb, 360 Kb, and 1.2 Mb) supported by previous DOS versions.

Big Disks

Up to now, DOS supported fixed disks with a capacity up to 32 Mb, but no more. If you added a larger disk to your PC, you needed a special program, such as a device driver from the disk's manufacturer, to go beyond 32 Mb. DOS 3.3 supports disk *partitions* of up to 32 Mb each—which is identical to the way OS/2 sub-divides disks—at least in its first release. A large fixed disk (like the 44, 70, 115, or 314 Mb drives used on the Personal System/2) is formatted as multiple partitions, or *logical drives*.

For example, using the DOS FDISK command, you could divide a 70 Mb fixed disk into three logical drives: 32/32/6 Mb, or 30/20/20 Mb, etc. Each partition can be no larger than 32 Mb, and receives a unique drive letter, starting with C:, then D:, E:, and so forth (on a two-disk system the drive letters continue alphabetically through the first drive, onto the second drive). So, if your first logical drive, "C:," became full, you could then begin using D: for storage on the second logical drive on the same physical disk. You could use logical drive C: for OS/2 and spreadsheet files, D: for word processing, and E: for others (Figure 5–2). The initial release of OS/2 uses the same logical drive support as DOS 3.3. One of OS/2 1.1's enhancements will remove the 32 Mb boundary and let you format the entire physical drive as a single, large partition.

PS/2 Serial Ports

The Personal System/2 models 50, 60, and 80 allow up to four serial or asynchronous communication "ports" or channels that can be used at the same time. Each port can support a serial printer, communication modem, or any one of many RS232-type input and output devices used in engineering, scientific, medical, and many other applications. DOS 3.3 also supports up to

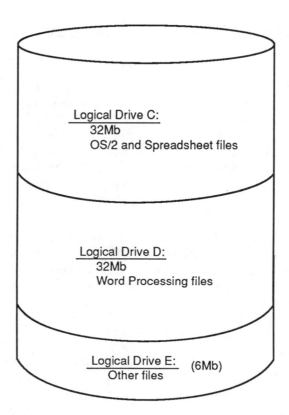

Figure 5–2 With OS/2 Standard Edition 1.0, a 70 Mb fixed disk, represented here, would have to be divided into at least three partitions, each no larger than 32 Mb. OS/2 1.1 removes the partitioning requirement. Partitions, or logical drives, are addressed with different drive letters (C:, D:, etc.), and can be used to store any DOS or OS/2 file.

the new maximum data rate of 19,200 bits per second (BPS) on those models. Port addresses are COM1:, COM2:, COM3:, and COM4:. Previous DOS versions supported two serial ports at no more than 9,600 BPS. Rate selection is done with the MODE command.

DATE and TIME Reset

Prior to DOS 3.3, when you used the DOS DATE or TIME commands, you set the current date or time maintained by the system (in memory)—but not on an installed clock chip or card. So, if you changed the time from standard to daylight savings, you may have been surprised the next morning when the machine came up in standard time again. That's because a PC clock/

calendar chip required a special program (such as the PC/AT's Diagnostic program or the PC Convertible's System Profile) to reset it. DOS 3.3's DATE and TIME commands are global in nature, resetting both software and hardware on the PC/AT, Convertible, and the Personal System/2.

IMPROVED APPLICATION CONTROL

Batch File Improvements

Batch files control the flow of most DOS applications, calling programs and commands in a prescribed sequence. Over time, DOS batch files have been enhanced, adding new commands to improve the flexibility and control of applications. But if batch file "B" was called from batch file "A," control would pass to "B" but would not return back to "A" when finished. DOS 3.3's batch file support now gives control to another batch file, returning to the calling file when finished. In fact, you can "nest" files up to 10 layers deep ("A" calls "B," which calls "C," which calls "D," etc.) (Figure 5–3). Batch file nesting uses the new CALL statement, which also supports parameter-passing of information from one batch file to the next.

In addition to parameter-passing, an area in DOS called the "environment" can also be used for program-to-program variables. It is a reserved memory space that is sometimes used to determine if the last program completed successfully, for instance. Now a batch file can also read environment variables. So, before passing control to the next program, the batch file can test a variable (IF ___ = ___, THEN ___) and branch around one or more steps if appropriate.

BOOSTING PERFORMANCE

Cache Memory

Several DOS 3.3 enhancements are aimed at performance. One program that improves Personal System/2 disk performance is not part of DOS, but complements it. That is the disk cache program, shipped on the Personal System/2 Reference Diskette with the Models 50, 60, and 80. IBMCACHE.SYS significantly boosts the speed of DOS programs with frequent and heavy fixed disk activity. It does this by setting aside memory where active fixed disk sectors are temporarily stored. Whenever a sector is accessed a second time, the cache program gets it straight from cache memory, eliminating the additional time required for another disk-to-memory

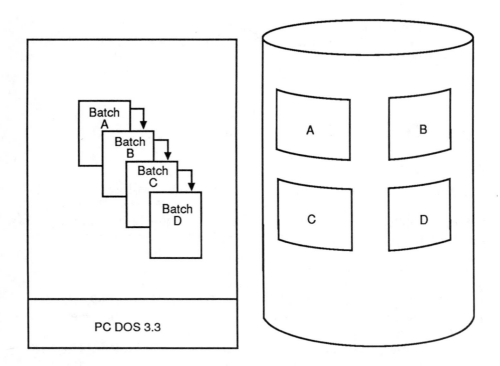

Figure 5–3   PC DOS 3.3 and OS/2 support batch file nesting, where one batch file can call another batch file, which can call another, and so on. Control always passes back to the "parent" file when a "child" is finished.

transfer. The cache program automatically saves sector changes back to the fixed disk. Cache memory performance improvements are especially dramatic on systems with heavy disk activity, such as a disk server on a local area network.

FASTOPEN

While IBMCACHE.SYS improves disk I/O performance, a new DOS command named FASTOPEN reduces the time it takes to *find* files. Using a relatively small amount of memory (approximately 3 Kb), it builds a table of files recently accessed and records precisely where they are located on the disk. On a fixed disk with many directories and subdirectories, this avoids the need to search for a file when it is accessed a second or third time. FASTOPEN can be used in conjunction with IBMCACHE.SYS, and is also particularly useful on a busy network disk server system.

Multi-Track I/O

Fixed disk drives are controlled by adapter cards or circuits inside a PC. IBM's drive adapters have a built-in feature which allows a full disk cylinder (tracks of data superimposed on parallel surfaces) to be read into memory at once. DOS versions 1.0 to 3.2 did not take advantage of this feature, instead reading or writing one track at a time. Because DOS 3.3 handles multiple tracks at once, fixed disk performance is improved for larger files.

File Buffers

The DOS configuration file, CONFIG.SYS, supports an optional DOS command, BUFFERS=___. File buffers are units of memory used to temporarily store disk sectors during reads and writes, similar to the disk cache program. If the BUFFERS command is not used, DOS sets a default value. With previous DOS versions, DOS would check to see what type of machine it was running on before setting the default. Now it checks the amount of memory on the system, and sets aside buffer memory according to the amount of memory installed.

BACKUP/RESTORE

The DOS 3.3 BACKUP program now compresses many files into a single backup file which is stored on each backup diskette. This results in higher speed backups (up to 40% improvement), more files backed up per diskette, and often fewer diskettes. Diskette formatting is now automatic on unformatted (new) diskettes. Each diskette now contains two files: CONTROL.xxx and BACKUP.xxx, where xxx is the diskette number (001, 002, etc.) and BACKUP.xxx contains the compressed files. Each diskette also has a label: BACKUP.001, etc. The BACKUP /L option prints a log of backed up files.

DOS 3.3: THE INTERNATIONAL OPERATING SYSTEM

PC DOS is now an international operating system. While this may not be obvious or important to most users in the United States, it is important to application developers creating software products for the worldwide PC marketplace, or for users as near as Mexico or French-speaking Canada. International language considerations involve things like keyboard layouts, date and time formats, use of the comma and decimal point, currency symbols, and the alphabet.

5 Code Pages

DOS 3.3 is translated into 11 languages, supports 17 different keyboards, and includes installation information for 19 countries. But to be truly international, other, more fundamental changes were needed. This meant adding characters such as some accented vowels that were not part of the original 256 PC characters. Four new character tables or code pages were created, based on local customs in many countries. In addition to the old PC standard character set "437" (which is still the default on all PCs, old and new), new Multilingual, Portuguese, French Canadian, and Nordic code pages have been added (Appendix A).

Code page 850 represents the International Standards Organization's (ISO) Multilingual character set for latin-based languages. The first 128 characters are the same as the PC's built-in code page 437, but some line-drawing and math symbols have been replaced with new letters.

The others are Code Page 860 (Portuguese), 863 (Canadian French), and 865 (Norwegian and Danish).

Any of the five code pages can be selected by a program or by the user. There is considerable overlap between the five pages (many letters and symbols are common to several languages), but each has a few unique characters of its own. When a code page is selected, only characters from its set can appear on the screen—you cannot mix characters from multiple pages. If you change code pages to get a special character, you may inadvertently replace other characters you did not intend to change. Several DOS commands support optional character sets: CHCP, GRAFTABL, KEYB, MODE, NLSFUNC, SELECT, and COUNTRY. Alternate code pages are supported on EGA and VGA-compatible displays, not CGA.

OTHER NEW AND ENHANCED PC DOS 3.3 COMMANDS

The first few pages in the DOS 3.3 Reference manual summarize changes to this release of DOS, and the various command descriptions go into more detail. We have already discussed many of these commands under performance, batch files, and international language support. Here are a few more.

APPEND

Many DOS users are familiar with the PATH command (and many others are unaware of it, since it is often buried in a batch file). PATH makes a list of fixed disk directories and subdirectories where programs are stored. When you ask for a program that is not in the current directory, DOS will search the PATH directories until it finds it. However, PATH was designed to find program, command and batch files only, and ignored data files that might be required by those programs, often residing in the same directories. The APPEND command supplements PATH by introducing a directory search for non-program files. The APPEND /X option searches for program and data files.

ATTRIB

The ATTRIB command has been enhanced to allow the file read-only and archive bits to be reset on all files in a directory and its subdirectories.

FORMAT

In order to support multiple diskette formats in a variety of drive capacities, the FORMAT command now has new arguments. For example, in order to format a 720 Kb diskette in a 1.44 Mb drive, you would enter: FORMAT B: /N:9 /T:80. The diskette would then be formatted for 9 sectors per track, 80 tracks.

BASIC

The BASIC language interpreter was originally designed in three versions: Cassette BASIC, Disk BASIC, and Advanced BASIC. Cassette BASIC was, and still is contained in ROM. It is no longer used to support cassette tape recorders as an output device, but it has been a base for the other two versions, which resided on the DOS diskette as files BASIC.COM and BASICA.COM. Since few programs used Disk BASIC (all of its function is contained in Advanced BASIC), that file has been removed from the DOS diskette. Now the BASIC command is automatically treated as BASICA.

The BASIC interpreter has not been upgraded for new hardware such as the Personal System/2 Displays' MCGA or VGA modes. The BASIC compiler product (see Chapter 8) has several enhancements.

DOS Packaging

DOS 3.3 is shipped on two 5.25-inch diskettes and one 720 Kb diskette. The LINK and EXE2BIN programs have been moved to the DOS Technical Reference diskette, and the DEBUG program is found on both.

PC DOS COMPANION PRODUCTS

OS/2 will eventually provide—especially in the Extended Edition—a full-function operating system that supports windowing, text, graphics, local area networks, host communications, and database management. Today most of these features are not part of DOS itself, but are available as operating system appendages, or extensions. These system software programs, which we will call DOS companion products, extend the operating system's function with additional layers of support that lie functionally between DOS and its application programs (Figure 5–4).

Many application developers will argue that these extensions should have been part of the operating system all along. They feel that general "overhead" functions like windowing and communications support should not be duplicated by each application program, and are done more effectively by a common control program, i.e., operating system. Since PC DOS simply did not have the basic architecture to provide such advanced functions, it used the "optional layer" approach instead. Most of the popular DOS companion products have been upgraded and enhanced for DOS 3.3, and can play an important role in long-range plans for conversion to OS/2.

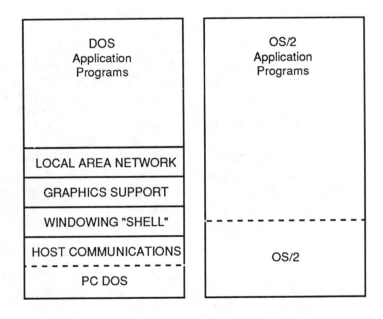

Figure 5–4 PC DOS (left), since it doesn't include support for graphics, windowing, database, or communications, often requires additional layers of software to provide missing function. OS/2 (right), through its two editions, provides such support uniformly for all application programs.

The following DOS companion products can be used with DOS 3.3 to ease the conversion to OS/2 for both the application developer and the end user. This is by no means an exhaustive list, but a sampling of software extensions to DOS. Since many of these products provide large memory management, multi-tasking, or an improved user interface, you may recognize them from Chapters 2, 3, and 4.

PC DOS MULTI-APPLICATION PRODUCTS

TopView 1.2.

TopView was created as a windowing, multi-programming layer for DOS that lets two or more applications be loaded into memory at the same time. The screen can be split into windows, and a cut-and-paste facility provides limited data exchange between them. Windowing is text-only, and any graphics programs must use the entire screen while they are running.

TopView supports extended memory above 1 Mb on 80286 or 80386-based machines as a temporary program storage area. When the program is needed, TopView copies it into memory under 640 Kb where DOS can run it. It also uses a roll-in, roll-out technique to access programs on fixed disk, although load time is much slower.

TopView's interface to DOS is being maintained through a new release for DOS 3.3. Users who have been running TopView with earlier versions of DOS may wish to continue doing so until OS/2 is available. OS/2's Presentation Services user interface, while it may resemble TopView in some ways, is still different. The TopView application program interface is also quite different from OS/2 and should not be relied on for application program conversion.

Microsoft Windows 2.0

Windows is another popular DOS shell, or user interface which supports multiple text and graphics programs with windowing. Its most recent version, Windows 2.0, reflects a user and application program interface (API) that is very similiar to OS/2's Presentation Services. Windows 2.0 may be used as a familiarization vehicle for future OS/2 users and as a program conversion aid for developers. Since the OS/2 Presentation Manager's graphics interface conforms to the new Systems Application Architecture, graphics programs will have to be modified for OS/2.

PC DOS GRAPHICS INTERFACE

Graphics Development Toolkit

In 1984, IBM introduced two new high-resolution displays, the Enhanced Color Display and the Professional Graphics Display, both with higher screen addressability (640 x 350 and 640 x 480, respectively) and more colors (16 or 256, respectively) than the old PC standard, the IBM Color/Graphics Adapter and Display (320 x 200, 4 colors). Fortunately, the new adapter/display combinations were designed to support existing software written for the popular PC Color/Graphics Adapter and Display. That meant that graphics programs would run on the new displays just as they did before. Unfortunately, without conversion they did not take advantage of the new resolutions and colors. A new graphics application interface was needed for DOS.

The DOS version available at that time, DOS 3.0, was text-based, not graphics (a limitation that is still true today). The BASIC language had a limited set of graphics functions that were not available to other languages and did not support the new displays. In order to provide a consistent, general graphics interface, IBM introduced its Graphics Development Toolkit product. Based on a new Virtual Device Interface (VDI), the Toolkit let programmers write applications to a general, "virtual" screen (Figure 5–5),

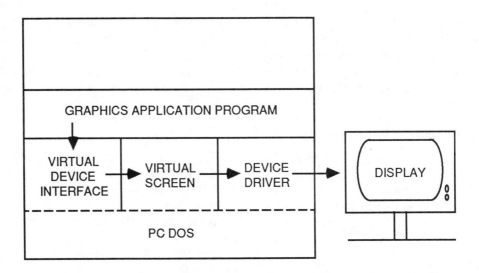

Figure 5–5   PC DOS provides graphics support via the Virtual Device Interface, or VDI. A program written for the VDI interface uses a 32,000-by-32,000 position virtual screen to draw each picture. This virtual screen is translated by a device driver into an image on a real display. A new, higher-resolution display can be used by simply installing a new driver.

which existed in memory and nowhere else. The dimensions of this virtual screen, 32,000 by 32,000, went far beyond the resolution of any physical PC display, but were scaled down to fit it. This conversion from virtual to real display was accomplished through a program called a *device driver*. Pre-PS/2 versions of the Graphics Development Toolkit included a set of device drivers for all of IBM's displays.

Programs written using previous versions of the Graphics Development Toolkit do not have to be changed to use the new IBM Personal System/2 display modes. By purchasing the Toolkit release 1.2 for DOS 3.3, one or more new device drivers can be added to the application, providing the necessary conversion from virtual screen to PS/2 display. Graphics output will appear on a Personal System/2 display in the selected mode, such as 640 x 480, 256-colors or 1024 x 768, 16-colors, etc.

Another version of the Graphics Development Toolkit (Release 2.0) will provide compatible VDI support and device drivers for OS/2. OS/2 Release 1.1's Presentation Services provides its own built-in graphics interface that is similiar in concept, but not compatible, to VDI. Many VDI-based application developers will want to change to the OS/2 1.1 Presentation Manager interface.

PC DOS COMMUNICATIONS PRODUCTS

Since OS/2 will not support some communications programs running in the PC DOS Mode, these programs will have to continue to run under PC DOS directly. Later, when the desired network or host communication support is available under the OS/2 Extended Edition, the conversion to OS/2 can be completed. In the meantime, whenever an OS/2 system needs to join a PC Network or Token Ring LAN, or communicate with a remote mainframe, any of the PC DOS companion products can be used. This will mean temporarily suspending OS/2 operations, booting up a DOS 3.3 diskette, running the communication session, and then rebooting OS/2 from fixed disk when finished. In the next chapter we will show how a dual DOS–OS/2 system can be set up.

3270 Communications

Several communications programs, some from IBM and some from other vendors, have been developed for 3270 communications. These products use software to make a personal computer "look like," or emulate a local or remote 3270-type communications terminal. To make a "dumb terminal" into an intelligent workstation, most programs add features like PC-host file transfer, automatic dial, program interfaces, and dual session support. Let's look at three updated 3270 emulation programs.

The *IBM PC 3270 Emulation Program, Entry Level 1.2*, has a High Level Language Application Program Interface (HLLAPI) which can be used by application developers for Personal System/2-to-host communications. Much of this HLLAPI will be contained in the Communications Manager of the OS/2 Extended Edition. This means that program development can take place (or program conversion started) using the DOS 3270 Emulation Program, and finished later on the OS/2 Extended Edition.

The Entry Level product is a low-cost, low-memory solution that runs on any Personal System/2 from the Model 25 on up. The PS/2, using a 3278 Emulation Adapter, is connected via a control unit to the mainframe computer. A single PC DOS session (running your favorite spreadsheet, word processor, etc.) is shared with up to five concurrent host sessions. The PS/2 can also run the IBM Local Area Network program at the same time.

The *IBM PC 3270 Emulation Program Version 3.0* is a more sophisticated version of the last program. Controller function is built in, so the PS/2 can be directly attached or remotely dialed into the host. On a PC Network or Token Ring network, this program provides gateway support, allowing multiple network users to share a single host communication line.

The *IBM 3270 Workstation Program 1.1* supports up to four host sessions, six PC sessions, and two notepad sessions. This versatile product uses the IBM Expanded Memory Adapter (XMA) card to multi-task up to six DOS programs, supporting up to 512 Kb for each one. The Workstation Program is much more than a communications program, becoming a multi-tasking DOS shell with windowing and cut-and-paste features.

When run on the PS/2 Model 80, the 3270 Workstation Program does not require the XMA card, instead using the 80386's Virtual 8086 mode for multi-tasking support. Later, when the Model 50 or 60 user migrates to OS/2, the XMA card becomes part of OS/2's extended memory.

PLANNING FOR OS/2

Selecting Hardware

Which System?

OS/2 will run on any IBM Personal Computer or Personal System/2 with an 80286 or 80386 microprocessor. That means a PC XT/286 or any model of the PC AT will work, but because of hardware features such as faster clock speeds, ABIOS, the Micro Channel Bus, and high-resolution graphics, the

Personal System/2 Models 50, 60, and 80 offer many advantages over older PCs. A PC AT or XT/286 can still be used as a lightly-loaded OS/2 system, or for OS/2 familiarization and training.

Other (Non-IBM) Systems

Microsoft Corp. is expected to license their MS OS/2 (similiar to IBM's OS/2 Standard Edition) to other manufacturers of 80286 or 80386-based PCs. Microsoft will then provide the necessary software interface to adapt MS OS/2 to a specific machine. While most OS/2 function is expected to be the same, performance will be dependent on many factors, such as the number, size, and processing demand of running applications, and hardware characteristics such as processor speed and bus architecture.

How Much Memory is Needed?

It really depends on what you are going to be doing with OS/2: the number and size of your application programs is the most important factor, but there are some guidelines for minimum memory size too. The OS/2 Standard Edition, with no PC DOS Mode, requires at least 1.5 Mb of RAM. Of this, the amount needed for the operating system itself will vary, depending on configuration (device drivers, cache memory, etc.). With the DOS Mode selected, up to 640 Kb is set aside for running DOS programs, increasing the recommended minimum memory to 2.0 Mb. The OS/2 Extended Edition will require at least 3.0 Mb. The minimum and maximum amounts of real memory that your programs need depend on how many segments are present at initial load and then how many additional segments are dynamically linked as the programs run. Swapping of segments to fixed disk takes place when the necessary real memory is not available, degrading overall performance. Adding more memory will eventually eliminate the need for swapping, and return performance to its previous level. At this point, adding more memory will not help.

The Personal System/2 Model 50 comes with 1 Mb of memory on the system board and three available card slots. Using three IBM 2 Mb Memory Expansion Adapters, a total of 7 Mb can be achieved. The Model 60, with seven empty slots, can be expanded to 15 Mb. A Model 80, with 2 Mb on the system board and seven slots, can support the maximum 16 Mb.

If possible, run a typical set of OS/2 application programs on systems with different increments of installed memory to see how performance is affected. For example, you may discover that the OS/2 Standard Edition with four concurrent applications provides acceptable performance on a 5 Mb Model 60, better with 7 Mb of memory, but no additional improvement with 10 Mb. That's because, in this case, 7 Mb was sufficient to support all of the activities on the system without swapping.

Fixed Disk

The total fixed disk storage, like memory, depends on the number and size of the applications stored there and the size of the swap area. A minimum of 20 Mb is recommended for the OS/2 Standard Edition, and 30 Mb for the Extended Edition. OS/2 Standard Edition 1.0 is shipping on four, 1.44 Mb diskettes or (for the AT version) four 1.2 Mb diskettes.

Data Files

Data file formats used by DOS programs are the same on OS/2. OS/2 applications will be able to read and write to old files, and create new ones that are DOS-compatible. Although the fixed disk storage requirements for OS/2 application program and data files should be roughly the same as for DOS, keep in mind that many OS/2 programs—and their data files—will be much larger, due to the additional memory available to them.

Got a Mouse?

The OS/2 Standard Edition 1.0, since it does not include the Presentation Manager, does not make full use of a mouse device as later versions do. Version 1.1's improved user interface is menu-oriented and window-driven, and a pointing device such as the IBM Mouse will be very helpful. You will still use the keyboard for entering data, program, and command names that are not menu-selectable. The cursor control keys can also be used in lieu of a mouse to move around the screen. Several mouse devices are supported, including the IBM PS/2 Mouse, Microsoft Mouse, PC Mouse, and Visi-On Mouse.

Displays

The improved graphics support in OS/2 version 1.1 will place demands on the display side of the user interface. OS/2 device drivers support a PC Color/Graphics Adapter and Display on a PC AT only in the 640 x 200, black & white graphics mode with an 8 x 8 character box size. This is far from what the new Personal System/2 displays are capable of. A PC AT user can support one of the PS/2 displays by installing an IBM Personal System/2 Display Adapter. While this will not improve OS/2 performance on an AT, the visual quality will at least be equivalent to a Personal System/2. The Enhanced Graphics Adapter supports OS/2 with 640 by 350, 16-color resolution, and the Color/Graphics Adapter provides only 640 by 200, black-and-white resolution.

OS/2 does not come with the device driver necessary to support the 1024 by 768 mode on the 8514 display. This driver is shipped with the display and must be installed on OS/2.

Serial and Parallel Devices

Printers, plotters, modems, and other popular PC devices are all OS/2-supported through device drivers, unlike the limited support they received from DOS. Most of the time, no program conversion is required, but in some cases it may be desirable. For example, on a PS/2 Model 50, 60, or 80, the serial port can operate at twice the rate (19,200 bits per second) as that of a PC. If an attached serial device can run at the higher speed, the program should take advantage of it. This may be accomplished as easily as using the MODE command to set the higher rate, but in some cases a program modification may be required.

Supported OS/2 printers are the Proprinters I, and II, XL, X24, and XL24; Quietwriter; and Wheelprinter. Plotters include the IBM models 6180, 6184, 6186, 7371, 7372, 7374, and 7375.

With some creative programming, the Personal System/2's parallel port can be used to input as well as output information, if the attached device supports it. The Data Migration Facility, described later in this chapter, uses the parallel port to receive files from an IBM PC.

One serial port is included on the PS/2 system board and the rest (two more supported by OS/2 alone) must be added on adapter cards such as the PS/2 Dual Asynch Adapter/A or PS/2 Multi-Protocol Adapter/A.

OS/2 SHIP GROUP PUBLICATIONS

PC DOS users have discovered the DOS User's Guide and Reference manuals to be an important source of information. The role of these publications for OS/2, while certainly still important, has changed somewhat. The new OS/2 tutorial, installation program, and on-line help facility now provide much of the assistance that an OS/2 user needs, on installation day as well as during daily operations. Hard copy documentation, while still helpful, will become more of a limited support tool.

OS/2 User's Guide

The approximately 50-page *Guide* serves as a brief introduction to OS/2, supplementing other ship group documentation rather than duplicating it. It begins by directing the new user to the screen that appears when you boot the first OS/2 Installation Diskette—the Program Selector menu. It then briefly summarizes the Introducing OS/2 Program and the Update selection for adding OS/2 or PC DOS programs. Using pictures of OS/2 screens, the User's Guide then shows you how programs are started or switched between, and how additions and updates are made to the Program Selector. Several common OS/2 commands are introduced in the section on Managing Information.

Appendixes are provided to list the various OS/2 key and key combinations, introduce the concepts of files and directories to a new computer user, and explain diskette compatibility. The OS/2 User Guide's Table of Contents lists the following sections:

Introduction
Installing the System
Installing Programs
Starting and Switching Between Programs
Updating the Program Selector
Managing Information
Appendix A. Keys
Appendix B. Computer Fundamentals

OS/2 User's Reference

The other ship group publication is the approximately 370-page User's Reference. Like the PC DOS Reference, this book gives detailed descriptions of the syntax and usage of each OS/2 command, complete with examples.

The User's Reference classifies commands in three major groupings: OS/2 Commands (those that can be entered directly from the keyboard or from inside a batch file), Batch File Commands (those that determine how a batch file controls an application), and Configuration File Statements (commands that set various OS/2 options at boot time). Command descriptions are also coded if they are exclusive to the DOS or OS/2 Modes, rather than working under both, as most commands do. Related, or associated commands are listed for each command, and diagrams are provided to illustrate the various required and optional arguments.

This is an example of a command diagram. FDISK, since it is an OS/2 external command, may be stored in a directory, which might require a drive letter and path name to precede the command name, like this: D:\DOS\FDISK. Its diagram looks like this:

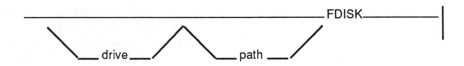

The straight line preceding the FDISK command name means that in some conditions (when you are already in the directory containing the command, or you have named the directory in the PATH command) you will not need to specify the drive or path. Otherwise the drive and path (the two options shown in parallel to the "no argument" case), must be entered prior to the PATH command name.

Internal commands never need a drive or path name, since they are built into the OS/2 command processor, and are always available. An internal command might be diagrammed in the User's Reference like this:

The VOL command (display disk volume label) is an internal command, and may be used alone or with an optional drive letter.

The first OS/2 User's Reference Table of Contents contains:

OS/2 OPTIONAL PUBLICATIONS

In addition to the publications packaged in the OS/2 ship group, others are available.

OS/2 Application Guide

This document lists various PC DOS programs that have been tested successfully by IBM under the DOS Mode.

Technical Documentation

The OS/2 Technical Reference and OS/2 Toolkit (which includes the OS/2 Programmer's Guide) are primarily of interest to the application developer. They will be described in Chapter 8, OS/2's Programming Interface.

SELECTING OS/2 APPLICATIONS

Each OS/2 user will run the operating system with a unique mix of application programs. Some may still exist in their original PC DOS format; others will be written or converted to take advantage of OS/2 features. Some will be user-written and others will be commercial application packages created by professional programmers. Most of the existing variety of old DOS programs and new OS/2 programs can be run on an OS/2 system.

But the Personal System/2 owner has to make some important decisions before installing OS/2. Which of my programs can be run as-is? Which ones need to be converted? Can I trade-in any of my old programs for a new OS/2 version? What new OS/2 applications do I need?

Three Application Types

During the first few months of OS/2 availability, many application programs will continue to be available only in PC DOS format. Over time, many developers will convert their software to either OS/2 Family or Full-Function formats. Family programs will be able to run in the extended memory above 1 Mb, but cannot be larger than 640 Kb, perform multi-tasking, or use other OS/2 exclusives that would make them non-DOS-compatible. Family programs do offer the advantage of being able to run under either PC DOS or OS/2. Full-function applications, on the other hand, can exploit all of OS/2's new features, but cannot run under PC DOS. A smart OS/2 Family program could be designed to check the environment it is running in. If under DOS, the program could limit itself to the proper subset of OS/2 function. When running under OS/2 Mode, the same program could take advantage of OS/2 exclusives such as large memory support and windowing. Up to 12 Family and Full-function programs can run in OS/2 Mode, while only one DOS Mode program can run at a time.

Most existing PC DOS programs can be easily installed under OS/2's DOS Mode. A few DOS programs with timing dependencies (such as communications applications) may not be able to run in the DOS Mode. Ill-behaved DOS programs (those that interface directly with hardware instead of through DOS) may also have difficulty running under OS/2. Such programs can still be run directly under PC DOS until OS/2 versions are available. The software manufacturer or dealer should be consulted to determine if a DOS program has been tested as OS/2-compatible.

Upgrades

Before installing your commercial DOS program under OS/2, it is a good idea to check with your software dealer or manufacturer to see if an upgrade to a new OS/2 version is offered. Some vendors have converted their best-selling programs to Family or Full-function versions, and are offering a trade-up plan for existing customers.

Conversions

If you or someone you work with write programs, chances are those programs are not protected against copying, so they can easily be transferred from a PC 5.25-inch diskette to a 3.5-inch diskette for a Personal System/2. The author of a program is always the best person to convert it to OS/2, which means making changes to its source code and recompiling. We will look at media migration and re-programming next.

CONVERTING FROM 5.25-INCH TO 3.5-INCH DRIVE SYSTEMS

The introduction of high-capacity, 3.5-inch diskettes on the Personal System/2 meant that many programs would have to be converted to the new media, even if no other changes were required. There are several ways to transfer programs from one diskette type to another, but they vary in cost and convenience. On the low-cost end of the range are the cable-connected schemes, and at the other end are the optional, external diskette drives. Communication networks can also provide a good data migration path. Before deciding on a conversion method, several questions need to be answered. Will this diskette-copying activity be a one-time startup occurrence, or a daily or monthly procedure? Will my company continue to have a mixture of 5.25-inch and 3.5-inch drive machines? Are the unlike systems used in the same office (where cabling between them is feasible)? How many of these machines share a common local area network or host system? Which of my existing PC DOS programs are resident on copy- protected diskettes?

Why 3.5-Inch Diskettes?

IBM chose 3.5-inch diskette drives for the Personal System/2 for several reasons. First, they provide additional storage today and a platform for even more in the future. The PS/2 Model 30 uses 720 Kb-formatted diskettes, twice the amount of storage provided by most 5.25-inch diskettes. The drives on the Models 50, 60, and 80 support both 720 Kb and 1.44 Mb-formatted diskettes, and future 3.5-inch drives promise an even greater capacity.

The size of the diskette drives makes the smaller Personal System/2 "footprint" possible. The diskettes can be conveniently carried in a pocket, purse, or briefcase. The diskette surface is protected from damage or dust, and it is kept stable during reading and writing, making possible high-precision, narrow-track data recording (Figure 5–6).

Diskette Write-Protection

A 3.5-inch diskette can be set to either of two physical modes: read/write or read/only. This is accomplished by changing the position of a built-in switch,

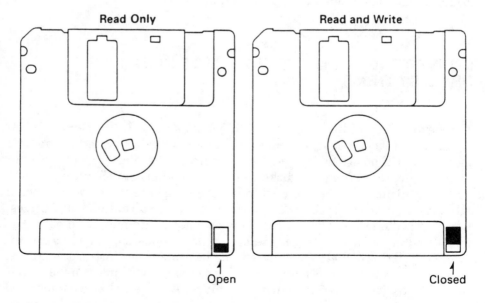

Figure 5–6 The 3.5-inch diskette is standard on the IBM Personal System/2. OS/2 is packaged on four, 1.44 Mb, 3.5-inch diskettes.

instead of searching for a "sticky tab" to put on the diskette jacket, as is done on 5.25-inch diskettes. The "open" position is read only and "closed" is read/write, just the opposite of 5.25-inch diskettes where "open" (no tab over the opening) is read/write and "closed" (tab in place) is read only.

Diskette Copy-Protection

Some 5.25-inch program diskettes will pose a problem, however. These have been safeguarded by the manufacturer to discourage illegal copying, even though their license agreement may allow it in some cases. That is because they permit a licensed copy of the software to be legally used on one machine at a time, and changing media format does not violate that kind of agreement. Data files produced by a program are never copy-protected or restricted, and can be copied or backed up without restriction. The best thing to do is read the license agreement that is included with each application package, to determine just what you can and cannot do.

Only a few PC XT and AT models support both kinds of diskette drives in the same system unit, which is the easiest and most convenient way to convert programs and data. Several other options are available.

IBM Personal System/2 Data Migration Facility

The parallel printer port on the Personal System/2 is fundamentally different from earlier PCs: it can *receive* as well as send information. No, the new Personal System/2 printers do not "talk" to the system unit, but the Data Migration Facility can. The DMF is nothing more than a cable adapter for an ordinary parallel printer cable. With it, you can connect the "printer end" of the cable to the parallel printer port on an IBM PC. Now you have a simple, high-speed cable link between the two computers. A word of caution: use an IBM parallel printer cable or an exact equivalent to make sure that all of the cable wires (needed for data transmission) are present.

A 5.25-inch diskette-based PC can now send files to a 3.5-inch based Personal System/2, using two programs. The SEND program is provided with the DMF on a 5.25-inch diskette, ready to be run on the PC. The RECEIVE program is already on the Personal System/2 Reference diskette that was shipped with the system. The Send program uses a form of the DOS COPY command to transfer files from PC to PS/2, a file at a time, or globally in groups. The Send program can also be used to send fixed disk files between machines. It does not break any of the copy-protection schemes used by software manufacturers to safeguard their applications. File copying takes place at roughly the same speed as it does between diskette drives on the same system, and error-checking is performed to insure accurate copying. File-copying cannot be done in reverse, from PS/2 to PC, since the PC's parallel port is incapable of receiving.

The DMF is designed as a low-cost data migration tool, for one-time diskette conversions or other occasional use. Since it uses the 6 ft. printer cable between two machines, it is inappropriate for diskette copying between offices.

IBM Personal System/2 5.25-Inch External Diskette Drive

One way to overcome the copy-protection problem is to install an external 5.25-inch drive on a Personal System/2. This way, a 5.25-inch program diskette that is "un-copyable" can be used directly on a PS/2. A possible complication can arise because the external drive always takes on the B: drive address. This can be a problem for a few applications that require a program diskette to be run from the A: drive only.

Copyable programs can be transferred from the external B: drive to either the internal A: diskette drive or the internal C: fixed disk. The external drive does not disrupt normal computer operations, making it suitable for long-term, periodic use in a mixed-system environment.

IBM PC 3.5-Inch External Diskette Drive

The IBM 3.5-inch external drive is designed for attachment to PCs, XTs and ATs, providing 3.5-inch capability in a mixed-system environment. It is only available with a 720 Kb diskette drive, and cannot read the 1.44 Mb formatted diskettes supported on the PS/2 Models 50, 60, and 80.

Media Transition Via Serial Port

Another method of diskette-copying uses a machine's communications capability. The oldest method, which has been used by application programmers for years, involves a serial-to-serial cable hookup. The asynchronous, or serial, port is capable of sending and receiving on almost every kind of computer. An ordinary serial cable can be modified by adding a cable adapter with some wires switched—actually, the send and receive wires are crossed so the two computers can talk and listen to each other. This adapter is known as a modem eliminator or null modem, since it replaces a serial communications modem. Using simple communication programs, most programmers "port" their programs to new machines this way. Today, commercial communication software such as Crosstalk XVI, PC Talk IV, and Procomm support this "local mode" of sending files between PCs. Communication speeds are usually slower than the Data Migration Facility.

A more sophisticated serial-to-serial hookup is The Brooklyn Bridge™ by White Crane Systems. It comes with the cable and software on both 3.5-inch and 5.25-inch diskettes. The Bridge runs at a communication speed of 115,200 BPS, copying files at a rated 10 Kb per second.

Over the Network

Another media conversion method is a little more indirect than a direct cable hookup, but can be practically "free" where PCs and PS/2s share a common communication network or mainframe. Most network and host communications software supports file transfers between PC and network file server or PC and host system. By uploading a program (on a 5.25-inch diskette, presumably) to a network file server or host library, it is available for downloading to other machines (with 3.5-inch diskettes) (Figure 5–7).

Modem to Modem

Finally, a common asynchronous communications modem makes a slower, but adequate data link between systems. Most popular communications programs support file exchanges. One system is designated as the answering machine, and the other as the originator. A phone call is placed over an ordinary telephone line, so the two computers can be in adjoining offices or thousands of miles apart. Typical modem speeds are 1200 or 2400 BPS, so data transmission times will be longer than with other methods.

REPROGRAMMING FOR OS/2

The lure of OS/2 and its potential will cause many programmers to convert DOS programs to OS/2. The amount of time and effort they put into this task will directly affect the function, usability, and power of the converted applications.

Program Migration

Sometimes the migration of a DOS program to an OS/2 system implies more than just simple file copying. The program may carry with it one or more batch files including AUTOEXEC.BAT, and those commands may have to be merged with the OS/2 AUTOEXEC file.

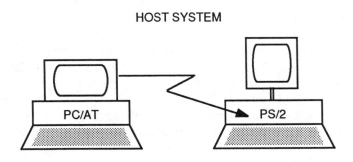

HOST SYSTEM

PC/AT

PS/2

Figure 5–7 The 3.5-inch diskette is standard on the IBM Personal System/2. OS/2 is packaged on four, 1.44 Mb, 3.5-inch diskettes.

Some DOS copy-protected programs use a timing-sensitive algorithm to foil illegal copying. When these programs are loaded, it should be done with no other programs running.

There may be device drivers and entries in the CONFIG.SYS file. You should examine those entries and determine if they should be entered in the OS/2 CONFIG.SYS file also. DOS device drivers may be a problem, since many will not work under OS/2. They may have to be replaced with new drivers that can be shared between DOS and OS/2 programs. OS/2 serial drivers, such as DEVICE=COM02.SYS, should be listed in the configuration file. Other considerations are discussed in Appendix B of the OS/2 User's Reference.

Program Conversion

Converting a PC DOS program to OS/2 Family or Full-Function format is a far more complicated task than simple media conversion. First of all, conversion can be performed only on the program's source code—the original set of language instructions used as input for the compiler. A compiler then translates the source file, producing executable, object code. You cannot reverse the process, making source code from object code. Second, program conversion can only be done by someone who knows a program language (like FORTRAN, COBOL, or C) quite well. Very few commercial program vendors distribute their source code to users, and few PC users are application programmers, so most conversions will have to come from the same software house that produced them originally.

DOS-to-OS/2 program conversions vary widely in complexity. The simplest conversions involve nothing more than copying programs to 3.5-inch diskettes. OS/2 Family programs require more work, but don't utilize OS/2 exclusive features. OS/2 full-function programs take the most time and effort, providing multi-tasking, windowing, and large memory support.

Compilers

Once modifications have been made to a program source file, it must be re-compiled using one of the six new IBM DOS-OS/2 language compilers. Their "DOS-OS/2" prefix indicates that these compilers run under either PC DOS or OS/2, and can generate program object code that runs under either one. The six new compiler products have the "/2" designation in their names: COBOL/2, FORTRAN/2, C/2, BASIC/2, Pascal/2, and Macro Assembler/2. The first three, COBOL, FORTRAN, and C, participate in IBM's Systems Application Architecture, assuring source code compatibility with compilers on other IBM mini and mainframe systems. More about the IBM language compilers in Chapter 8.

OS/2 Toolkit

IBM offers a set of programming tools for OS/2, called the OS/2 Toolkit. Toolkit 1.0, which coincides with the release of OS/2 Standard Edition 1.0, includes the OS/2 Programmer's Guide and software tools for creating applications using features such as dynamic linking and external message files. It also assists in the programming of OS/2 Family Applications. Programming tools and sample programs are provided for the IBM Macro Assembler/ 2 and C/2 languages. The Toolkit 1.1 version will provide additional tools for Presentation Manager functions such as graphics and windowing. The Toolkit is discussed in more detail in Chapter 8.

BASIC Interpreter Programs

Most application programs today are written in one of the above six languages, and are distributed in an object code format. Programs written using the BASIC language interpreter are an exception. An interpreter is a program that stores programs in an intermediate format somewhere between source and object code. When an interpreted BASIC program is displayed or printed, it looks like source statements: 10 PRINT "Hello" or 20 INPUT X are examples. Interpreter programs do not need to be compiled to run, you just type RUN.

The BASIC interpreter comes "free" with DOS and OS/2. It has been especially popular with novice and amateur programmers. Programs are easy to write, the compiling steps are eliminated, and debugging is easier. The biggest drawback is performance: compiled BASIC programs often run 10 to 30 times faster than interpreted programs.

The BASIC interpreter does not run in OS/2 Mode, but in DOS Mode it can run interpreter programs just as it does under PC DOS alone. The BASIC interpreter lets you optionally save a program in a source format which can then be compiled with the BASIC/2 compiler for OS/2 Mode. Few commercial programs are distributed in interpreter format, but many "home grown" BASIC interpreter programs can be converted to OS/2 this way. The BASIC 3.3 Reference is not shipped with OS/2; it must be ordered separately as part number 6280189.

Ill-Behaved Programs

PC DOS programs that use a software interface outside of the "official" published DOS documentation may require additional changes before they will run with OS/2. That is because such program shortcuts are not permitted under OS/2, which protects program segments from accessing unauthorized system calls or memory segments. This includes high-performance techniques such as sending output directly to a display. OS/2 allows such direct hardware access through its Input-Output Privilege Level

(IOPL). The OS/2 Call-Return command interface is used to read and write to system devices.

Text and Graphics

Text-based programs such as spreadsheets and word processors do not require changes to take advantage of the higher-resolution character box size on the Personal System/2 displays. Graphics is another story. Existing PC DOS programs that use the PC Virtual Device Interface (VDI) may be converted to OS/2 by using a new version of IBM's Graphics Development Toolkit.

DOS Hotkey (terminate and stay resident) programs can exist as OS/2 "detached" background sessions after conversion. A keyboard device monitor can be used to trap certain keystrokes and use them to bring the detached program to the foreground.

New OS/2 Programming Features

Once all of the necessary changes have been made to a program (enough to get it to run under OS/2 without embellishments), further modifications can begin which truly exploit OS/2. Exclusive features like device monitors, dynamic loading, multi-tasking, timer functions, interprocess communications, separate message files, Presentation Services, code page support, and more will be discussed in Chapter 8 on programming.

Bridge Products

To ease the conversion to OS/2, certain programs can be used with DOS to get a head start on the conversion process. Microsoft Windows 2.0 has an application program interface that is similar to OS/2, particularly in its windowing interface. Software in IBM's 3270 emulation family, such as the 3270 Workstation Program, have a communications interface that will be similar to the OS/2 Extended Edition.

Chapter 8 will have more information on the OS/2 programming interface.

6

OS/2 Installation:
Up and Running

Once the necessary hardware has been purchased, programs have been upgraded or converted, and diskettes have been copied, OS/2 and its applications can be installed. Most users will want to run a mix of DOS and OS/2 applications, and some may want to have both operating systems installed, at least for the time being. The OS/2 installation process is easy, and a familiarization program is provided for the first-time user. Applications can be easily installed, started, and switched between, from OS/2 menus. Maintenance, configuration changes and performance tuning may be done on occasion.

DEFINING SOME TERMS

Startup Diskette.   When installing both DOS and OS/2 on the same system, only one operating system (usually OS/2) is bootable, or set up to load at power-on. DOS would be booted from a Startup diskette, containing DOS and some configuration commands.

Configuration File.   This file, named CONFIG.SYS, contains DOS and OS/2 options that are read by the operating system during power-on initialization (system boot).

Initialization Files. DOS uses the AUTOEXEC.BAT batch file to issue commands and/or run a program, when the DOS Mode is first started. OS/2 has a similar file, named OS2INIT.CMD, which runs when each OS/2 session is started.

Autostart File. OS/2 recognizes a batch file named STARTUP.CMD that can pre-load multiple OS/2 applications at power-on.

GETTING READY

Purchasing OS/2

A DOS user—with any version of DOS—can upgrade to the OS/2 Standard Edition 1.0 for less than the full purchase price, thanks to a special introductory upgrade offer from IBM. OS/2 Standard 1.0 users can also upgrade to release 1.1 for no additional cost.

Ship Group Components

The OS/2 Standard Edition 1.0 package contains four high-capacity diskettes. 1.44 Mb, 3.5-inch diskettes are shipped with the Personal System/2 version and 1.2 Mb, 5.25-inch diskettes come with the Personal Computer AT version. A relatively brief User's Guide and a larger User's Reference are provided as documentation. Documentation can also be ordered separately.

DUAL OPERATING SYSTEMS

Sometimes, especially during the initial DOS-to-OS/2 conversion period, it may be necessary to have both PC DOS and OS/2 installed on the same system. This is a requirement for some time-dependent programs, such as communications applications, that run under DOS (by itself) but not under the DOS Mode of OS/2. Both operating systems can share the same fixed disk and even some of the same programs and data files, but only one can run at a time (Figure 6–1).

Creating a DOS Startup Diskette

Although you can run either OS/2 or PC DOS from the same fixed disk, only the primary operating system is bootable, and in our example this will be OS/2. The secondary operating system (in this case DOS) must be booted from a diskette in drive A. Once loaded, it has access to the entire fixed disk, including all OS/2 files. Just as OS/2 may not be able to run some DOS pro-

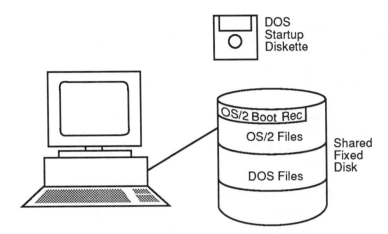

Figure 6–1 OS/2 and PC DOS can co-reside on the same system . OS/2 is booted from the fixed disk, and DOS is booted from a Startup diskette containing DOS, its configuration file, and any required device drivers. Other OS/2 and DOS files can reside anywhere on the fixed disk, although care should be taken to store duplicant files in separate directories.

grams, the reverse is also true: OS/2 Full-function programs don't run under DOS. The DOS Startup diskette can be created as a copy of the original DOS diskette or it can be any diskette that has been formatted with the FORMAT/S (system) option.

In your DOS needs are relatively simple, you may be able to get by with a standard DOS diskette that can be booted whenever DOS programs need to run. After changing the default drive to the fixed disk (enter C:), the name of a resident DOS program can be entered. However, if you have an installed DOS system with a CONFIG.SYS and AUTOEXEC.BAT file, you should review the following procedure. It shows you how to create a Startup diskette and a fixed disk directory that provide the same DOS conditions that existed before OS/2 installation.

A PC DOS Directory

The Startup diskette is designed only to start DOS, and then you will want to remove it and run from the fixed disk as before. The various DOS external commands and other files from the DOS diskette should be stored in a unique fixed disk directory, with a name like \PCDOS. Make sure that the DOS command processor, COMMAND.COM, is included in that directory. The \PCDOS directory will provide the user and some DOS programs with commands and other files they may need. With the DOS diskette in drive A:, the new DOS directory can be created and loaded like this:

```
MKDIR C:\PCDOS
COPY A:*.* C:\PCDOS
```

Make sure that any DOS command files, device drivers, or any other application components are copied to either the Startup diskette or the new \PCDOS directory. This will avoid the possibility of OS/2 confusing old DOS files with its own.

If PC DOS is Already Installed

If PC DOS has already been installed on the system, copy its \CONFIG.SYS configuration file (if there is one) from the root directory of the fixed disk to the root directory of the DOS Startup diskette. The DOS \AUTOEXEC.BAT file should also be copied from the fixed disk to the Startup diskette. These two files will allow DOS to be booted with the same options, drivers, and programs that were set when it was booted from the fixed disk. The COPY commands are:

```
COPY C:\CONFIG.SYS A:
COPY C:\AUTOEXEC.BAT A:
```

Examine the two files (TYPE A:\CONFIG.SYS, for example). If any additional files in the C:\ root directory are used, such as device driver files in DEVICE statements, those files should also be copied to the Startup diskette, as above.

A:\CONFIG.SYS and A:\AUTOEXEC.BAT may require some changes. During the boot sequence, DOS reads the configuration file first, then goes on to load the COMMAND.COM command processor, and finally looks for the AUTOEXEC.BAT file. This sequence will not change, but a few file changes will help make an orderly transition from Startup diskette boot to fixed disk operation. The files can be edited with DOS's EDLIN line editor, a full-screen editor such as IBM's Personal Editor, or with many word processing programs which are capable of reading and writing ASCII-format DOS files.

Configuration File Changes

A new command in the CONFIG.SYS file will point DOS to the new location of its command processor:

```
SHELL=C:\PCDOS\COMMAND.COM /P
```

If there is no configuration file to modify, you should create one containing this command. If any DOS device drivers are referenced in the configuration file, they should be modified to show the new PCDOS directory name, as in this Virtual Disk example:

```
DEVICE=C:\PCDOS\VDISK.SYS 128
```

Remember to re-save the modified configuration file in the Startup Diskette's root directory: A:\CONFIG.SYS.

AUTOEXEC.BAT File Changes

Up to now, DOS has been booted from the fixed disk, so drive C: has been the default system drive. Since the Startup diskette is booted from drive A:, it temporarily becomes its default drive. Using the editor, modify the Startup diskette's AUTOEXEC.BAT file to add three new statements (at the beginning) that (1) tell DOS where to find its files on the fixed disk and (2) change the default drive to C:. If the DOS command directory is named \PCDOS, they would look like this:

```
PATH C:\PCDOS
SET COMSPEC=C:\PCDOS\COMMAND.COM
C:\
```

If AUTOEXEC.BAT already contains a PATH command, you should add \PCDOS to its directory list. If there are any remaining batch file commands already in the file, such as the name of a program to load, they should be left alone. Re-save the modified file as A:\AUTOEXEC.BAT.

During the OS/2 installation, some files will be copied or added to the fixed disk root directory that have the same names on a PC DOS system, such as CONFIG.SYS. This should present no problem, since DOS now has everything it needs on the Startup diskette and the fixed disk \PCDOS directory for booting. After booting, DOS will automatically go to the \PCDOS directory for its command processor and other files.

Adding PC DOS to OS/2

If OS/2 is already installed on the system, the dual-system installation procedure is essentially the same. Make a new directory (using the OS/2 MKDIR, or MD command) for the PC DOS diskette files. Create a DOS Startup Diskette as described above, containing the revised AUTOEXEC.BAT and CONFIG.SYS files.

Testing the Startup Diskette

With the DOS Startup Diskette in drive A:, reboot the system by pressing the <Ctrl + Alt + Del> key combination. PC DOS should come up normally, and then switch to the fixed disk. You should then either see the C> prompt on the screen or an AUTOEXEC.BAT-loaded program will appear.

INSTALLING OS/2

Installation Program

Once you are ready to proceed with the actual OS/2 installation, you begin by booting the OS/2 Installation Diskette. The installation program formats (if necessary) the fixed disk, creates directories, copies files from the four OS/2 diskettes, and creates the Configuration and Startup files. It will skip the formatting step if the fixed disk was previously formatted by DOS. (While OS/2 can be booted from diskette, as it is at the start of installation, it isn't practical to run the operating system this way. Fixed disk storage capacity is needed to hold large files, such as the swap file.)

Partitions

If the fixed disk is unformatted, OS/2 Install creates a primary DOS-type partition (OS/2 and DOS share the same kind of partition). The primary partition can be up to 32 Mb in size; any remaining space is used for the extended partition, which can be further subdivided into logical drives of up to 32 Mb. For example, on a 70 Mb disk there could be a 32 Mb primary partition and two additional logical drives totalling 38 Mb (32 Mb and 6 Mb or 19 Mb and 19 Mb, etc.). In OS/2 Standard Edition 1.1 and Extended Edition 1.1, the entire fixed disk capacity can be used as a single partition.

OS/2 Directories and Files

Next, the Install program creates directories where OS/2 files are stored. The user is prompted to insert, in turn, each of the other three diskettes in the OS/2 package. Some of the files go into the disk's root directory, and the others are copied into subdirectories.

OS/2 Directory	Contents
\ (root)	CONFIG.SYS, AUTOEXEC.BAT, OS2INIT.CMD, STARTUP.CMD, device drivers
\OS2	OS/2 Main Directory

OS/2 Directory	Contents
\OS2\INTRO	OS/2 subdirectory for Introducing OS/2 Familiarization program.
\OS2\INSTALL	OS/2 subdirectory for OS/2-DOS External Commands.

System Files

Install creates three special files in the root directory that the operating system uses to set options or start programs. They are:

File Name	Purpose
CONFIG.SYS	OS/2 Configuration File. Contains special commands to set general system options. Takes effect before any OS/2 or DOS Mode programs are started.
AUTOEXEC.BAT	DOS Mode Initialization File. Batch file containing PC DOS commands or programs to be executed when DOS Mode is selected. This file is ignored in OS/2 Mode.
OS2INIT.CMD	OS/2 Mode Initialization File. Batch file containing OS/2 commands or programs to be executed when each OS/2 Mode session is started. Initially contains PATH and DPATH commands. Ignored in DOS Mode.

Since these files play such an important role in the behavior of the operating system, it is a good idea to look a little closer at each of them.

OS/2 CONFIGURATION FILE

The OS/2 Installation program creates a configuration file derived partly from system defaults and partly from user-selected options. The OS/2 configuration file has the same name and is similar in function to the configuration file on PC DOS systems. PC DOS's configuration file had to be created by the user or generated by an application program; OS/2 creates its own.

The configuration file establishes certain universal conditions that apply to both DOS and OS/2 Mode programs. Any changes made to this file do not take effect until the system is rebooted. CONFIG.SYS contains special commands (different from those in batch files) that are executed during OS/2 loading. The two initialization files, on the other hand, are DOS-like batch files that are executed every time a DOS or OS/2 Mode *session* is started. Their commands and options can be superseded by other batch files or user commands anytime during a session.

OS/2 Install puts several commands in the original CONFIG.SYS file. For example, answering "yes" to the Install program question about DOS Mode causes the command PROTECTONLY=NO to be placed in the file (translation: "NO" Protect Mode Only means that low-memory space will be allocated for DOS Mode programs). Later in this chapter we will look at some of the configuration file options and see how they can be used to modify system characteristics.

OS/2 BATCH FILES

OS/2 batch files are similar in concept to PC DOS's. OS/2 Mode sessions only recognize batch files that have a filename ending in .CMD. DOS Mode, like DOS itself, recognizes batch files that end in .BAT. While the OS/2 Mode and DOS Mode batch file commands are sometimes different, the logic commands used to control application flow (IF, FOR, GOTO) are the same.

Initialization Files

The Install program creates two batch files used to issue commands at the beginning of each program session. AUTOEXEC.BAT runs when DOS Mode is started, and OS2INIT.CMD performs a similar function for each OS/2 Command Prompt session. Neither of these should be confused with CONFIG.SYS which sets global operating system options that apply to all applications. These special batch files set session defaults that can be overridden by the user or another batch file.

AUTOEXEC.BAT

The DOS Mode Initialization File contains a single PATH statement, directing the session to search the root and \OS2 disk directories for programs and commands when they are not found in the current directory:

```
PATH C:\;C:\OS2
```

Additional DOS commands can be added, and the PATH command can be modified to include other user directories. A DOS menu program might be called next, or a favorite DOS application program could be run. Remember that only one DOS Mode session can run under OS/2.

OS2INIT.CMD

The OS/2 Mode Initialization File is run each time an OS/2 Mode session (OS/2 Command Prompt) is started from the Program Selector menu (OS/2 sessions auto-started at system initialization are found in the STARTUP.CMD file to be discussed next). The Install program creates an OS2INIT.CMD file with two entries: one is a directory search list for commands, and the other is for data files:

```
PATH C:\;C:\OS2;C:\OS2\INSTALL;
DPATH C:\;C:\OS2;C:\OS2\INSTALL;
```

These commands can be extended to include application paths. OS2INIT.CMD does not take effect when an OS/2 program is started from the Program Selector.

The OS/2 Autostart File

You do not have to manually select your favorite set of OS/2 applications every time you start the system. A special batch file, named STARTUP.CMD, can be created by the user to autostart several OS/2 programs. The START command, new to OS/2, is used in STARTUP.CMD to start each program session as soon as OS/2 is booted. STARTUP. CMD runs immediately after CONFIG. SYS, at the beginning of an OS/2 session.

Introducing OS/2 Tutorial

When the installation process is finished, the Program Selector menu contains a single entry: *Introducing OS/2*, the OS/2 on-line tutorial, or familiarization program (Figure 6–2). Since this program describes many of the operating system functions, it is a good idea to take this short course before going further.

INSTALLING APPLICATION PROGRAMS

Building the Program Selector

Now that OS/2 itself is installed, it is ready to install the application programs which will run under it. After each OS/2 application is copied onto the fixed disk, it can be added to the Program Selector menu. DOS Mode programs can be started from a batch file or a DOS shell program.

```
                     Introducing OS/2

         These are the main topics covered in this program.

                  Getting Started
                     Overview
                     Using Special Keys

                  Running Programs
                     Overview
                     Using Multitasking
                     Using the Program Selector
                     Using Help

                  Managing Information
                     Overview
                     Using Commands and Messages
                     Learning Other Commands

                               Press the Enter key to continue.

         Enter    F3=Exit
```

Figure 6–2   The Introducing OS/2 program is a short tutorial on the operating system. Its first screen is shown here.

OS/2 PROGRAM INSTALLATION

OS/2 Command Prompt

The *Program Selector OS/2 Command Prompt* entry initiates the OS/2 command processor, a blank screen containing the default [C:\] prompt. Now OS/2 commands (most are the same as DOS's) can be used to create directories, copy, and run programs.

Loading the Application

Consult the installation documentation that comes with each OS/2 program. You may find that a batch file on the program diskette has been provided to automate the program installation. This is the way most DOS applications are loaded today. If no batch file is provided, the procedure may be as simple as (1) creating a subdirectory and (2) performing a global file copy from diskette to the new directory. You can use OS/2 commands such as COPY or

XCOPY to copy the OS/2 application programs over from diskette. Here is an example:

```
MKDIR C:\FINANCE (Create the directory)
COPY A:*.* C:\FINANCE   (Copy files into directory)
```

Testing the Application

If the documentation gives you a program or batch file name, you should try running it before finishing the installation. In our example, let's say the program name is MONEY. You could run the program from outside of its directory by entering:

```
C:\FINANCE\MONEY
```

or, from inside the directory, by first changing directories:

```
CHDIR C:\FINANCE
MONEY
```

Once you are satisfied that your application is working properly, all that remains to be done is to add the program to the Program Selector menu. Then you will be able to run it anytime you want to. Type *EXIT* to leave the current OS/2 session or place the *EXIT* command at the end of the batch file that calls the program.

Adding a Program Title

Now you should be back at the Program Selector menu. Press F10 or use the mouse to select the *Update* menu. It appears as a window in the upper-left hand corner of the screen. Of the four Update choices (1. *Add a Program Title*, 2. *Delete a Program Title*, 3. *Change Program Information*, and 4. *Refresh Switch List*), we will select *1. Add a Program Title*.

The Add a Program Title screen appears next (Figure 6–3). Now you will have three items of information to provide about the program.

The *Program Title* is the descriptive name (not the filename) that will appear on the Start A Program menu. It can be up to 30 characters long. In the example we have been using, the name of the program might be something like "Personal Financial Investment."

The *Program Pathname* is the complete program filename, including drive and directory. In our example it could be something like: C:\FINANCE\MONEY.

Program Parameters are optional information that some programs require. This information would normally be entered just to the right of the program name, like this: MONEY 7 88 which might mean "run the MONEY

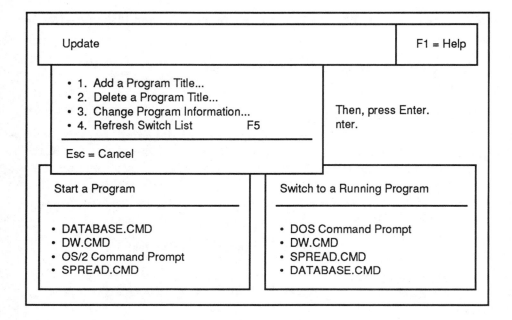

Figure 6–3 Installing an OS/2 application is easy. Press F10 from the Program Selector menu. Select Option 1 from the Update menu (shown here). Next OS/2 will ask for the Program Title and its file name.

program and process data for July, 1988." The two parameters are 7 88. You could substitute question marks for the optional parameters (MONEY ? ?) and OS/2 will ask you for the parameters each time you run the program.

Press Enter and the title will be added to the Start a Program list, and you will be returned to the Program Selector menu. All installed OS/2 Programs (such as the example in Figure 6–4) can be started from the left-hand menu.

DOS PROGRAM INSTALLATION

Installing a DOS program is a much simpler procedure. From the Program Selector screen, move the highlighted bar to the box on the right marked "Switch to a Running Program." At this point, unless your OS/2 configuration file said otherwise, you will have one selection in the box: *DOS Command Prompt*. This will bring you to the DOS Mode C>_ prompt.

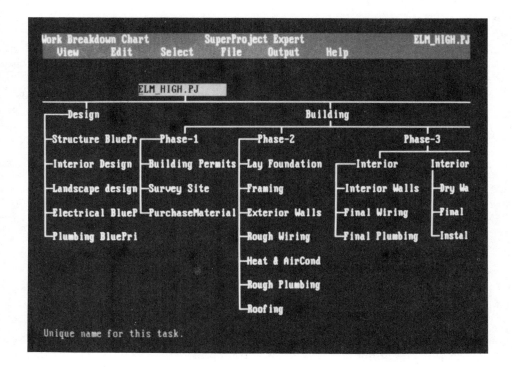

Figure 6–4 Once a program has been added to the Start a Program menu, it can be selected and run. Here, Super Project Expert™ is used to display a Work Breakdown Chart.

Loading the Application

Consult your application documentation to determine the installation steps. As with the OS/2 programs described in the last section, DOS application installation is mostly a matter of copying files into a directory on the fixed disk. Enter the program's name (which may be a batch file) to run it.

That is all there is to installing DOS applications. Remember, only one DOS program at a time can run under OS/2. The DOS Command Prompt is the only DOS option on the Switch to a Running Program list—no DOS program descriptions or filenames appear. If you want to run a different DOS program, you must finish the first one (which returns you to the DOS prompt) and start the second one by entering its program name. When you are finished with a DOS program and want to return to the Program Selector, press <Ctrl + Esc>.

Deleting Programs

To erase an OS/2 program from the Program Selector menu, press F10 or use the mouse to select the Update screen, then 2. *Delete a Program Title.* From the list of installed programs, remove the program's descriptive name. Then go to the OS/2 command prompt, ERASE all program and related data files and remove the directory (RD).

USING OS/2

Once OS/2 installation is complete, you should test the system by running various combinations of the installed applications in a multi-application environment.

PC DOS Mode

First select the DOS Mode and run one or two of your old PC DOS applications. Return to the DOS command prompt by ending the program. Enter some DOS commands such as CD \ or TYPE \AUTOEXEC.BAT. (The DOS Mode session cannot be removed or terminated.)

OS/2 Mode

Now return to the Program Selector menu (<Ctrl + Esc>) and start one or more of your OS/2 applications (either Family or Full-function). From the OS/2 command line, try some OS/2 commands such as TYPE \CONFIG.SYS or DIR. If you can, run a couple of OS/2 Mode programs and hotkey (<Alt + Esc>) between each of them and the DOS Mode. (An OS/2 Mode session can be terminated with the *EXIT* command.)

MAINTAINING AN OS/2 SYSTEM

An OS/2 system requires a minimum of post-installation care and feeding. As with DOS systems, OS/2 system fixed disk drives—at least the important data you are currently working on—should be backed up frequently. But other steps may be taken to perform routine tasks such as maximizing performance or adding new output devices.

Software Warranty

IBM warrants both the media and the programs on its OS/2 diskettes for three months. The Service Coordinator at a PC dealer or a large IBM customer can report OS/2 problems and receive assistance by calling either of two special telephone numbers. One is a voice hotline, and the other is an asynchronous communications port. OS/2 provides system tracing and dumping features to assist in locating problems. More on these later in the chapter.

Administrative Support

Many OS/2 users will be able to install and maintain their own systems without outside help. In some companies with multiple systems installed, a technical coordinator may be responsible for general PC support. This person's role may include training, consulting, program selection and distribution, troubleshooting, and installation support.

Backups

Whether performed by an individual user or by an administrative person assigned to the task, file backups are too important to be put off. Depending on the size, importance and frequency of file changes, backups should be selective and scheduled. Whether backups are performed daily, weekly, or monthly, there are several ways to go about it.

BACKUP/RESTORE

The standard way to backup fixed disk files is to use the OS/2 BACKUP command, which condenses and copies files to diskette. The RESTORE command does the reverse, copying backup files to the fixed disk. Once on diskette, files copied with the BACKUP command cannot be used directly. That means that if you try to read or copy one of them, you will not be able to. They will remain there until you reuse the diskette for your next backup. Hopefully you will not have to use those backup diskettes, but they are good insurance for all of that work that took so many hours to do. (The DOS 3.3 and OS/2 level BACKUP/RESTORE programs have been improved to compress backed up files, thus improving performance and reducing diskette space).

Backups can and should be done selectively; you do not backup unchanging application program and batch files, for example, at least not more than once. Since they are constant, there is no need to repeatedly make copies of them. Files that contain critical, hard-to-recreate data are good candidates for regular backup. Their selection is easier if they are stored in identifiable directories or subdirectories. For example, all of your current Writing Assistant documents might be saved in a directory named \WRITE\ACTIVE or \LETTERS\1988. Or, if your Lotus 1-2-3 spreadsheets are all stored with file names ending in .WKS, they could be referenced with a file specification like \LOTUS*.WKS. The BACKUP command can copy only selected files, saving time and diskette space.

XCOPY

The COPY and XCOPY commands can also be used for transferring fixed disk files to diskette and back. Unlike BACKUP, they don't compress files, keeping them in their original form: same names, same size, etc. The XCOPY command has an optional feature that works like BACKUP; its /M option marks source files (those on the fixed disk) when they are copied. Files previously marked but not modified are not copied. Each time a file is resaved or changed in any way, the mark, or attribute is removed. The next time you XCOPY your files, only the ones that have changed will be copied.

Adding New I/O Devices

OS/2 comes with a set of device drivers for many popular printers and other output devices. Additional hardware devices can be easily installed, provided that the new device is software compatible with an existing one or is shipped with a new driver. OS/2 1.1 provides an installation procedure for adding such device drivers to its collection and a menu for the user to redirect program output to a different device. OS/2 device drivers work with either OS/2 or DOS programs, but old DOS drivers are restricted to DOS programs.

CHANGING OPERATING SYSTEM OPTIONS

Several new or enhanced configuration and batch file commands are used in OS/2. We've already mentioned a few (DEVICE, PATH, DPATH) that are placed in OS2INIT.CMD and AUTOEXEC.BAT by the Install program. These and several others can be added or altered by the user for the purpose of improving performance, designing a specific hardware configuration, adding international character set support, or performing system troubleshooting.

In this section, commands fall into two categories. Configuration file commands (those that are placed in CONFIG.SYS by the Install program or later by the user) are read during OS/2 initialization. If any of these commands are changed, the system must be rebooted for them to take effect. DOS and OS/2 commands, on the other hand, are operating system internal (built-in) and external commands that can be issued anytime from the command prompt or from inside a batch file. They take effect immediately.

PERFORMANCE

Once the OS/2 system is up and running with a reasonably stable set of everyday applications, you may want to do some performance tuning. Sometimes one or two relatively simple adjustments can make a big difference in performance.

Running in a Multi-tasking Environment

Almost any PC DOS program running under OS/2's DOS Mode will show at least a slight decrease in performance from standalone PC DOS—all other things equal. That's because the operating system itself carries additional overhead because of its complexity; even in the simple DOS single-program example, the program will still run slightly slower. That's because OS/2 still "grabs control" of a time-slice now and then to perform system management tasks. Since many OS/2 users will be running on faster Personal System/2 hardware, this small performance decrease will often be offset.

As time goes on, many converted OS/2 programs will show performance increases over their DOS versions. This can be attributed to the use of multi-tasking techniques, where several threads, or tasks, can run in parallel. But many users will want to load and run several programs, and OS/2 will distribute system resources—including processor time—among them, slowing down individual application programs while increasing overall user productivity and system throughput.

Understanding Throughput

Figure 6–5 is a diagram illustrating a typical personal computer work session, first using DOS (top), and then with OS/2 (bottom). The shaded bars are used to show "person time": steps that the user must perform. The unshaded bars are steps that run unattended, performed entirely by the computer, without user interaction.

First the DOS scenario

A spreadsheet program is loaded, a small change is made to it, and the sheet is recalculated. The modified sheet is then saved and printed. Next a word

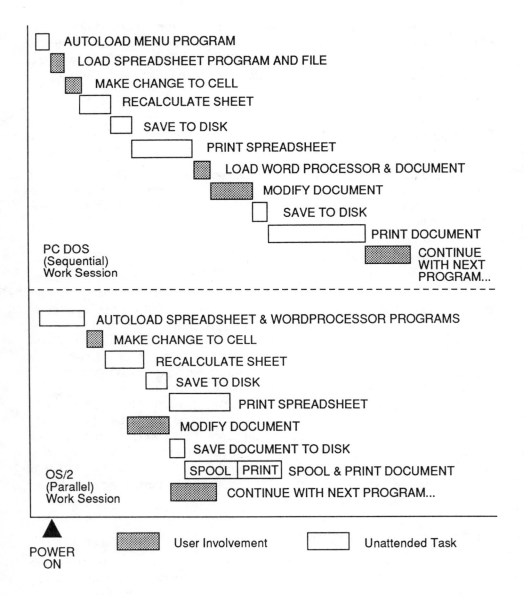

Figure 6–5 Both application program design and user work habits can aid productivity on a multi-tasking system. In the top example, a work session is performed in a sequential manner, just as if PC DOS were used. User-interactive tasks (load file, make changes, etc.) are shown in dark. In the bottom example, the same work session is repeated, with user-interactive foreground tasks overlapping with background jobs (recalc, save, print). This lets the user do more productive work in less time, without waiting.

processing program and document file are loaded. The document is modified, saved, and printed.

Now the OS/2 scenario

The same spreadsheet is loaded and changed. While the sheet is recalculating (background job), the user begins to work on the document. When the sheet is finished recalculating, it is saved and printed as a background job. While the document is being saved and printed, the user starts the next job, and so on. Notice how user functions (shaded bars) now can be performed without interruption, where under DOS there were times when the user had to wait for other work to finish. The total throughput—the elapsed time from start to end of a work session—can be drastically reduced. This savings in "people time" is potentially much greater than what could be gained by an increase in processor performance alone.

There are other things that you can do to improve throughput. Several configuration and batch file commands can be used to fine-tune OS/2. Using a full-screen editor or word processing program, you can examine and modify the \CONFIG.SYS and \OS2INIT.CMD files. The IBM OS/2 User's Reference describes the use of each command in much more detail. Most commands have (1) default values that OS/2 uses if the command does not appear, (2) Install program values that are placed in a configuration or initialization file, and (3) a range of user-selected options to override (1) and (2). Only significantly changed or new commands are discussed here.

BUFFERS

File buffers are blocks of memory used to move data from and to a disk. The BUFFERS command, if not present in CONFIG.SYS, defaults to three 512-byte blocks. The Install program overrides this with a BUFFERS=30 entry in the file. On a system with heavy disk activity, increasing this number may improve performance.

DISKCACHE is another configuration file statement that sets aside memory to improve fixed disk performance. The Install program's default for CONFIG.SYS is DISKCACHE=64, where 64 Kb of memory is used. On a busy system, increasing this number may improve performance. DISKCACHE works only on the Personal System/2 Models 50, 60, and 80.

MAXWAIT

When several applications are running at various priority levels, sometimes a program may be deprived of enough processor cycles to do useful work. This command sets a time limit for any program. When the limit is reached, OS/2 gives the process a temporary boost in priority. The initial CONFIG.SYS file command is MAXWAIT=10, where 10 is the time in seconds.

MEMMAN

OS/2 swaps program segments to disk unless told otherwise. It also takes time to perform storage compaction, where memory segments are moved to free up space. In a time-critical application, either swapping or compaction can be suspended by placing this command in CONFIG.SYS.

PRIORITY

OS/2 can change program priority, or relative performance levels dynamically, as programs run, or by using absolute, fixed priority levels established by the programs. PRIORITY=DYNAMIC is the default, but PRIORITY=ABSOLUTE can be set in the configuration file.

TIMESLICE

This CONFIG.SYS option establishes the minimum and maximum values, in milliseconds, of processor time-slices that are allocated to each program thread. The default is TIMESLICE=32, 248.

Adding Memory

OS/2 gives programmers the ability to segment programs in smaller parts, allowing them to run in less memory than the sum of those parts. Segments are copied into memory from the fixed disk, either at program load time, or later, as needed. As memory is required for new segments, old ones can be discarded (if they haven't been altered) or swapped to a temporary disk file. When memory becomes fragmented, OS/2 will move segments around to free up additional space. All of this activity adds to system overhead and decreases performance. Of course, if enough memory is available, none of this activity is necessary.

The best way to find out just how much additional memory will improve performance on such a system is to simply try it. Create a stable test environment, one in which you are actively using a typical set of programs and data. Time yourself as you run a specific scenario, trying to reduce variable factors such as typing time, to a minimum. Now add a memory increment (512 Kb or 1 Mb would be best) and repeat the test to see if it takes less time to run. You should find that, at some point, additional memory will not make much difference, since no more segment loading or swapping is taking place.

OTHER SYSTEM CONFIGURATION OPTIONS

The following commands are all related to various system options affecting the user interface, supported devices, memory utilization, and other OS/2 characteristics.

DEVICE

OS/2 includes a set of standard device drivers (keyboard, display, printer, diskette, fixed disk, and clock) that don't require DEVICE statements in the CONFIG.SYS file. Before any additional device drivers can be used, their filenames must be specified in configuration file statements. Optional drivers are provided for serial devices, diskette/disk drives (those not supported by built-in drivers), mouse devices, and virtual disk support.

IOPL

Some OS/2 programs use a "fast path" to hardware in order to improve performance, such as when animated graphics images are sent directly to a display. Such programs "take over" the system, suspending all others. IOPL programs can be allowed or disallowed with the CONFIG.SYS command IOPL=YES or IOPL=NO.

LIBPATH

This configuration file command identifies a set of directories to be searched when loading dynamic link program segments. Since dynamic link segments can be used by more than one program, this command takes effect globally. Batch file commands like PATH and DPATH apply to a single program session. The Install program places this statement in CONFIG.SYS:

```
LIBPATH=C:\;C:\OS2;C:\OS2\INSTALL;
```

PAUSEONERROR

This configuration file command enables or disables the pause that occurs when an error message appears. This allows an unattended background program to continue processing in spite of errors.

PROTECTONLY

The DOS Mode can be selected or skipped by using this command in the configuration file. If PROTECTONLY=YES is used, no DOS Mode memory area will be set aside, and the entire system is used for OS/2 Mode programs only.

PROTSHELL

This configuration file command specifies an alternate user interface to OS/2's CMD.EXE command processor. The Install program inserts PROT-SHELL into CONFIG.SYS, naming the Program Selector files.

```
PROTSHELL=DMPC.EXE SHELL11F.CNF SHELL11F.EXE
CMD.EXE /K OS2INIT.CMD
```

RUN

Background programs that serve multiple applications are called system programs. An example is OS/2's print spooler, SPOOL.EXE. Such programs can be started in the configuration file before any of the DOS or OS/2 sessions with the RUN command.

SWAPPATH

This configuration file command specifies the drive to be used for swapping program segments in and out of memory. The default is SWAPPATH=C:\, but you could change it to a specific directory (SWAPPATH=C:\SWAPDIR) or another logical drive (SWAPPATH=D:) on a partitioned fixed disk.

THREADS

This CONFIG.SYS command specifies the maximum number of threads, or program execution units, that can exist at one time. The default (THREADS=64) allows for 24 OS/2 threads and 40 for applications.

The following commands are OS/2 or DOS-OS/2 commands that can be entered at the command prompt or used in a batch file.

DETACH

This OS/2 command is used to run background, non-interactive programs independently from the command processor. Such programs are similar to the "hotkey," terminate-and-stay-resident commands that run with DOS programs.

FDISK

This old DOS command has been upgraded to support large fixed disk drives. Storage can be formatted as partitions of up to 32 Mb in size. The OS/2 kernel, or bootable portion must reside in the primary partition, but extended partitions can be used for program and data storage. Each extended partition can be further divided into logical drives, of no more than 32 Mb apiece, that are addressed as drives D:, E:, etc.

HELP

This user command is used to get additional assistance when an error message is received. Each OS/2 message is first displayed in its short form, such as:

```
SYS0123 LOCK VIOLATION
```

The user could then enter:

```
HELP 123
```

and receive:

```
Explanation: A file is currently locked against reading.

Action: Wait a short time and try again.
```

SETCOM40

This command enables a DOS Mode program to use one of the system serial ports to support a serial device such as a printer or modem. Normally OS/2 Mode programs share these ports unless this command is used. The serial device driver must be listed first in the configuration file (see DEVICE).

SPOOL

This OS/2 command is used to set up a print spooler, a background program that intercepts output destined for a printer, temporarily stores it on disk if necessary, and then prints a job at a time. The spooler can also be started from the RUN or DETACH commands.

START

This command is used in a ".CMD" OS/2 batch file to start one or more OS/2 programs. If a program title is given, it will appear on the Program Selector menu.

INTERNATIONAL CHARACTER SETS

Several new configuration and batch file commands support the new international language features of OS/2. They will be of interest to programmers who are planning to distribute programs outside of the U. S., and OS/2 users in other countries.

Code Page Switching

If you are using OS/2 outside of the U.S., you may need to modify your system to use an alternate keyboard and/or character set. This may mean adding or changing commands in your CONFIG.SYS and STARTUP.CMD files.

The CODEPAGE, COUNTRY, and DEVINFO commands in the CONFIG.SYS configuration file select the character set(s) that will be used, provide the country code, and name the keyboard and output devices. The CHCP and KEYB commands are used in the STARTUP file to select a predefined code page (character set) to support a language like Canadian French or Portuguese, and the keyboard mapping for the IBM keyboard used in that country.

CODEPAGE

This configuration file command selects two code pages that can be alternated between by the user or from batch file commands.

COUNTRY

This CONFIG.SYS command selects a country for which character set and other information has been predefined. This affects several options for non-U.S. users: date and time format, decimal/comma separators, character set, sort collating sequence (alphabetical sorting rules for that language), and additional information for double-byte (oriental) character set support.

DEVINFO

This configuration file command prepares the system keyboard, display, and printer for alternate code page support.

CHCP

This command can be used in a DOS or OS/2 batch file or given at the command prompt. It selects one of two code pages (character sets) previously specified in the configuration file. It does not change the keyboard mapping, except where a character occupying a position in the new table is different from the previous table.

KEYB

This command is used to select alternate keyboard mapping. Alternate keyboards must have been first listed in the configuration file, using the DEVINFO command. Keyboard mapping assigns character positions from the current character set to keys (upper and lower shift positions). It does not change the current character set.

TROUBLESHOOTING

Some commands are intended for use by a trained Service Coordinator in troubleshooting the system.

TRACE. This configuration file command is used to turn system tracing on and off. The Install program puts the TRACE=OFF command in the file.

TRACEBUF. This CONFIG.SYS command sets the size of the trace buffer. Default is TRACEBUF=4, or 4 Kb.

CREATEDD. This OS/2 external command initializes a dump diskette for use by the stand-alone dump facility. A storage dump may span several diskettes.

TRACE. This command selectively enables or disables system tracing. It is used in conjunction with TRACE in the CONFIG.SYS file.

TRACEFMT. This command formats the contents of the system trace buffer, including time stamps, and outputs it to a display or printer for further analysis.

Servicing OS/2

When an OS/2 problem is suspected during the warranty period, the user should contact the local OS/2 Service Coordinator, who can be either a dealer service representative or a designated member of a large company's PC support organization. Once an OS/2 problem is suspected, the Service Coordinator can call a special IBM OS/2 hotline, either voice or online database (ServiceLine). He or she may be asked to do some further troubleshooting, such as taking a system memory dump to send to IBM. In return, IBM may provide a fix (in the form of a replacement file), or if appropriate, a restriction or bypass to the problem.

IBM may, on occasion, provide Service Coordinators with documentation corrections, warnings, or other forms of preventative maintenance. Troubleshooting procedures are covered in the Service Coordinator's Guide.

OS/2 AND DOS MODE COMMANDS

Appendix A of this book lists all OS/2 and DOS Mode commands, and also indicates which ones work in only one mode.

7

OS/2's Extended Edition: Tying it all Together

The Operating System/2 Standard Edition provides a sufficient software base for many OS/2 application programs: large addressable memory, multi-application support, and an improved user interface. These operating system enhancements are encouraging software developers to upgrade DOS applications with features that were once impossible. But many DOS users—particularly those who live in the modern business world of mixed PC, mainframe, and minicomputers—argue that a "real" operating system must be able to communicate easily with other computers. To the intelligent workstation user, an operating system should provide a global interface, not only to programs and data that reside locally, but also with remote network and host systems.

That is a pretty tall order, when you consider the complexities of computer communications and data management, especially for a personal computer. And this would still be a difficult challenge if it were not for Systems Application Architecture. Because now, with SAA, IBM has defined not only the operating system interface to programs and the end user, but also to the communication links and databases used by large and small systems alike.

But not everyone will need the full OS/2 Extended Edition; some will be quite content without communications and database support. So, IBM is offering a choice: Standard or Extended Edition. The price differential is significant (the original offerings are priced at $325 and $795), but so is the function. For those who purchase OS/2 Extended, or trade up to it later, micro-to-mainframe compatibility takes a giant leap forward.

The OS/2 Standard Edition, or base operating system, is a product of the IBM/Microsoft Joint Development Agreement. The IBM-logo version of OS/2 is licensed for IBM systems. The Microsoft-logo version, called MS OS/2, will be licensed by Microsoft to run on non-IBM 80286 and 80386-based systems, through various hardware manufacturers. OS/2 Extended Edition, on the other hand, was written by and is licensed solely by IBM. The base operating system portion of Extended Edition is the same as the Standard Edition, but the communication and database managers are new (Figure 7–1).

Previous chapters have dealt with the base operating system. In this chapter we will summarize the other two of OS/2 Extended's three major components. The Communication Manager and Database Manager are the two additional modules, developed by IBM. I am assuming that most readers are not experts in either communications or relational databases, so we will try to keep it simple, starting with a few definitions.

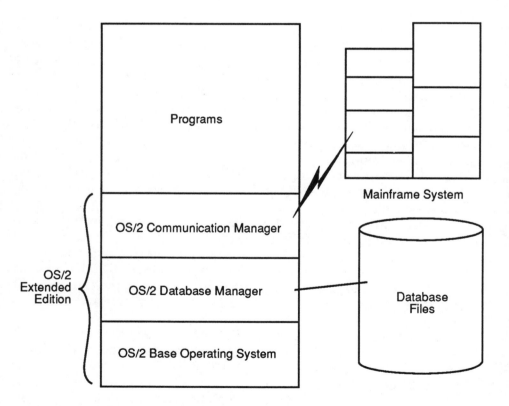

Figure 7–1   OS/2 Extended Edition is made up of three main components. Its base operating system is identical to the OS/2 Standard Edition. Its Communication and Database Managers are exclusive to the Extended Edition.

DEFINING SOME TERMS

Intelligent Workstation. The original computer workstation was the "unintelligent" or dumb communications terminal, capable only of input and output with the host. Then came the PC, and "smarts" provided by terminal emulation programs. Today's PC-based intelligent workstation can support multiple DOS and communication sessions, upload and download files with the host, and run programs that "talk" to programs on other systems.

Terminal Emulation. Before a PC can communicate with a host computer, it must "look like" something that a host is familiar with: a communication terminal. A PC terminal emulation program, with the help of a communications adapter card, changes the PC's identity so that it "appears" (over a cable or telephone line) as a host-supported terminal.

Asynchronous communications. One of the earliest forms of computer communications is still very popular today. Although relatively unsophisticated, asynch software and hardware lets many PCs communicate with each other and with remote mainframes over ordinary voice-grade telephone lines. A low-cost asynch modem, which generally runs at 1200 or 2400 bits per second, can be installed as a PC adapter card.

Communication Link. An electrical cable, telephone line, or radio signal can be used to carry computer signals. Communication links exist between terminals and computers and also interconnect computers.

Data Stream. The content and format of information on a communication link is more than just letters and numbers. It must also contain formatting commands (such as carriage-returns and page breaks), control information (display colors or printer commands), and identifying information (filename or destination address).

Communication Protocol. In order for two computer devices to communicate with each other, data must be sent and received in a standard protocol, or format and sequence. While the data stream deals with the content of data, its protocol covers specific format-related characteristics such as transmission speed, size of data blocks, and parity-checking.

Network Management. A network management program on a host system can monitor the status of remote local area networks, logging errors, and other status information.

Gateway. A gateway on a local area network is a communication link between one of the network stations and a host computer. It provides a low-cost means of host access by users of the network.

Relational Database. A relational database manager provides a means of entering and accessing large data files. Data from multiple files can be merged, as long as a common field of information (such as customer number) relates them.

Structures Query Language (SQL). SQL is used to select, sort and arrange data for display or printing. SQL commands can be imbedded in a program or entered directly by the user.

OS/2 COMMUNICATIONS MANAGER

First we will examine the OS/2 Extended Edition's Communications Manager. PC communications are nothing new, but they have become much more sophisticated and complex over the past few years. Most PC owners did not know this, but a simple 300 bits-per-second asynchronous communications program (named COMM) can be found on the PC DOS diskette. This program, a very simple terminal emulator without the ability to automatically establish a host connection or transfer data files, was considered usable a few years ago. Today, full 3270 communications capability is often considered the minimum. To get a better idea of where PC communications are going, let's see where we are today.

PC DOS COMMUNICATIONS

Layers on DOS

Several dozen popular PC communication packages are in use today, with hundreds of other commercial and home-grown programs satisfying a variety of needs. While most of these programs are designed to operate under DOS control, each of them had to initiate and maintain a communications link that DOS is incapable of alone. That is because PC DOS (like the OS/2 Standard Edition) is not a communicating operating system by itself. Either an additional layer of system software must be added to supply the missing function, or the application program itself must provide it.

HLLAPIs

Three examples of DOS companion products are the 3270 Emulation Programs (Entry Level 1.1 and Version 3.0) and the 3270 Workstation Program. The user interfaces built into these packages qualify them as application programs, but they also provide a program interface for application developers. This interface is called a High Level Language Application Program Interface, or HLLAPI. The HLLAPI makes it easier for a software developer to create a communications program without being a communications "guru." A disadvantage is that the HLLAPI-providing software package must be purchased as a prerequisite to running the application. On the other hand, if the communications interface was built into the operating system, the application developer could be confident that more potential customers could run the program without the need for prerequisite software (Figure 7–2).

Avoiding Conflicts

The OS/2 Extended Edition, like the more modest Standard Edition, avoids many of the multi-application conflicts that plagued DOS. That is because

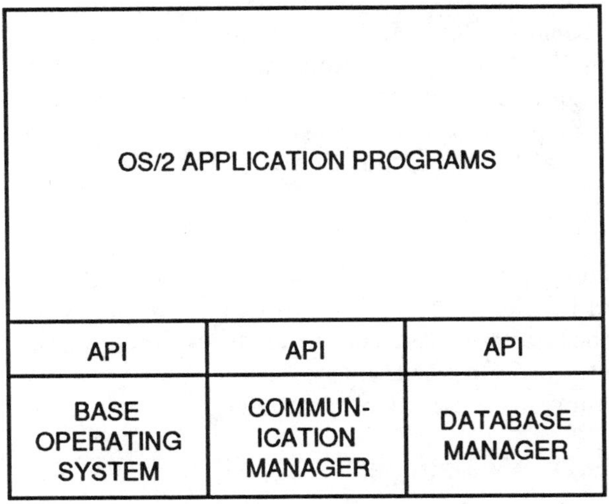

OS/2 APPLICATION PROGRAMS		
API	API	API
BASE OPERATING SYSTEM	COMMUN-ICATION MANAGER	DATABASE MANAGER

Figure 7–2 OS/2 provides a common application program interface (API) for all of its programs. The API for communications and database support requires the OS/2 Extended Edition.

when even two simple DOS programs attempt to share the same computer, there is a chance of a system-crashing collision. Imagine two or three complex communication sessions (such as a local area network link and two remote host connections) sharing memory and other system resources with standalone, or non-communicating programs. It is much better to let the operating system arbitrate this situation rather than leave it up to individual programs to work it out for themselves.

Asynchronous Communications

Many relatively simple asynchronous communication programs serve thousands of PC users. Programs like PC Talk®, Crosstalk™, and Telecommuter™ were designed primarily for accessing popular data services like the Dow Jones News Service®, CompuServe®, The Source®, MCI Mail®, and the on-line Official Airline Guide™. While it is not especially difficult to write a "dumb terminal" emulation program, it takes some sophistication to exchange data files between a Personal System/2 and a host system, and even more "smarts" to maintain the connection while other programs are running.

OS/2 Compatibility Problems

Some PC DOS communication programs will not run in OS/2's PC DOS Mode. That is because DOS Mode programs are suspended during the brief intervals when OS/2 or its programs gain control of the processor. These periods, although short, can cause havoc with programs that have timing dependencies. Such interruptions can cause communication programs to drop the line, breaking the connection with the host.

The Solution

Some DOS communications programs will be converted to run under the OS/2 Standard Edition, where the timing problems of the DOS Mode can be avoided. Without built-in OS/2 communications support, the job of writing a communications program will be no easier than it was under DOS, and many programmers will not attempt it.

Microsoft OS/2 LAN Manager™

One example of an OS/2 Standard Edition communication product is Microsoft's OS/2 LAN Manager. This program lets the OS/2 user participate in a local area network interconnecting DOS-based and OS/2-based systems. File and print servers share programs, data files, and printers across the network, and users can communicate with each other.

Many communications applications are expected to utilize the capabilities of OS/2 Extended Edition. In addition to the base the Communications Manager provides for new software, it promises even more sophisti-cated applications in the future. These programs will implement IBM's Systems Application Architecture, bringing a compatible communications interface to the IBM Personal System/2, System/3X, System/370, and other participating systems.

Hardware Requirements

In addition to the necessary network or host communication adapter cards, a Personal System/2 running the OS/2 Extended Edition requires a mini-mum of 3 Mb of memory.

SYSTEMS APPLICATION ARCHITECTURE

IBM's System's Application Architecture addresses cross-system communi-cations compatibility in its *Common Communications Support* section. Not all of the pieces are in place yet, and SAA/CCS content will increase in fu-ture communications products. Much of the Common Communications Support already has been defined by an earlier IBM standard called Sys-tems Network Architecture (SNA), and has guided the development of OS/2's Extended Edition.

Data Streams

SAA deals with more than just how computers are connected to each other and what communications protocol they share. It also addresses the content of the data—the data stream. A stream of data between a terminal and a computer contains more than just text: there are imbedded characters used for controlling a terminal's display and printer. A personal computer, in order to join a network or connect to a host, must be able to send and receive a data stream in the same way. The 3270 Data Stream is supported on all SAA systems. For compatibility purposes, future System/3X systems will continue to support the 5250 Data Stream.

Document Content Architecture (DCA) defines the way a text docu-ment is stored and transmitted, insuring compatibility between different word processing programs and systems. The Intelligent Printer Data Stream (IPDS) is used with page printers.

Application Services

Application program interfaces in a communications environment are de-fined through SNA Distribution Services (SNADS), Document Interchange Architecture (DIA), and SNA Network Management Architecture.

Other SAA communication-related specifications deal with communication protocols such as the program-to-program Session Services, PC-to-PC networking, and the popular SDLC, token-ring, and X.25 protocols.

INTEGRATED COMMUNICATIONS SUPPORT

Combining LAN and Host Support

The Extended Edition combines and enhances the function found in many of the popular IBM DOS-based packages. It does this by bringing the features and functions of several DOS companion products into the operating system.

Like the OS/2 Standard Edition, multiple programs or tasks within a program can run at the same time. Depending on a system's communications hardware (adapter cards, cabling, etc.), several communication sessions can run concurrently. For example, a user might simultaneously work with a spreadsheet file on a nearby LAN file server while reading electronic mail from a remote data service. Multiple communication sessions can simultaneously use different terminal emulation and communication protocols. Application programs on standalone workstations, local area network, and remote mainframe systems can "talk" to each other and exchange information without user intervention or involvement. Distributed processing, once a dream of computer engineers, can be achieved.

User Interface

The OS/2 Extended Edition has two interfaces: one for the application developer and another for the user. The first release of OS/2 Extended, like OS/2 Standard 1.0, is based on the simple Program Selector interface (Figure 7–3). Both of the release 1.1 versions use the OS/2 Presentation Manager, which can window a variety of communicating and non-communicating programs. The Clipboard "cut and paste" facility, for instance, can transfer data between standalone and communicating programs. An inactive communication session can be reduced to a small background window so the user can keep an eye on it. That way, for instance, you can work on a word processing report until an electronic mail system "Mail Waiting" message appears. Switching sessions, the electronic message is read and then downloaded to a subject matter file. You then return to the report you were working on.

As communication capabilities and needs change, the OS/2 Extended Edition is adaptable to a variety of new environments. The user can configure the system to support any of several network and host protocols. In most cases, no additional software is required.

One way for an OS/2-based intelligent workstation to be able to communicate with a host computer, whether it is the company's corporate main-

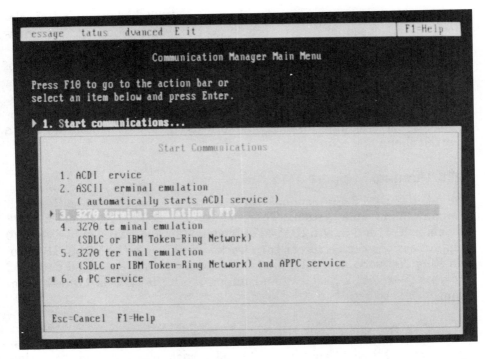

Figure 7–3   The OS/2 Extended Edition's Communications Manager provides a variety of network and host communication support with a menu-driven user interface (shown here) and an application program interface.

frame or an outside data service, is for the computer to take on the personality of a data terminal. The Extended Edition's Communication Manager emulates several popular terminal types.

HOST TERMINAL EMULATION

IBM 3101 and DEC VT100™ Terminal Support

Asynchronous communications are still the most common in use, while not a very sophisticated form of PC communications. The early teletype terminal evolved to the cathode ray tube "glass teletype" to terminals like IBM's 3101 Model 20. The standard features of IBM 3101 and DEC (Digital Equipment Corp.) VT100 terminals have been enhanced in PC software to include intelligent terminal emulation features such as file upload/download, automatic logon, and program-to-program communication.

Asynchronous communication lines can be switched (regular dial telephone lines), leased, or directly connected between computers. The industry-standard RS232C protocol is used.

The XMODEM technique is used for checking the validity, or parity, of file exchanges. Data is sent in 128-byte blocks, and a one-byte check-sum record is transmitted back to the sending computer at the end of each block. If the transmitted and received numbers agree, the next block is sent. Otherwise, it is sent again. This method improves transmission accuracy over a poor telephone line connection.

3270 Terminal Support

The popular IBM 3270 terminal can be emulated, for communication with company mainframe systems. This includes the IBM 3178 Model 2, 3278 Models 2, 3, 4, and 5, and IBM 3279 Models S2A and S2B. Up to five 3270 display sessions can be run at each workstation, using the SDLC, IBM Token-Ring Network, or DFT links. OS/2 Extended can exchange data and program files with a host system running the 3270-PC File Transfer Program.

Keyboard Remap

The Keyboard Remap facility can be used to customize terminal emulation, changing key assignments to make a PC or PS/2 keyboard behave more like a custom data terminal.

The Extended Edition is compatible with several communication environments:

CATEGORY	PROTOCOL	LOCAL/REMOTE
Data Service	Asynchronous	Local
Mainframe		Remote
Local Area	PC Network	Local
Networks	Token Ring	Remote (Gateway)
Mainframe	Synchronous (SDLC, DFT)	Remote

The Communications Manager supports combinations of these sessions depending on the limitations of installed adapter cards, available memory, and processor speed.

APPLICATION PROGRAM SUPPORT

OS/2 Extended Edition is designed to support a variety of communicating programs. A special operating system interface is provided for developers who wish to write their own terminal emulation or file transfer programs. It is called the Asynchronous Communications Device Interface (ACDI).

APPC

An application program interface is provided for Advanced Program-to-Program Communications (APPC). A pair of programs can run on separate computers, communicating with each other over a data link. Applications can run on IBM System/370 mainframes running either MVS-CICS or VSE-CICS, or an IBM System/36, System/38, Personal System/2, Personal Computer, RT PC, System/88, or Series/1.

SRPI

Another API is provided to support IBM's Enhanced Connectivity Facilities (ECF). The Server-Requester Programming Interface (SRPI) supports simple "requester" programs which communicate with host server programs on a mainframe System/370.

Languages

Application programs may use the Communication Manager if written in IBM Pascal/2, IBM Macro Assembler/2, or IBM C/2. C/2 is also compatible with Systems Application Architecture.

LOCAL AREA NETWORK SUPPORT

Both IBM PC Network and Token-Ring Network support is provided, using the LU6.2 standard communication protocol. A maximum of 255 concurrent network sessions are supported over remote (SDLC) or local networks. The IBM Net BIOS and IEEE 802.2 Data Link Control application program interfaces are provided for LAN communications.

Network Management

Communications and Systems Management (C&SM) support for a System/370 host network is part of the Communications Manager. This allows a mainframe computer to monitor one or more Communications environments including asynchronous, SDLC or local area networks (PC Network or Token Ring). Network program and data file activity can be monitored, and error logs and system dumps displayed or printed. As a management tool, C&SM provides information on program, session, and resource usage. It can start and stop remote programs.

PLANNED ENHANCEMENTS TO COMMUNICATION MANAGER

Future versions of the OS/2 Communications Manager will include SNA local area network gateway support, Enhanced Connectivity Facility (ECF) enhancements, 5250 workstation support, and X.25 communication protocol support. A 3270 API will be added, compatible with the API for the PC 3270 Emulation Program, Entry Level 1.1.

OS/2 DATABASE MANAGER

Large relational database systems, using IBM's Structured Query Language, have grown in popularity on IBM host systems (DB2, SQL/DS) while DOS programs such as dBase III and RBase supported the PC user. The Personal System/2 can have as much as 628 Mb of on-line fixed disk storage and up to 1600 Mb of optical disk storage, making it capable of supporting a large, sophisticated database. IBM is bringing the function of a host relational database system to the PS/2 user.

The third element of the OS/2 Extended Edition, the Database Manager, simplifies the development of new applications that can access large quantities of information distributed throughout a corporation: on a local PS/2 disk, on a departmental network server, or on the corporate mainframe. A built-in user interface provides users with a means of reviewing, merging, sorting, and printing information without the need for an application program.

INTEGRATED DATABASE SUPPORT

User Interface

The OS/2 Database Manager, more so than the Communications Manager, can be used without the addition of any application software. Its built-in user interface supports the direct entry of data, as well as its access, manipulation, and report generation. The user can enter simple *ad hoc* queries, write query procedures for repetitive use, or use the interactive, prompted interface.

Application Interface

Database Manager application program interfaces (APIs) are provided to aid the software developer in accessing and managing data. Applications can range from full-blown database managers to occasional file access. The Structured Query Language may be used in programs written in C/2. The API enables data migration from DOS programs, shared network file support, and Systems Application Architecture compatibility. Database procedures, which can be built without writing and compiling a program, are written in the REXX procedure language, also defined in SAA.

RELATIONAL DATABASES

Relational databases consist of data distributed across two or more files. Often the information needed to prepare a report is not wholly contained in a single file. Instead, it exists in several files, or tables. Each table consists of rows (records) and columns (fields). As long as two or more tables are *related* to each other by a common element (such as a customer number), data can be combined, sorted, and displayed.

In the following example, two tables contain information about football teams. The first table, named LEAGUE, lists team names, divisions, and cities (NAME, DIV, CITY). The second table, named RECORDS, lists team names, wins, and losses (NAME, WIN, LOSS). Both tables were created first as spreadsheets and later migrated to the Database Manager table format.

Table: LEAGUE			Table: RECORDS		
NAME	DIV	CITY	NAME	WIN	LOSS
Chargers	AFC	San Diego	Jets	3	13
Dolphins	AFC	Miami	Broncos	14	2
Browns	NFC	Cleveland	Dolphins	16	0
Jets	AFC	New York	Giants	10	6
Giants	NFC	New York	Chargers	8	8
Broncos	NFC	Denver	Browns	6	10

Since the team names are common to both tables, we have a relational database. Now we can enter a SQL query using data spanning both tables: list the team cities, ranked in order of their season record:

```
SELECT CITY, WIN FROM LEAGUE, RECORDS
WHERE LEAGUE.NAME = RECORDS.NAME ORDER BY WIN
```

This SQL instruction identifies the two fields to be printed, the tables containing them, and the two related fields, LEAGUE.NAME and RECORDS.NAME.

The result is sorted in order by the number of wins. The result looks like this:

CITY	WIN
Miami	16
Denver	14
New York	10
San Diego	8
Cleveland	6
New York	3

Structured Query Language

This is a simple example of SQL, a high-level data definition and manipulation language. Arithmetic operations can also be performed on data. SQL can be learned by many OS/2 users and used through the Query Manager to access and display reports. SQL instructions can also be imbedded in C language application programs.

SYSTEMS APPLICATION ARCHITECTURE

SAA specifies that the Structured Query Language (SQL) is the user and program interface to a relational database. It does not define *how* the system performs the data entry or retrieval—just the command language. The SAA specification is compatible with the versions of SQL used in the DB2 and SQL/DS mainframe systems as well as OS/2 Extended Edition.

DATABASE MANAGER UTILITIES

Import/Export

The Database Manager provides a set of useful utility programs. Import/Export programs are used to convert such files as Lotus 1-2-3, Symphony, dBase III, and IBM Personal Decision Series formats to relational database tables. This way a user can continue to work with a familiar spreadsheet or DOS database file under the OS/2 Extended Edition.

Backup/Restore/Unload/Load

A set of utility programs are provided for backing up an entire database or selected portions of it.

Reorg/Runstats

Database tables can be reorganized by the user. By resorting some tables, frequently-accessed data can be obtained more quickly. Statistical information about table characteristics can also improve efficiency.

QUERY MANAGER

Using the Query Manager, the user can enter and update data, enter queries, and print formatted reports. Queries can be built by using an interactive, prompted interface or by issuing SQL commands directly. Once the correct command syntax or report format has been established, it can become part of a stored procedure query that can be repeated at any time.

The Forms facility lets the user define input screen formats that are used to simplify the entry of data. Forms can be made to resemble their real-life paper counterparts. Form-collected data can be saved in multiple database tables, and form-assisted queries can access multiple tables. This way, a more experienced Database Manager user can define query formats for occasional users.

The Report Generator guides the user through a selection process leading to a finished report. Data columns (fields) are selected and formatted. Titles and headings can be added. Calculations can be inserted (totals, subtotals, etc.). Printer options can be used. The report-building process is interactive; you can stop anytime to test the format before continuing.

Finally, menus can be created to assist the user in selecting from any of the available queries, procedures, forms, reports, or other menus.

DATABASE MANAGEMENT

The Database Manager provides password protection for database security. Record-level and table-level locking is performed during a file update, to prevent a second update from starting before the first one is finished. Commit and Rollback features help ensure that a database will be properly updated by an application transaction.

APPLICATION INTERFACES

In addition to SQL itself, OS/2 system calls can be written into a program to access data. Programs written in Macro Assembler/2, Pascal/2, and C/2 are supported. Of these three, C/2 is part of Systems Application Architecture.

Supported Data

The Database Manager supports a variety of file formats and sizes. Data types include integer, floating point, packed decimal, fixed and variable-length character strings, date and time. Files can be any size up to the current OS/2 logical fixed disk partition of 32 Mb. OS/2 1.1 will remove the 32 Mb logical drive limit.

PLANNED ENHANCEMENTS TO DATABASE MANAGER

In a future version of the OS/2 Database Manager, its Remote Data Services will provide support for both Token Ring and PC Network local area networks. This will let multiple network users share a common database, or a single user can serially access multiple network (server) databases.

Language support will be extended to the IBM Pascal/2 and COBOL/2 compilers, for SQL statements imbedded in programs (today only C/2 is supported). The Import/Export programs will also support non-delimited DOS ASCII format files. (Delimited ASCII files were supported in the original OS/2 versions.)

GETTING READY FOR EXTENDED EDITION

The OS/2 Extended Edition will be used by many large companies with a need to interconnect their PCs with larger systems. More than the Standard Edition, it requires planning to prepare for a smooth installation and incorporation into existing computing environments. Several key people will be affected.

The System Administrator

This person, usually a member of the Management Information Services (MIS) department, could also be a computer dealer or consultant. Typically, he or she would plan the overall installation, and provide guidance and assistance to people who will be installing, configuring and using the OS/2 Extended Edition in their jobs. This person should have a good knowledge of the operating system's features, and be able to guide other users in learning more about it through the documentation, the on-line tutorial, and in-house training programs. For example, an introductory course in the Structured Query Language might be appropriate. A workshop could be given to assist users in converting spreadsheet and other data files to Database Manager format.

Since communication and database management are two key features of the Extended Edition, the System Administrator should have a good working knowledge of the company's mainframe and network communications, and the location and type of data users require. The application and communications needs of each user should be determined, in order to plan for host system support and to prepare the user for OS/2. In some cases the administrator may have to assist with or customize a user's system. This may include things like establishing power-on, default communication sessions for a workstation, or determining which database files a user is allowed to access. Additional memory and application programs may be needed to support and exploit OS/2 Extended. Some in-house application software may have to be modified or written. Some users may have requirements for databases and services provided only by an outside data service such as MCI Mail, the Source, or the IBM Information Network, and subscriptions will have to be obtained.

System support should be provided. An in-house OS/2 hotline could provide early support for new OS/2 Extended Edition users, to answer questions and provide troubleshooting assistance. Coordination is essential between the System Administrator and the organization or dealer Service Coordinator to insure quick problem reporting and fix distribution.

The Programmer

Members of the company programming staff should become familiar with OS/2 on a technical level, using documentation such as the OS/2 User Reference, Technical Reference, and Programmer's Guide. A book related to this one, *OS/2: Features, Functions, and Applications* published by John Wiley & Sons, provides more information about OS/2. One or more of the six IBM OS/2 language compilers may be purchased in order to convert existing DOS programs or write new ones. The OS/2 Programmer's Toolkit may shorten the programming time and assist with some programming jobs such as application windowing, dialog sessions, and creating Family programs that will run under either DOS or OS/2.

Since there are so many application interfaces supported by the Communication Manager, the programmer should be familiar with the communication protocols offered by the host system. For example, programs written to the APPC or SRPI interfaces could be used to access host data. An existing DOS program, written to the 3270 API, may be converted to OS/2 with little effort. DOS programs written to interface with a local area network will also require conversion to OS/2.

The Structured Query Language should be considered for new applications requiring database access. SQL statements can be imbedded in a program (written in C/2), greatly simplifying its design. Or, SQL procedures can be built in some cases, in lieu of programs, to access data and compile reports.

8

OS/2 Programming
Interface: A Look Inside

I have saved this chapter until last for two reasons. First, not everyone will care about the OS/2 application program interface. Second, there are other manuals and books which go into much more detail than you will find here. But there are good reasons for taking the time to learn a little bit about OS/2's API, language compilers, Toolkit, and SAA compatibility. The more you understand the technical side of OS/2, the more you will appreciate its potential and the role of the programmer in exploiting it.

The period following the announcement of OS/2 has seen much DOS program conversion activity and the creation of several new OS/2 applications. Some programs will continue to exist in their old PC DOS format, unable to take advantage of OS/2 functions like multi-tasking or windowing. Others will undergo a relatively minor re-write to the Family application subset. Then there will be the "superstars" that exploit multi-tasking, large memory, dynamic linking, presentation services, and a host of other new OS/2 features.

The OS/2 programmer has an array of options to choose from. Release 1.1's Presentation Manager will fulfill OS/2's commitment to windowing and graphics support. The OS/2 Toolkit reduces the programming effort, assures Systems Application Architecture compatibility, and makes Family applications easier to produce. OS/2 international support is not just for foreign programmers; many U.S.-written applications will find their way overseas. The Extended Edition will enable advanced communication and database functions for OS/2 software.

DEFINING SOME TERMS

API.   Application Program Interface. A set of operating system commands and functions used by programs to access system resources. OS/2 uses a CALL program interface.

Language Compiler.   A program which translates instructions written in a computer language like FORTRAN or COBOL into an executable program. A source file is used as input to the compiler, and an object file is the result.

Application Generator.   A program used by an application developer to generate program instructions or executable code. The OS/2 Toolkit is an example of an application generator.

Process.   An OS/2 process (usually a single program) owns a set of computer resources (memory, files, display, printer), and will have one or more executing threads executing under its control. Multiple processes are supported in OS/2.

Thread.   A unit of execution (or task) running in a process. Multiple threads can run in a process, sharing the resources assigned to it. A properly designed multiple-thread program can improve throughput over a traditional single-task version.

Scheduler.   The OS/2 Scheduler divides a critical resource—units of processor time—among concurrent tasks, based on program priorities.

Keyboard Monitor.   Some applications use special key combinations (unknown to OS/2) to invoke a background program or perform other functions. A keyboard monitor can be written to intercept key combinations.

PC DOS PROGRAMMING

Before getting into OS/2's programming interface, we should understand the software base that supports most of today's applications: PC DOS 3.3. Its API, which has evolved from a rudimentary 1981 version, has been exploited, extended, and enhanced beyond what many programmers (and users) ever thought possible. OS/2 preserves this latest DOS interface for the sake of compatibility. At the same time it removes old DOS barriers and provides the means for much greater application function and usability.

RUNNING PROGRAMS IN PC DOS

Booting PC DOS

When a PC DOS diskette or fixed disk is booted, a startup sequence loads the operating system and sometimes through a batch file, an application program. Before DOS's command processor is loaded into memory, the DOS nucleus, or kernel program, checks for the existence of a file named CONFIG.SYS. If present, its commands establish system options such as disk buffers, country support, and device drivers. If the configuration file is not there, default settings are assumed and COMMAND.COM is started.

PC DOS Batch Files

The command processor first looks for a batch file with the name AUTOEXEC.BAT. If found, its commands and program names complete the initial boot sequence—usually by loading a DOS shell (like a menu) or an application. PC DOS loading is now complete; in OS/2 terms, this is a single PC DOS Mode.

Running PC DOS Applications

Sometimes the AUTOEXEC.BAT file loads more than one program. It may first load one or more "terminate and stay resident" programs such as a printer buffer or a pop-up calendar. All DOS programs have a filename extension of .COM (based on DOS's *com*mand file structure) or .EXE (*executable* program). There are subtle internal differences between these two formats. The program called by a fixed disk's AUTOEXEC.BAT file may be a DOS shell program such as TopView or Windows, since the operating system's user interface (the familiar "C>_") does not do much to assist the user in listing or selecting programs.

In Chapter 6 we looked at DOS and OS/2 program installation, paying particular attention to the three files which establish a program's operating environment. The DOS CONFIG.SYS file, or at least its suggested set of commands, may undergo several changes when a program is migrated to OS/2's multi-application world. The OS/2 configuration file controls both the DOS and OS/2 Modes, and cannot be modified to suit every program. A DOS program's AUTOEXEC.BAT initialization batch file may undergo fewer changes, or eliminated altogether, since only one DOS program at a time can run in OS/2's DOS Mode. An OS/2 initialization file, named OS2INIT.CMD, performs the same function for each OS/2 Mode application. But the major changes take place in the program itself.

PC DOS PROGRAMMING CONSIDERATIONS

There is a lot more to programming, in DOS or OS/2, than the configuration and startup files. We mentioned them here because quite often a PC user will have to get his or her hands "dirty" by going into one or both of these files to change an operating system option or install a new device driver. Programs themselves are another matter entirely; if you do not have the original program source code and a good knowledge of programming, you will not be able to change anything on your own. Yet it may be helpful to know a few basics.

The OS/2 API

The OS/2 Application Program Interface is the official, published interface for programs written in Macro Assembler, BASIC, FORTRAN, Pascal, C, and COBOL. Unlike DOS, it is difficult for a programmer to circumvent the API and write "ill-behaved" programs. OS/2, with the help of the 80286/386 processors, strictly enforces its API. Unlike DOS, this API gives the programmer much more flexibility and power than ever before. Because of the richness of the OS/2 API, the programmer does not have to devote hours of program design and coding to unnecessary overhead.

The API is actually made up of several components, based on the various OS/2 managers. The windowing and graphics API is part of the Presentation Manager, OS/2 1.1. The communication and database APIs are found only in the Extended Edition.

PC DOS Interrupts

The IBM Personal Computer and Personal System/2 are interrupt-driven systems. Hardware interrupts include priority signals in the keyboard and display interface that are hard-wired into system board circuits and programmed into ROM BIOS. Software interrupts are used to invoke operating system services such as disk read and write routines. One of the DOS interrupts, decimal number 33 or *hexadecimal 21*, is used to initiate secondary commands, or functions. Some programmers add their own functions and *vector*, or redirect, interrupts to them.

Interrupts are part of the DOS programming interface and are used by many programs, particularly those written in the DOS Macro Assembler language. They have serious drawbacks, though. Interrupts are very hardware-specific, unique to the IBM PC, its derivatives and clones. This makes such programs difficult to migrate to other types of computers. They require programming at a detailed, "bits and bytes," level which should be managed by the operating system. Also, interrupts sometimes occur nearly simultaneously (such as when two or three background programs are running) and can overload DOS. The "lost interrupt" condition is a common cause of a "hung system" that can only be restarted by turning the computer off and back on again.

The OS/2 CALL interface between programs and the operating system replaces the interrupt interface, leaving interrupt-handling up to the operating system—of no concern to the programmer. Both hardware and software interrupts are managed efficiently by OS/2 and the hung system condition is averted.

PC DOS Video Interface

PC display programming presents other problems. Programs which use only text are relatively easy to manage. Every PC display adapter, whether a card on an older PC or a chip on the new Personal System/2, contains the standard 256-character PC character set. Programs do not have to be concerned with the way characters are formed. Graphics programs, on the other hand, place little colored dots of light on the screen to create pictures and animated sequences. The resolution (number of horizontal and vertical dots) and number of colors vary widely between the PC's standard 320-by-200, 4-color Color Graphic Adapter (CGA) and the Personal System/2's maximum 1024-by-768, 256-color 8514 display.

PC DOS has no built-in graphics support. IBM instead offers a set of DOS programming tools (such as the Graphics Development Toolkit) that use the Virtual Device Interface (VDI). A graphics program designed for the VDI "standard" can run on any of several different displays by replacing its device driver. A user can purchase a new (and better) display, copy a new device driver file from a ship group diskette, and the program is ready to go. No program changes are needed, and the program's graphics output now takes advantage of a display's best resolution and range of colors.

OS/2's release 1.1 Presentation Services will, like VDI, provide a built-in standard programming interface for graphics as well as text. In fact, graphics and text begin to merge in OS/2 1.1. You will be able to select alternate character fonts and styles in addition to the standard PC characters. New fonts are generated as groups of dots, graphics-style, that are sent to the screen. Both monospaced and proportional fonts are possible.

SYSTEMS APPLICATION ARCHITECTURE

Like other aspects of OS/2 such as its user, communications, database, and graphics interfaces, the OS/2 programming interface is also impacted by IBM's SAA. The Common Programming Interface (CPI) portion of Systems Application Architecture deals with two general categories: (1) language compilers, application generators, and procedural languages, and (2) operating system services, including the database, dialog, presentation, and query interfaces.

The Common Programming Interface is key to SAA, since it enables the migration of applications between unlike systems. It will give application developers a consistent, portable interface across several operating systems, rich in advanced programming tools. SAA/CPI will also benefit the end user, whose software is now richer in function and easier to use. Much of the SAA CPI was implemented in OS/2's Standard Edition 1.0, OS/2 Toolkit 1.0, and three of its language compilers. Some elements, such as the programming interface for graphics and windows, will appear in the Standard Edition 1.1 and OS/2 Toolkit 1.1, through the OS/2 Presentation Manager. Other portions of CPI, such as the database interface, will be satisfied in the OS/2 Extended Edition and its Toolkit. The following summary describes the impact of CPI on OS/2 and its applications.

SAA: LANGUAGES

Application Generators

This includes code-producing tools such as found in the OS/2 Toolkit. These create application code for difficult-to-write segments such as interactive dialog screens, help message libraries, and menus. SAA-conforming application generators make programming easier, improve application usability, and create programs that migrate easily to other systems.

Languages

Three of OS/2's six language compilers are participating in SAA: C/2, COBOL/2, and FORTRAN/2. Each language's interface to the programmer is source-compatible between compilers of the same language on the Personal System/2, System/3X, and System/370, so that only recompilation is often necessary. The actual hardware interface of each language compiler is not defined by SAA, allowing it to take advantage of underlying machine features. The six new IBM OS/2 language compilers will be described later in this chapter.

The C language itself is relatively simple, with many functions provided through its library. SAA defines many of the functions in this library that are needed to create consistent, portable applications, including I/O, math, dynamic memory management, and other routines. The C interface specification has been developed in accord with the draft proposed American National Standard Programming Language—C (X3J11).

The COBOL language interface will allow many mainframe and mid-range programs to migrate downward to the Personal System/2. The SAA/CPI includes the ANSI standard X3.23-1985; ISO standard 1989-1985, Intermediate Level; and some elements of ANSI X3.23-1985, High Level. SAA also contains some language features above the industry standards, for enhanced programmer productivity and ease of use.

The FORTRAN language interface is based on ANSI standard X3.9-1978 (FORTRAN 77), ISO standard 1539-1980, and some enhancements.

Procedures Language

DOS batch files, which can issue commands and call programs, are a form of procedure language. SAA has defined the VM/370 REXX implementation as its standard for procedures languages.

SAA: SERVICES

Database Interface

The SAA program interface to databases is IBM's Structured Query Language, or SQL (see Chapter 7). Based on ANSI standard X3.135-1986, the SQL specification is almost identical to the mainframe DB2 (Release 3) and SQL/DS (Version 2) implementations. The OS/2 Database Manager (OS/2 Extended Edition) provides both a programming interface and a user interface for SQL.

Dialog Interface

The SAA Dialog Interface deals with user-interactive display panels such as menus, help screens, data input screens, and program messages. OS/2 support is provided via the OS/2 Toolkit.

Presentation Interface

This interface, supported by the OS/2 Presentation Manager and OS/2 Toolkit 1.1, defines a set of functions for windowing, mouse and keyboard interaction, graphics support, and some image support. Most of this interface is already available on IBM mainframe systems through the Graphical Data Display Manager, GDDM/MVS and GDDM/VM products, with the exception of window support.

Query Interface

The OS/2 Database Manager will implement a query interface for accessing data and writing reports. Unlike SQL, which responds to commands, the query interface consists of a menu-interactive series of screens which guide the user through data selection, manipulation, and printing. The SAA standard is based on the existing System/370 Query Management Facility (QMF).

OS/2: SOMETHING DIFFERENT

Programming for OS/2 can be easier than writing a PC DOS program, or it can be quite complex. This complexity depends partly on the sophistication of the program: the functions it can perform (power) and the richness of its user interface (usability). But the programming job can be simplified, without the loss of function or usability, through the use of programming tools.

STARTING UP

The Configuration File

A programmer writing an OS/2 program should be aware of the various options controlled by the OS/2 configuration file, or CONFIG.SYS, which is read and acted upon at boot, or IPL time. This file may include several commands which determine how the operating system responds in both DOS and OS/2 Modes. CONFIG.SYS is initially created by the installation program, and its contents may vary somewhat, depending on user responses to that program. Also, a user can modify CONFIG.SYS with an editor. Since some of the configuration file options may affect the way a program runs, the application documentation may want to suggest certain options. Configuration file changes do not take effect until the system is rebooted. Chapter 6 describes new or modified configuration file commands.

OS/2 Mode

Each time an OS/2 program is started, it runs in its own OS/2 Mode session. The OS/2 Mode initialization process loads a copy of CMD.EXE, the OS/2 command processor, and then looks for a batch file named OS2INIT.CMD. If present, OS2INIT loads a program or executes other batch file commands. This is analogous to DOS's AUTOEXEC.BAT batch file. Like CONFIG.SYS, this file can be examined and modified by a user in order to affect OS/2 performance and other characteristics. Unlike CONFIG.SYS, an application can provide a batch file of its own to override conditions set by OS2INIT.CMD. The program name may also be included in the STARTUP.CMD file among those to be loaded at power-on.

PC DOS Mode

If the command PROTECTONLY=NO is found in the configuration file, OS/2 will set aside a low memory area for PC DOS programs, and a DOS Mode session can be started by the user. If an AUTOEXEC.BAT file exists in the root directory, it assumes control and may be used to load an application. If no AUTOEXEC.BAT file is found, the DOS command processor, COMMAND.COM, takes over. Now PC DOS applications can be loaded and run exactly as they would under PC DOS itself, using the same commands, batch files, and programs. The user can switch back to the Program Selector and start one or more OS/2 Mode sessions.

Only one DOS Mode session is ever running, and it is suspended whenever OS/2 or one of its OS/2 Mode programs is executing. Program suspension and a few other unique DOS application characteristics can cause problems in the DOS Mode.

PROBLEM PROGRAMS

Suspended Programs

Program suspension, however briefly, can pose problems for time-dependent software. This includes programs that count cycles or loops as a measure of time, and those that maintain communications with other computers. For this reason, many DOS programs will not be supported in the PC DOS Mode, which is always suspended when an OS/2 Mode program is running or brought to the foreground. DOS program suspension can even take place when no other programs are running; OS/2 still receives occasional time-slices for its own administrative functions. Such programs must be converted to run in the OS/2 Mode.

Ill-Behaved Programs

DOS Programs that are not written to the published DOS application program interface are sometimes referred to as "ill behaved." That is because they exploit hardware and software below the DOS level: hardware I/O ports, memory addresses, internal BIOS routines, etc. Not only will such programs require major modifications to run under the OS/2 Mode, but they may not work correctly in DOS Mode either. For example, some programs send their output directly to the video buffer, to improve text or graphics performance. They should be able to keep their performance advantage if the OS/2 IOPL feature is used.

Non-OS/2 Device Drivers

Some relatively well-behaved programs use device drivers as an interface between DOS and a printer or plotter. Such programs may not work in the DOS Mode. That is because OS/2 manages all of the resources on a system, including the sharing of attached devices, thus blocking any attempt by a program or driver to bypass it. IBM Virtual Device Interface (VDI) device drivers are less of a problem. The programmer can purchase the IBM Graphics Development Toolkit version 2.0, which contains a full set of DOS-OS/2 compatible device drivers. DOS graphics programs and converted OS/2 programs can use the new drivers, including those for the Personal System/2 Display family.

Other Problems

Programs that check for the DOS version number may be in for a surprise. The OS/2 version number is 10.0. Programs that manipulate device controllers are taboo. Self-modifying programs are not supported, either. OS/2 segregates program and data segments, and only data segments can be modified. DOS .COM files (which contain code and data) must be converted to .EXE format (code only). The safest and easiest-to-migrate programming interfaces are those in the high-level language compilers. Not only are C/2, FORTRAN/2, and COBOL/2 programs compatible between DOS and OS/2, but their SAA participation makes them easier to migrate to other systems.

The Alternative: PC DOS 3.3

Programs that do not work under the DOS Mode, and have not yet been converted to OS/2, can still run as they always have, under PC DOS itself. This requires booting up from a DOS Startup diskette and then running the communications or ill-behaved program. When finished, OS/2 can be restarted with <Ctrl + Alt + Del>. This procedure is described in Chapter 6.

LOADING PROGRAMS

OS/2 Application Control

In addition to AUTOEXEC.BAT (DOS) and OS2INIT.CMD (OS/2), the application may include other batch files to perform other tasks. For example, a file named INSTALL.CMD could be used to automate the program installation process. This could include the creation of a new directory and the copying of program files.

CMD.EXE recognizes most of the same commands familiar to the DOS command processor, COMMAND.COM, with a few enhancements. Some commands can be grouped in multiple command statements, separated by AND (&&), OR (|), or separator (&) operators.

Detached Programs

Some programs can be designed for background-only operation, such as "pop-up" or "hotkey" programs that remain out of sight to perform non-interactive tasks like printing or communications, or can be called on demand, like calendar programs. The OS/2 DETACH command is used to start such programs.

OS/2 APPLICATION TYPES

There are three types of programs that run under OS/2. Most PC DOS programs (other than the exceptions just mentioned) are fine as they are, requiring no conversion in order to run under the DOS Mode. OS/2 Full-Function and Family applications must, at a minimum, undergo minor changes and recompilation before they will run under OS/2. Full-function applications, in order to take advantage of all that OS/2 has to offer, will probably undergo major revision prior to final compilation and testing.

Full-Function Applications

As you have seen, OS/2 programs can do a lot more than old DOS programs ever could—if a programmer takes advantage of the API. Writing large, segmented, multi-tasking applications is a far cry from small, single-thread DOS programs. Each of the six new language compilers and the new OS/2 Programmer's Toolkit support these new features, and the investment in time will produce an application that has more features, is easier to use, and can be multi-tasked with other programs.

Family Applications

OS/2 Family Applications are programs designed to run almost anywhere—directly under PC DOS, or in a DOS or OS/2 Mode session. Family applications benefit the programmer (only one version to maintain), the dealer (only one version to take up shelf space), and the user (a program can run under DOS today and OS/2 later).

But there are disadvantages to OS/2 Family applications. They are written to a "lowest common denominator" level: a subset of OS/2 function that will also work on DOS. This means that OS/2-exclusive features like large memory support, multi-tasking, threads, graphics calls, interprocess communications, and dynamic linking cannot be used in a Family application, since PC DOS does not support them. Only 8088/86 instructions can be used; 80286-specific instructions would disqualify a program as a true Family application. Also, Family applications are 10—30 Kb larger on disk, and because of their larger size, take a little longer to load. The OS/2 Programmer's Toolkit is an important prerequisite for writing Family programs. While technically it is not always required, the Toolkit certainly makes Family application development much easier. The Toolkit's BIND utility is used with the program's .EXE file so that OS/2 CALLS are converted to DOS interrupts when running under DOS.

MULTI-TASKING PROGRAMMING

Segment Sharing

The OS/2 programmer will have to learn some new tricks if this new operating system is going to be used effectively. Programs are divided into code segments of between 1 Kb and 64 Kb in size. Data segments are separate. Programs can modify data segments, never code segments. Both code and data segments can be shared between tasks within a program or even two concurrent programs.

Processes and Threads

A DOS program converted to OS/2 can reduce its overall run time and increase throughput, through the judicial use of processes and threads. An OS/2 process "owns" a collection of resources: memory, files, I/O devices, display. It is usually a single program, an .EXE file. It can also generate its own child processes. A thread is a basic unit of execution, a path within a process. Every process has at least one thread, but several threads can run within a process. Multiple processes and threads can run concurrently to overlap I/O and maximize throughput.

For example, a DOS spreadsheet program is used repetitively by a bank's financial officer to update spreadsheets, recalculate them, save to disk, and print them. This DOS program was converted to OS/2, and now it uses multi-tasking, or multiple threads in the program. The spreadsheet is still updated first, but now, while the recalculation is taking place, the user can immediately start working on the second spreadsheet. The recalculation continues in the background, and when finished, the spreadsheet is saved to disk and printed—without interruption to the user.

The results might look like this:

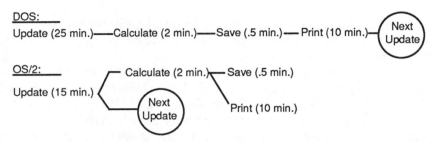

Under DOS, the average update/calculate/save/print cycle takes 27.5 minutes before the next one can begin. In OS/2 the cycle has been reduced to 15 minutes, since the next update can begin without waiting for recalculation, file saving, and printing.

Scheduler

Much of an application's performance is outside the control of the program itself. Hardware (processor speed, bus capacity) and other software (number of concurrent programs, design of each) have a big impact on how a program performs. Yet there is still much that a program can do to affect its own performance. As Chapter 6 showed, several configuration file commands can be adjusted. Within a program, one of three priority levels are available.

Priority 1 programs are the highest level, including time-critical applications such as communications. Priority 2 programs are mid-range, "average" applications. Their priority is variable, dependent on such things as foreground or background status. Priority 3 programs get what is left over, usually reserved for background programs that do not require fast response.

OS/2 uses a time-slicing scheduler. Each thread executes for a short time before the scheduler starts the next one. If multiple threads are running at the same priority level, each one receives an equivalent amount of time on a round-robin basis.

OS/2 detached programs replace the old DOS Terminate and Stay Resident programs. They reside out of sight, as background programs, until the user brings them to the foreground. They are usually accompanied by a keystroke monitor routine, since a specific key combination (like <Ctrl + F9>) is needed to invoke them.

COMMUNICATING BETWEEN PROGRAMS

Much attention is paid in OS/2 to protecting, or insulating, programs from each other. But sometimes two processes or applications need to communicate with each other or share relevant information. There are several ways that this can be done.

Pipes

Pipes are a simple method of moving information between two programs, much as data is copied to disk. DOS already supports pipes; the symbol " I " between two program or command names indicates that data is being passed from the one on the left to the one on the right. For example, the DOS SORT command can sort a list of names in alphabetical order. It can sort them from a file, by typing NAMES I SORT and the results will appear on the screen, or it can sort directly into a file, NAMES I SORT > NEWNAMES. These are examples of redirected I/O. Piping means that a program (or command in this case) passes data to another program. DIR I SORT says "list the current directory, sort the file names in the directory, and display them on the screen." Command DIR "pipes" its output directly to command SORT (without first sending it to the screen).

Pipes usually work in a First In, First Out (FIFO) manner: the data arrives in the same order in which it was sent. Multiple processes may pipe into a single shared process. An example is a print spooler which receives documents piped from several programs and prints them in the order received. Another is the piping of messages to the display by multiple applications. A characteristic of piping is that data is temporarily stored in a memory file, long enough to pass it to the next program or process. That file is a 64 Kb code segment.

Queues

Data can be "sent" between processes through a queue without actually copying it, as pipes do. Code segments are simply shared between programs. The receiving program does not have to take the data in a FIFO order; it can "pick and choose" whatever it needs. And data is not limited to one segment, either, it could take up most of available memory if necessary. Performance is also improved since no data movement or manipulation takes place during the process.

Semaphores

Semaphores do not send or receive data themselves, but act as traffic lights to keep order. An example is a printer device driver or spooling program. Multiple programs cannot all use the printer at the same time, since incoming text from several sources might get jumbled together. A semaphore can be set to tell waiting tasks that the printer is busy. When one document is finished, the next one can begin.

OS/2 SEGMENT MANAGEMENT

PC DOS programs are static in nature; they are loaded into memory and stay there until another program is loaded on top of them. Some applications, in order to conserve memory, maintain a swap area within a program: a place where disk-resident program subroutines can be copied in as needed. By swapping pieces of a program, the total memory required at any point in time is reduced. A segment can be as large as 64 Kb, but is usually between 16 — 32 Kb for best performance.

OS/2 performs a similar function for its programs, but the programmer does not have to design a swap area or subroutine calls. Since programs are already segmented, OS/2 can start running a program with only a few of its segments in memory. When a program instruction references a segment that is not currently in memory, the operating system issues a program *fault*, something like an error. The fault tells OS/2 to look up the segment in its file descriptor table, which points to its fixed disk location. The segment is loaded into memory (after a brief pause for the disk activity) and the program continues.

This is called dynamic linking, since program segments can be linked dynamically to the main program during execution, not prior to it. Certain segments, for performance reasons, might be pre-loaded into memory first, saving the dynamically linked ones for less frequently used routines like error messages. Main program files can be identified by their .EXE filename extensions, and dynamic link library files by .DLL. If enough memory is available, all segments might remain resident. Otherwise, OS/2 can swap them out to disk temporarily to make room for other segments. This file, which is constantly expanding and contracting in size, is named SWAPPER.DAT. Sometimes very large programs can be written, knowing that they are larger than available memory. This is called memory over-commit, and is a form of virtual memory management. Dynamic linking, swapping, and memory overcommit, like all disk activity, are slower than memory-bound programs.

Dynamically linked segments can be shared by multiple programs requiring a common function. They can be maintained as separate files, so that an entire program will not require modification or recompilation if a segment changes.

Segment Activity

Since each segment must have a contiguous block of memory, OS/2 moves segments around occasionally to free up space. Both segment swapping (to disk) and segment motion (in memory) can be turned on or off with a configuration file command. Segment discard takes place when an inactive segment has not changed and can be thrown away.

OS/2 RESOURCE MANAGEMENT

Operating System/2 manages a lot more than memory segments; it keeps track of multiple programs, their individual user interfaces (keyboard and display), disk space, and output to a printer or other device. The operating system shares these resources among the applications, relieving the programmer of unnecessary work and improving overall system efficiency.

Multi-Tasking

A programmer does not have to provide for multi-programming several programs at once—OS/2 handles that. Sharing of system resources (memory, disk files, displays, printers, etc.) among concurrent programs is far too complicated for programs to work out among themselves—the operating system must keep track of disk file usage, memory segments, spooled print jobs, multi-application windowing, etc.

OS/2 Device Drivers

OS/2 depends on device drivers to provide the interface between the operating system and the various internal and external devices a computer system uses. This lets a programmer design a program against the standard OS/2 output interface, without concern for device specifics. The user, in turn, does not have to purchase a special version of a program to support a particular device. A new device driver, matching the installed device, can be installed (copied) to the OS/2 disk, and then selected from a menu of available drivers.

Device drivers service requests in both DOS and OS/2 Modes. Drivers manage devices so as to improve overall system performance. They are re-entrant, which means that several programs can use one at the same time. OS/2 drivers are bimodal, so that they can be shared by both DOS and OS/2 programs. Devices are shared among programs in an efficient manner. For example, a fixed disk device driver can queue several read and write requests from multiple programs, and handle the disk activity in a way that minimizes the amount of read/write head travel across the disk surface. The programmer also has several OS/2 device driver helper routines available to help manage the request queue. Special drivers, not otherwise known to OS/2, must be listed in the configuration file.

Creating a Device Driver

Although OS/2 is shipped with a set of device drivers for common PC and Personal System/2 I/O devices, occasionally a programmer will have to write one for a new device. The OS/2 Programming Guide and the OS/2 Technical Reference tell how to create a device driver that is bimodal, supporting both DOS and OS/2 programs.

Video Input and Output

OS/2 Standard Edition 1.0 uses a text-based, full-screen VIO interface to the display. VIO does not support all-points-addressable graphics or windowing within a program; that support will be part of the Presentation Manager in Standard Edition 1.1 and Extended Edition 1.1. Release 1.0-level programs will run under 1.1, can be windowed on the screen with other applications, but will not make their own windows. Many additional display I/O functions will be available in Presentation Manager to utilize its improved text/graphics interface. The IBM Graphics Development Toolkit 2.0 can be used to design and run graphics programs in release 1.0.

Presentation Manager

In addition to graphics and windowing support, the OS/2 Standard Edition 1.1's Presentation Manager provides an interactive user dialog interface, alternate character font styles, and bitmaps for moving and reproducing graphics images.

Message Files

Program messages can be kept in a separate text file. Instead of including prompts and error messages inside the program, they can be called from the external file as needed. This way, rarely-used text such as help information, tutorials, or error conditions can remain on fixed disk until needed, without taking up memory space. Frequently-used messages can be bound, or attached, to program segments. The OS/2 Toolkit provides tools for implementing both methods.

The OS/2 Print Spooler

The OS/2 printer spooler (SPOOL) supports one printer, either serial or parallel type, at a time. Multiple copies of the spooler can be started at once to drive multiple printers. The spooler can receive print-image output directly from any of several concurrent programs or via pre-saved disk files. Print output is segregated by process number so that lines from several jobs are not intermixed. Some application programs, such as word processors, may require the user to start SPOOL, or they may do it themselves.

Keyboard Monitor

OS/2 has its own set of keyboard and mouse rules, but some key combinations are not used. These can be assigned to special functions, such as invoking a calendar program which is normally hidden in the background. A keyboard monitor program can be written to intercept special key combinations or to translate characters as they are typed. This gives OS/2 programmers a way to filter keystrokes and perform functions normally unrecognized by the operating system.

Input/Output Privilege Level (IOPL)

DOS programs that interfaced with hardware directly were called "ill-behaved." When an OS/2 program requires maximum performance from a device, the operating system provides a "fast path" to move data to and from it directly. An IOPL code segment "grabs control" of the device, bypassing normal OS/2 device drivers and temporarily suspending other processes. The OS/2 Programmer's Guide describes how an IOPL segment is written.

OS/2 APPLICATION PROGRAM INTERFACE (API)

CALL

PC DOS required application programmers to deal directly with hardware and software interrupts, but OS/2 uses a higher-level CALL interface, which it translates internally into the necessary hardware interrupts. This not only relieves the programmer of an unnecessary level of detail, but it makes a program more transportable to other systems. This is consistent with IBM's Systems Application Architecture. The OS/2 Application Program Interface provides a stable base for applications with underlying room for growth and expansion. For example, if OS/2 were to exploit unique 80386 function, or if new device support were added, the API and its application programs would not have to change.

Operating System/2 uses a CALL-RETURN interface between high-level languages like C or COBOL and OS/2. CALL parameters are first PUSHed on the stack, and are passed to OS/2 when the CALL is issued. A RETURN code is passed back to the program for each CALL (and checked to confirm normal completion of the CALL). The 80286/386 hardware assists in the CALL parameter-passing, improving performance. A CALL Gate is used for special IOPL routines, which have direct hardware access.

A detailed listing and description of OS/2 API function calls is beyond the scope of this book. You can read *OS/2: Features, Functions, and Applications* by Krantz, Mizell, and Williams (Wiley, 1988) for more information on the OS/2 programming interface. In addition, the two-volume OS/2 Reference is the "bible" where all functions are listed. They have descriptive names like KbdCharIn, MouOpen, and VioPrtScreen, covering all of the interfaces listed below.

The following table gives the total number of OS/2 Standard Edition API functions in each of several categories. Since Family applications use a subset of the available Full-function application calls, the number of functions in each "Family" category is never more than the "Full-Function" total. The numbers in some categories (particularly those controlling the user interface) will increase under OS/2 1.1.

Function Category	Family	Full-Function
Tasking	3	13
Asynchronous Notification	2	3
Interprocess Communication	0	21
Timer	3	6
Memory Management	10	13
Dynamic Linking	0	5
Family API	2	2
Device I/O Services	33	63
Device Monitors	0	5
File I/O	27	33
Errors and Exceptions	1	3
Messages	3	3
Program Startup	2	2
National Language Support	5	5
TOTAL	91	177

OS/2 Standard Edition 1.1

While the Standard 1.1 API is much richer in function than the 1.0 version, it will run 1.0 programs compatibly. The OS/2 Toolkit 1.1 provides assistance to the developer wishing to take advantage of the new SAA-compatible graphics/window interface.

A variety of new functions fall into the Windows, Messages, and Graphics categories:

Windows

Various types of windows can be created, depending on the needs of the application: main application windows, child or task windows, and user dialog boxes. Within a window, the position, size, border, pointer shape, title bar, action bar, and other characteristics can be established.

Messages

Both program input and output text are called messages. Message display and input is usually done through one of the windows or dialog boxes. A message can originate at the keyboard in the form of a function key or text input, or as a signal from a mouse button. Messages can also be sent between programs. If two or more applications are waiting for input, only the current foreground program will be able to enter information. Message output can be sent to the screen either through the 1.0-level VIO interface, or the Advanced VIO of the Presentation Manager. AVIO supports text output in multiple windows within an application.

Graphics

The Presentation Manager API offers a rich set of graphics primitives, or functions, for drawing graphs, charts and various line drawings. Various font styles can be used to describe the graphics pictures. Bitmaps support the moving and copying of graphics pictures around the screen. Presentation Manager release 1.1 API programs can be windowed on the display with other OS/2 text and 1.1 graphics programs.

Images (such as pictures captured through a scanner or video camera) can be used in an OS/2 application, but they are highly device dependent and may limit the portability of the application.

Programs using the Graphics Development Toolkit graphics interface will run as they did in version 1.0, as full-screen programs. They are not compatible with the enhanced Presentation Manager graphics, and will have to be rewritten before they can be windowed with other programs or migrated to other SAA systems.

THE FINAL STEPS

Once a program's source code has been migrated and modified for OS/2, the program must be compiled. For this you need one of the six IBM OS/2 language compiler products: Macro Assembler, COBOL, FORTRAN, Basic, C, or Pascal.

Object File

Figure 8–1 illustrates the steps a program goes through during compiling and linking. The final source file becomes input to a language compiler, and the object file (with a filename extension of .OBJ) is the result.

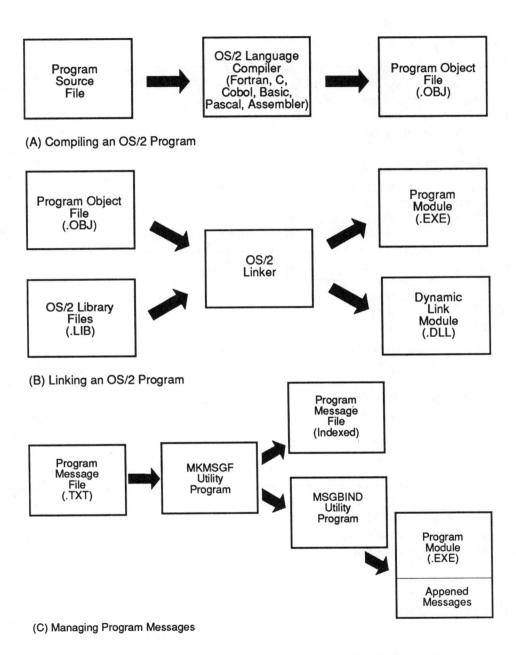

(A) Compiling an OS/2 Program

(B) Linking an OS/2 Program

(C) Managing Program Messages

Figure 8–1 The OS/2 application program compile and link procedure includes three main subtasks. First, (A) the source code (which might be a modified DOS program) is compiled using one of the six language compiler products. An object file is the result. Next, (B) the program is linked into a final program file, which can also call memory segments from a dynamic link module. Last, (C) a separate message file can be prepared or combined with the program file.

Linking

Next, the program object file is run through the OS/2 linker, where it is prepared for loading. Various library files (.LIB) are used in the process. The output is either a program module (.EXE) or a dynamic link module (.DLL). If the program is a Family application, a .MDF file is used. The OS/2 Bind utility is used to convert the program so that it can run under DOS or OS/2.

Message File

A program can be designed with messages (prompts, errors, help, etc.) stored in a file separate from the program. Using an OS/2 utility program, a text file (.TXT) is then converted to a message file (.MSG) using the MKMSGF utility. This file can be used by the program as needed, selecting the indexed messages by number. A disk-based message file saves memory, and the file is easier to maintain and translate, if necessary. Messages can also be appended directly to a program file (.EXE) with the OS/2 MSGBIND utility to improve access time.

Loading

The program module file is loaded by the user, who selects it from a menu of previously installed programs or calls it from the OS/2 Mode command line. If the application was designed with dynamic link modules, they are automatically loaded by the operating system as necessary. If memory becomes full, old modules are temporarily swapped out to a swap area to make room for new ones.

Family Applications

Family applications are a special case. In order to be able to run under DOS or OS/2, they may not use any OS/2 exclusives, such as dynamic link modules or message files. The program module must be run through a BIND utility program, which adds a PC DOS interface to the OS/2 program. This allows it to run under either operating system or either mode of OS/2.

OS/2 TOOLS

Operating system tools are important to programmers because they provide time-saving utilities and program libraries while enforcing good programming practices and software standards. Some tools, like language compilers, are essential to programming while others, like application code generators, are optional. Tools are especially important in the early stages of a new operating system, as developers rush to convert their programs.

Tools also include maintenance aids such as program debuggers, editors and tracers, and cosmetic enhancements such as picture libraries and font generators. Program performance can be improved with tools such as indexed file support and code optimizers. An application can be made much easier to use when a programmer uses code-generating tools for menus, help messages, and dialog screens.

TOOLKITS

The OS/2 Toolkit 1.0 is provided to assist programmers in application development, particularly in writing programs that use OS/2 features such as large memory, multi-tasking, dynamic linking, and in creating Family Applications. It consists of a Toolkit diskette and the OS/2 Programmer's Guide.

The Toolkit diskette contains various utility programs and libraries used in the program compiling process. It also contains several sample programs in the Macro Assembler and C languages. An installation program guides the user through various options, creating disk directories and copying files to them.

The Programming Guide is shipped only with the Toolkit, and is not available separately. Its table of contents is listed later in this chapter. The OS/2 Technical Reference is not part of the Toolkit, but is a prerequisite for using the Toolkit.

OS/2 Toolkit 1.1

The release 1.1 Toolkit will add several new features for use in creating programs that use the Presentation Manager. This includes tools for designing windows and graphics output. The Dialog Editor helps a programmer design interactive program screens that run in a pop-up or child window. The Icon and Font Editors are used for modifying or creating character fonts and images of various sizes (an application can use up to four simultaneous fonts). A Resource Compiler is provided to collect icons, fonts, menus, and dialog box templates in a program resource file. A full-screen debugger shows original program source code with a live program dump. Owners of the Tookit 1.0 version will be entitled to a free upgrade to Tookit 1.1 when it is available.

OS/2 LANGUAGE COMPILERS

Six new language compilers are available from IBM for DOS and OS/2 programmers. All run as Family applications, which means they can be used to compile programs under either operating system and produce executable programs that run under DOS or OS/2. Each compiler is upward-compatible from earlier versions, supports the Personal System/2 models, and three of them (C/2, COBOL/2, and FORTRAN/2) participate in IBM's Systems Application Architecture. The OS/2 Toolkit is recommended for use with any of these compilers, in order to take advantage of OS/2 facilities and produce SAA-compatible applications.

C/2

The C/2 Compiler is highly compatible with previous C versions and participates in IBM's Systems Application Architecture. It is in partial compliance with the proposed C language standard. C/2 features Math Co-Processor support and an interactive debugging tool.

FORTRAN/2

IBM FORTRAN/2 is a high-function compiler that is highly compatible with earlier FORTRANs and participates in the new SAA standard. It was designed according to the ANSI X3.9-1978 standard, and will be submitted for compliance testing against that standard. FORTRAN/2 features Math Co-Processor support, multi-tasking support of both the compiler and the code generated by it, and an interactive debugger.

PASCAL/2

The new Pascal/2 Compiler is highly compatible with previous versions. It also provides network support via the IBM LAN Manager 1.2 version, including file sharing and record-locking. Pascal programs can call programs written in Assembler or C, or they can be called from Assembler, BASIC, or C programs. An interactive debugger is provided.

Macro Assembler/2

The latest IBM assembler supports the full 80286/80287 instruction set, including 80286 Protect Mode instructions.

BASIC/2

The latest BASIC language compiler is upward-compatible from previous versions. It features a common language for calling programs written in C, Pascal, or Assembler; an interactive debugger; Math Co-processor support, and extended Indexed Sequential Access Method (ISAM) file support.

COBOL/2

IBM COBOL/2 is a high-level COBOL compiler that is compatible with earlier COBOL versions as well as SAA. For example, COBOL programs can be written, compiled, and tested on an IBM Personal System/2 and then migrated to a System/370 mainframe for recompilation and further testing. IBM intends to submit COBOL/2 for certification against the ANSI X3.23-1985 Intermediate Level and X3.23-1974 High Level standards.

COBOL/2 includes data and procedure divisions larger than 64 Kb, the Animator interactive debugging tool, PC Network support, and many other features.

TECHNICAL PUBLICATIONS

OS/2 Programmer's Guide

This publication, packaged as part of the OS/2 Toolkit, is for the OS/2 application developer. It deals with function calls, tools and utility programs, and will be updated for release 1.1. Its table of contents reads as follows:

IBM OS/2 Programmer's Guide
Table of Contents

OS/2 Technical Reference

Like its predecessor, the DOS Technical Reference, this two-volume set describes the "official" OS/2 application program interface. It gets under the covers of OS/2, describing in detail its architecture, control structures, data structures, and I/O formats. The Technical Reference is a prerequisite for using the OS/2 Toolkit. It will be updated for the Standard Edition 1.1, and 1.0 Tech Ref owners will receive a free upgrade to the 1.1 version.

IBM OS/2 Technical Reference
Table of Contents
Volume 1

IBM OS/2 Technical Reference
Table of Contents
Volume 2

IBM BASIC Reference 3.3

The latest BASIC Reference describes the operation and use of the BASIC interpreter shipped with DOS 3.3 and OS/2 versions. (The BASIC interpreter runs only in the DOS Mode under OS/2).

A Quick Reference to OS/2 Commands

This appendix provides an overview of Operating System/2™ (os/2™) commands.

Source: IBM OS/2 User's Reference, 84X1896. Used with permission.

Commands for One Mode Only

os/2 has two modes of operation:

- OS/2
- DOS.

There are some commands that provide functions specific to one mode. In this book, these symbols identify commands that work in only one mode:

OS/2 only   **DOS only**

If you enter a command that has a symbol for one mode while you are in the other mode, an error message is displayed.

OS/2 Commands

Command	Purpose
ANSI	Enables or disables extended display and keyboard support in OS/2 mode
APPEND	Locates data files outside of the current directory
ASSIGN	Assigns a drive letter to a different drive
ATTRIB	Turns on or off the read-only and archive attributes of a file
BACKUP	Backs up one or more files from one disk to another
BREAK	Sets on or off the check for Ctrl+Break in DOS mode whenever a program issues system calls
CHCP	Displays or changes the current system character set
CHDIR	Changes the current directory or displays its name
CHKDSK	Scans the disk and checks it for errors
CLS	Clears the display screen
CMD	Starts another OS/2 command processor
COMMAND	Starts another DOS command processor
COMP	Compares the contents of two files

Command	Purpose
COPY	Copies one or more files and also combines files
CREATEDD	Creates a dump data diskette
DATE	Displays the system date
DETACH	Starts a noninteractive program in OS/2 mode
DIR	Lists the files in a directory
DISKCOMP	Compares the contents of two diskettes
DISKCOPY	Copies the contents of one diskette to another diskette
DPATH	Locates data files outside of the current directory
ERASE	Deletes one or more files
EXIT	Ends the current command processor
FDISK	Creates and deletes partitions and logical drives, changes the primary partition, displays partition data, and selects next fixed disk drive for partitioning
FIND	Searches for a specific string of text in a file
FORMAT	Formats the disk to accept OS/2 files
GRAFTABL	Allows the extended character set to be displayed when using display adapters in graphics mode
HELP	Provides help information related to a warning or error message

Command	Purpose
JOIN	Joins a disk drive to a specific path
KEYB	Specifies a special keyboard layout that replaces the default U.S. keyboard layout
LABEL	Creates, changes, or deletes the volume identification label on a disk
MKDIR	Creates a new directory
MODE	Sets operational modes for devices
MORE	Sends output from a file to the screen one full screen at a time
PATCH	Allows you to apply IBM supplied patches
PATH	Locates commands outside of the current directory
PRINT	Prints or cancels printing of one or more files
PROMPT	Set the OS/2 command prompt
RECOVER	Recovers files from a disk containing defective sectors
RENAME	Changes the name of a file
REPLACE	Selectively replaces files
RESTORE	Restores one or more backup files from one disk to another
RMDIR	Removes a directory
SET	Sets one string value in the environment equal to another string for later use in programs

Command	Purpose
SETCOM40	Sets the COM port for DOS mode
SORT	Reads data from standard input, sorts it, and writes it to standard output
SPOOL	Intercepts and separates data from different sources going to the printer so printer output is not intermixed.
START	Starts an OS/2 program in another session. Can be used in STARTUP.CMD autostart facility
SUBST	Substitutes a drive letter for another drive or path
SYS	Transfers the OS/2 hidden files IBMBIO.COM and IBMDOS.COM from one diskette or fixed disk to another diskette or fixed disk.
TIME	Displays and sets the system time
TRACE	Selects system trace
TRACEFMT	Displays formatted trace records in reverse time stamp order
TREE	Displays all of the directory paths
TYPE	Displays the contents of a file
VER	Displays the OS/2 version number
VERIFY	Confirms that data written to a file is correct
VOL	Displays the disk volume label
XCOPY	Selectively copies groups of files, including those in subdirectories, from one disk to another

Batch Commands

Command	Purpose
CALL	Nests a batch file within a batch file
ECHO	Allows or prevents display of OS/2 commands while a batch file is running
ENDLOCAL	Restores the drive, directory, and variables that were in effect before a SETLOCAL command was issued
EXTPROC	Defines an external batch file processor
FOR	Allows repetitive processing of commands within a batch file
GOTO	Transfers control elsewhere in the batch file
IF	Allows conditional processing of commands within a batch file
PAUSE	Suspends processing of the batch file
REM	Displays remarks from within a batch file
SETLOCAL	Sets the drive, directory and variables that are local to the current batch file
SHIFT	Allows more than 10 replaceable parameters in a batch file

Statements for the CONFIG.SYS File

Statement	Purpose
BREAK	Turns on or off the check for Ctrl+Break during program processing in DOS mode
BUFFERS	Sets the number of disk buffers for use
CODEPAGE	Selects system character sets to be prepared by OS/2 for character set switching
COUNTRY	Sets the country dependent information
DEVICE	Specifies the path and filename of a device driver to be installed
DEVINFO	Prepares a device for character set switching
DISKCACHE	Assigns storage to be used for disk cache
FCBS	Sets File Control Block information for DOS mode
IOPL	Enables I/O privilege to be granted or denied to requesting processes in OS/2 mode
LIBPATH	Identifies the locations of dynamic link libraries in OS/2 mode
MAXWAIT	Sets time limit for lack of access to processor resource in OS/2 mode
MEMMAN	Selects storage allocation options for OS/2 mode

Statement	Purpose
PAUSEONERROR	Enables or disables pausing when error or warning are issued during the processing of CONFIG.SYS
PRIORITY	Selects priority calculation in scheduling regular class threads in OS/2 mode
PROTECTONLY	Specifies an OS/2-only operating evironment
PROTSHELL	Specifies the user interface program and the OS/2 command processor
REM	Allows you to add remarks to your CONFIG.SYS file
RMSIZE	Sets the amount of storage used for DOS programs
RUN	Loads and starts a system program during system startup
SHELL	Loads the command processor for DOS mode
SWAPPATH	Identifies the location of the file that keeps track of segments swapped out of storage in OS/2 mode
THREADS	Determines the maximum number of independent actions, known as threads, in OS/2 mode
TIMESLICE	Sets amount of processor time each process receives
TRACE	Selects system trace

Statement	Purpose
TRACEBUF	Sets the size of the system trace buffer

Index